THE TRUE NAME

VOLUME I

◆

OSHO

২৫ সাহিত্য

DISCOURSES ON
JAPUJI-SAHEB OF
GURU NANAK DEV

PUBLISHING FOR ONE WORLD

WILEY EASTERN LIMITED
*New Delhi • Bangalore • Bombay • Calcutta • Guwahati
Hyderabad • Lucknow • Madras • Pune
London*

Books for NEW AGE

W I L E Y   E A S T E R N   L I M I T E D

NEW DELHI: 4835/24 Ansari Road, Daryaganj, New Delhi 110 002

BANGALORE: 27, Bull Temple Road, Basavangudi, Bangalore 560 004

BOMBAY: Post Box No. 4124, Saraswati Mandir School, Kennedy Bridge, Nana Chowk, Bombay 400 007

CALCUTTA: 40/8, Ballygunge Circular Road, Calcutta 700 019

GUWAHATI: Pan Bazar, Rani Bari, Guwahati 781 001

HYDERABAD: 1-2-412/9, Gaganmahal, Near A V College, Domalguda, Hyderabad 500 029

LUCKNOW: 18, Pandit Madan Mohan Malviya Marg, Lucknow 226 001

MADRAS: No. 6, First Main Road, Gandhi Nagar, Madras 600 020

PUNE: Flat No. 2, Building No. 7, Indira Co-op. Housing Society Ltd. Indira Heights, Paud Fatta, Erandawane, Karve Road, Pune 411 038

LONDON: Wishwa Prakashan Ltd., Spantech House, Lagham Road, South Gladstone, Surrey, RH9 8HB, U.K.

Editing by   Dolly Diddee
Swami Anand Nirgrantha
Swami Anand Robin B.A. (Cantab.)

ISBN: 81-224-0606-8

Published by H.S. Poplai for Wiley Eastern Limited, 4835/24, Ansari Road, Daryaganj, New Delhi 110 002. Typeset by Jay Compusoft, New Delhi and printed at S.P. Printers, Sector IX, Noida, U.P.

Printed in India.

Production: M.I. Thomas

इधर से गुजरा था सोचा सलाम करता चलूं

About Osho

M OST OF US live out our lives in the world of time, in memories of the past and anticipation of the future. Only rarely do we touch the timeless dimension of the present — in moments of sudden beauty, or sudden danger, in meeting with a lover or with the surprise of the unexpected. Very few people step out of the world of time and mind, its ambitions and competitiveness, and begin to live in the world of the timeless. And of those who do, only a few have attempted to share their experience. Lao Tzu, Gautam Buddha, Bodhidharma... or more recently, George Gurdjieff, Raman Maharshi, J. Krishnamurti — they are though by their contemporaries to be eccentrics or madmen; after their death they are called "philosophers". And in time they become legends — not flesh-and-blood human beings, but perhaps mythological representations of our collective wish to grow beyond the smallness and trivia, the meaninglessness of our everyday lives.

Osho is one who has discovered the door to living His life in the timeless dimension of the present — He has called Himself a "true existentialist" — and He has devoted His life to provoking others to seek this same door, to step out of the world of past and future and discover for themselves the world of eternity.

Osho was born in Kuchwada, Madhya Pradesh, India, on December 11, 1931. From His earliest childhood, His was a rebellious and independent spirit, insisting on experiencing the truth for Himself rather than acquiring knowledge and benefits given by others.

After His enlightenment at the age of twenty-one, Osho completed His academic studies and spent several years teaching philosophy at the University of Jabalpur. Meanwhile, He traveled throughout India giving talks, challenging orthodox religious leaders in public debate, questioning traditional beliefs, and meeting people from all walks of life. He read extensively, everything He could find to broaden His understanding of the belief systems and psychology of contemporary man. By the late 1960s Osho had begun to develop His unique dynamic meditation techniques. Modern man, He said, is so burdened with the outmoded traditions of the past and the anxieties of modern-day living that he must go through a deep cleansing process before he can hope to discover the thought-less, relaxed state of meditation.

In the early 1970s, the first Westerners began to hear of Osho. By 1974 a commune had been established around Him in Poona, India, and the trickle of visitors from the West was soon to become a flood. In the course of His work, Osho has spoken on virtually every aspect of the development of human consciousness. He has distilled the essence of what is significant to the spiritual quest of contemporary man, based not on intellectual understanding but tested against His own existential experience.

He belongs to no tradition — "I am beginning of a totally new religious consciousness," He says. "Please don't connect me with the past — it is not even worth remembering."

His talks to disciples and seekers from all over the world have been published in more than six hundred volumes, and translated into over thirty languages. And He says, "My message is not a doctrine, not a philosophy. My message is a certain alchemy, a science of transformation, so only those who are willing to die as they are and be born again into something so new that they cannot even imagine it right now...only those few courageous people will be ready to listen, because listening is going to be risky.

"Listening, you have taken the first step towards being reborn. So it is not a philosophy that you can just make an overcoat of and go bragging about. It is not a doctrine where you can find consolation for harassing questions. No, my message is not some verbal communication. It is far more risky. It is nothing less than death and rebirth."

Osho left His body on January 19, 1990, as a result of poisoning by US government agents while held incognito in custody on technical immigration violations in 1985.

His huge commune in India continues to be the largest spiritual growth center in the world attracting thousands of international visitors who come to participate in its meditation, therapy bodywork and creative programs, or just to experience being in a buddhafield.

Introduction

W HEN THE FULL moon night spreads over the bosom of the ocean, who can know the limits of feelings that begin to wave in its waters! Something similar happens when Osho's voice descends into the inner strata of the listener and one does not know how much and what begins to overflow and soak into one's inner being.

A rustling sound is born when the wind passes through the leaves of a tree, but that rustle is born out of a collision—the collision of the wind and the leaves. If you sit on the banks of a river you hear the sweet rippling sound of the running water, but this sound is born out of the collision between the water and the rocks. When the strings of the veena are played upon, the sound is born because of the collision between the fingers and the strings.

Using all these metaphors, Osho takes us towards Ek Omkar, the sound of Om alone, of Nanak, where all collisions disappear, where duality itself disappears, where energy particles take a shape...the shape of a sound, the shape of the sound of Omkar. It is this sound Nanak called Satnam, The True Name. It is a hint towards a space where all names attributed by the world disappear. Only one reality remains: Omkar, the sound of Om.

Ek Omkar Satnam, the sound of Om alone, is the true name.

Osho's voice leads us into the difference between reality and truth. Where science seeks truth through the medium of mind alone and a poet seeks through the medium of the heart, and the mind and the heart both fall short, Osho becomes a pointer to that inner experience of Nanak where the two meet and merge, where the duality of science and art is lost and we enter the Omkar.

When Osho's voice rustles in one's interior like a soft breeze, when overburdened like a rain cloud it showers drop by drop, and when it descends into one's being like a ray of the sun, I can say on my own authority that the dormant seed of consciousness starts sprouting. Then the flower of countless colors that blooms can have any name to it. It blooms also as a Gautam Buddha, it blooms also as a Mahavira, it blooms also as a Nanak.

Symbols are used to convey the otherworldly truths which are difficult to grasp for the people of this world. Some sagas, some parables are put together which travel down through the centuries as pointers toward the reality. These stories are for awakening the dormant inner potentialities of man. But when sects form, the vision and outlook contract into smaller and smaller units; the symbols remain but their meanings are lost. With empty gestures people go on bowing down to all these symbols in the same manner as before but remaining as miserable as ever.

To speak plainly, what Osho has given to the world is a revolution of consciousness, which unfolds the meaning of each such story. While talking of Nanak moving towards Ek Omkar, Osho talks of many such sagas. It may be Nanak's drowning in the river for three days, it may be the stream of milk coming out of Laloo's bread when squeezed, it may be the story of Nanak agreeing to perform *namaz*, the Mohammedan prayer, along with a Mohammedan ruler when asked by him, or it may be the story of Kaaba in Mecca moving in the same direction wherever Nanak's feet were moved. Going through each of these stories, Osho goes on making a direction, a dimension available that penetrates the very being, the dormant potential in everyone for awakening their consciousness.

No truth becomes one's own until it becomes one's experience. Talking of such an experience I can say that whenever I want to understand Nanak, I see Osho standing there. His words point the way and lead me to where I can gain a glimpse of an encounter with Nanak. When I want to understand Krishna, I find Osho standing in front of me, and then with a smile He moves behind Krishna. He hides in the silence of Gautam Buddha also, and speaks in the tinkling anklets of Meera.

If one has to enter the very soul of Japuji, my feeling is that in this age we have been given the voice of Osho as a boon through which the seed of our consciousness can sprout so that Nanak would flower within us, Ek Omkar would flower within us.

AMRITA PREETAM,
Member, Rajya Sabha

Contents

Contents

Chapter 1

The Singer

He is one, He is Omkar, the supreme truth.
He is the creator, beyond fear, beyond rancor.
His is the timeless form,
Never born, self-creating.
He is attained by the guru's grace.
He was truth before the ages and as time ran its course.
Nanak says, Now is He truth eternal, and forever will He be.
We cannot comprehend Him though we think a million times;
Nor quiet the mind by silence, however long we sit;
Nor a mountain of bread appease the hunger of the soul;
Nor one hundred thousand feats of mind achieve unity with Him.

How can truth be attained and the veil of falsehood torn?
Nanak says, By submission to the divine order which is preordained.

I T WAS A DARK moonless night; the clouds were heavy with rain because it was the monsoon season. Suddenly thunder sounded and lightning flashed as a few rain drops started to fall. The village was asleep. Only Nanak was awake and the echo of his song filled the air.

Nanak's mother was worried because the night was more than half over and the lamp in his room was still burning. She could hear his voice as he sang. She could restrain herself no longer and knocked at his door, "Go to sleep now, my son. Soon it will be dawn." Nanak became silent. From the darkness sounded the call of the sparrowhawk. "Piyu, piyu, piyu!" it called.

"Listen, mother!" Nanak called out. "The sparrowhawk is calling to his beloved; how can I be silent, because I am competing with him? I will call my beloved as long as he calls his—even longer, because his beloved is nearby, perhaps in the next tree! My beloved is so far away. I will have to sing for lives upon lives before my voice reaches Him." Nanak resumed his song.

Nanak attained God by singing to him; Nanak's quest is very unusual—his path was decorated with songs. The first thing to be realized is that Nanak practiced no austerities or meditation or yoga; he only sang, and singing, he arrived. He sang with all his heart and soul, so much so that his singing became meditation; his singing became his purification and his yoga.

Whenever a person performs any act with all his heart and soul, that act becomes the path. Endless meditation, if halfhearted, will take you nowhere; whereas just singing a simple song with all your being merged in it, or dancing a dance with the same total absorption and you will reach God. The question is not what you do, but how much of yourself you involved in the act.

Nanak's path to supreme realization, to godliness is scattered with song and flowers. Whatever he has said was said in verse. His path was full of melody and soft, filled with the flavor of ambrosia.

Kabir says: "My enchanted mind was so intoxicated that it drained the filled cup without caring to measure the quantity." So it was with Nanak: he drank without caring how much he drank; then he sang and sang and sang. And his songs are not those of an ordinary singer; they have sprung from within one who has known. There is the ring of truth, the reflection of God within them.

Now another thing about the Japuji. The moonless night described at the beginning was an incident from Nanak's life when he was about sixteen or seventeen years of age. When the Japuji was conceived, Nanak was thirty years, six months and fifteen days old. The first incident refers to the days when he was still a seeker in quest of the beloved. The call to the beloved, the refrain, "Piyu, Piyu, Piyu..." was still the sparrowhawk calling; he had not yet met the beloved.

The Japuji was his first proclamation after the union with the beloved. The sparrowhawk had found his beloved; the call of "Piyu, Piyu," was now over. The Japuji is the very first words uttered by Nanak after self-realization; therefore they hold a very special place in the sayings of Nanak. They are the latest news brought back from the kingdom of heaven.

The incident preceding the birth of the Japuji needs to be understood also. Nanak sat on the bank of the river in total darkness with his friend and follower, Mardana. Suddenly, without saying a word, he removed his clothes and walked into the river. Mardana called after him, "Where are you going? The night is so dark and cold!" Nanak went further and further; he plunged into the depths of the river. Mardana waited, thinking he would be out soon, but Nanak did not return.

Mardana waited for five minutes; when ten minutes had passed he became anxious. Where could he be? There was no sign of him. Mardana began to run along the shore calling to him, "Where are you? Answer me! Where are you?" He felt he heard a voice saying, "Be patient, be patient!" but there was no sign of Nanak.

Mardana ran back to the village and woke everyone up. It was the middle of the night, but a crowd collected at the riverside because everyone in the village loved Nanak. They all had some sense, a glimpse, of what Nanak was going to be. They had felt the fragrance of his presence, just as the bud gives off its fragrance before the flower has opened. All the village wept. They ran back and forth the whole length of the river bank but to no avail.

Three days passed. By now it was certain that Nanak had drowned. The people imagined that his body must have been carried away by the swift current and perhaps eaten by wild animals. The village was drowned in sorrow. Though everyone thought him dead, on the third night Nanak appeared from the river. The first words he spoke became the Japuji.

So goes the story — and a story means that which is true and yet not true. It is true because it gives the essential truth; it is false in the sense that it is only symbolic. And it is evident that the more profound the subject matter, the greater the need for symbols.

When Nanak disappeared in the river, the story goes that he stood before the gate of God. He experienced God. There before his eyes stood the beloved he pined for, for whom he sang night and day. He who had become the thirst of his every heartbeat stood revealed before Nanak! All his desires were fulfilled. Then God spoke to him, "Now go back and give unto others what I have given unto you." The Japuji is Nanak's first offering after he returned from God.

Now, this is a story; what it symbolizes must be understood. First, unless you lose yourself completely, until you die, you cannot hope to meet God. Whether you lose yourself in a river or on a mountaintop is of little consequence, but you must die. Your annihilation becomes his being. As long as you are, he cannot be. You are the obstacle, the wall that separates you. This is the symbolic meaning of drowning in the river.

You too will have to lose yourself; you too will have to drown. Death is only completed after three days, because the ego does not give up easily. The three days in Nanak's story represent the time required for his ego to dissolve completely. Since the people could only see the ego and not the soul, they thought Nanak was dead.

Whenever a person becomes a sannyasin and sets out on the quest for God, the family members understand and give him up for dead. Now he is no longer the same person; the old links are broken, the past is no more, and the new has dawned. Between the old and the new is a vast gap; hence this symbol of three days before Nanak's reappearance.

The one who is lost invariably returns, but he returns as new. He who treads the path most certainly returns. While he was on the path he was thirsty, but when he returns he is a benefactor; he has left a beggar, he returns a king. Whoever follows the path carries his begging bowl; when he comes back he possesses infinite treasures.

The Japuji is the first gift from Nanak to the world.

To appear before God, to attain the beloved, are purely symbolic terms and not to be taken literally. There is no God sitting somewhere on high before whom you appear. But to speak of it, how else can it be expressed? When the ego is eradicated, when you disappear, whatever is before your eyes, is God himself. God is not a person—God is an energy beyond form.

To stand before this formless energy means to see Him wherever you look, whatever you see. When the eyes open, everything is He. It only requires that you should cease to be and that your eyes be opened. Ego is like the mote in your eye; the minute it is removed, God stands revealed before you. And no sooner does God manifest, than you also become God, because there is nothing besides Him.

Nanak returned, but the Nanak who returned was also God Himself. Then each word uttered became so invaluable as to be beyond price, each word equal to the words of the Vedas.

Now let us try to understand the Japuji:

Ek Omkar Satnam
He is one. He is Omkar, the supreme truth.
He is the creator, beyond fear, beyond rancor.
His is the timeless form,
Never born, self-creating.
He is attained by the guru's grace.

He is one: Ek Omkar Satnam.

In order to be visible to us, things must have many levels, many forms. That's why whenever we see, we see multiplicity. At the seashore we see only the waves, we never see the ocean. The fact is, however, only the ocean is, the waves are only superficial.

But we can see only the superficial because we have only external eyes. To see within requires internal eyes. As the eyes, so the sight. You cannot see deeper than your eyes. With your external eyes you see the waves and think you have seen the ocean. To know the ocean, you must leave the surface and dive below. So in the story Nanak did not remain on the surface, but dived deep into the river. Only then can you know.

Waves alone are not the ocean, and the ocean is much more than a mere collection of waves. The basic fact is that the wave that is now, after a moment no longer will be; nor did it exist a moment ago.

There was a Sufi fakir by the name of Junaid. His son, whom he loved dearly, was killed suddenly in an accident. Junaid went and buried him. His wife was astonished at his behavior. She expected him to go mad with grief at the death of the son he loved so dearly. And here was Junaid acting as if nothing had happened, as if the son had not died! When everyone had left, his wife asked him, "Aren't you sad at all? I was so worried you would break down, you loved him so much."

Junaid replied, "For a moment I was shocked but then I remembered that before, when this son was not born, I already was and I was quite happy. Now when the son is not, what is the reason for sorrow? I became as I was before. In between, the son came and went. When I was not unhappy before his birth, why should I be unhappy now to be without a son? What is the difference? In between was only a dream that is no longer."

What was formed and then destroyed, is now no more than a dream. Everything that comes and goes is a dream. Each wave is but a dream; the ocean is the reality. The waves are many, the ocean only one, but we see it as so many waves. Until we see the unity, the oneness of the ocean, we shall continue wandering.

There is one reality, truth is only one: Ek Omkar Satnam. And, says Nanak, the name of this one, is Omkar. All other names are given by man: Ram, Krishna, Allah. These are all symbols, and all created by man.

There is only one name that is not given by man and that is Omkar, and <u>Omkar means the sound of Om</u>.

Why Omkar?—because when words are lost and the mind becomes void, when the individual is immersed in the ocean, even then the strain of Omkar remains audible within him. It is not a man-made tune but the melody of existence. Omkar is the very being of existence; therefore Om has no meaning. Om is not a word but a resonance that is unique, having no source, no creation by anyone. It is the resonance of the being of existence. It is like a waterfall: you sit beside a waterfall and you hear its song but the sound is created by the water hitting against the rocks. Sit by a river and listen to its sound; it is caused by the river striking against the banks.

We need to go deeper to understand things. Science tries to break down the whole of existence. What it first discovered was energy in the form of electricity, and then charged particles like the electron of which all of existence is made. Electricity is only a form of energy. If we ask a scientist what sound is made of, he will say that it is nothing but waves of electricity, waves of energy. So energy is at the root of everything. The sages say the same thing; they are in agreement with the scientists except for a slight difference of language. Sages have come to know that all existence is created out of sound, and sound is only an expression of energy. Existence, sound, energy— all are one.

The approach of science is to analyze and break things down, to reach the conclusion. The sage's approach is absolutely different: through synthesis they have discovered the indivisibility of the self.

The wind rises creating a murmur in the branches of the tree, a collision of air against the leaves. When the musician plays a chord on an instrument, the sound is produced by a blow. All sound is produced by an impact, and an impact requires two—the strings of the instrument and the fingers of the musician. Two are necessary to form any sound.

But God's name is beyond all separateness. His name is the resonance that remains when all dualities have faded and cease to exist. Within this indivisible whole you come across this resonance. When a person reaches the state of samadhi, Omkar resounds within him. He hears it resounding inside him and all around him; all creation seems to be vibrating with it.

He is struck with wonder when it first happens knowing that he is not creating the sound. He is doing nothing and yet this resonance is coming—from where? Then he realizes that this sound is not created by any impact, any friction; it is the anahat nad, the frictionless sound, the unstruck sound.

Nanak says: Omkar alone is God's name. Nanak refers to name a great deal. Whenever Nanak speaks of His name—"His name is the path," or "He who remembers his name attains"—he is referring to Omkar, because Omkar is the only name that is not given to Him by man, but is His very own. None of the names given by man can carry you very far. If they do go some distance towards Him, it is only because of some slight shadow of Omkar within them.

For instance the word Ram. When Ram is repeated over and over it begins to transport you a little, since the sound "m" in Ram is also the consonant in Om. Now if you keep repeating it for a long time, you will suddenly discover that the sound of Ram subtly changes into the resonance of Om, because as the repetition begins to quieten the mind, Omkar intrudes and penetrates Ram; Ram gradually fades and Om steps in. It is the experience of all the wise men that no matter with what name they started their journey, at the end it is always Om. As soon as you start to become quiet, Om steps in. Om is always there waiting; it only requires your becoming tranquil.

Says Nanak: "Ek Omkar Satnam."

The word *sat* needs to be understood. In Sanskrit there are two words: sat means beingness, existence, and *satya* means truth, validity.

There is a great difference between the two, though both contain the same original root. Let us see the difference between them.

Satya is the quest of the philosopher. He seeks truth. What is the truth? It lies in the rules whereby two plus two always equals four, and never five or three. So satya is a mathematical formula, a man-made calculation, but it is not sat. It is logical truth but not existential reality.

You dream in the night. Dreams exist. They are sat/reality, but not satya/truth. Dreams are—or else how would you see them? Their being is there but you cannot say they are true, because in the morning you find they have evaporated into nothingness. So there are happenings in life which are true but not existential. Then there are other occurrences that are existent but are not logically true. All mathematics is true but not existential; it is satya but not sat. Dreams are; they are existential, but they are not true.

God is both. He is sat as well as satya, existence as well as truth. Being both, He can neither be fully attained through science, which probes truth, nor through the arts, which explores existence. Both are incomplete in their search, because they are directed only towards one half of Him.

The quest of religion is entirely different from all other quests. It combines both sat and satya: it is in quest of that which is more authentic and true than any mathematical formula. It is in quest of that which is more existential, more empirical, than any poetic imagery. What religion seeks is both. Looking from any one angle, you will fail; from both directions, then only shall you attain.

So when Nanak says "Ek Omkar Satnam," both sat and satya are contained in his expression. The name of that supreme existence is as true as a mathematical formula and as real as any work of art; it is as beautiful as a dream and as correct as a scientific formula; it contains the emotions of the heart, and the knowledge and experience of the mind.

Where the mind and the heart meet, religion begins. If the mind overpowers the heart, science is born. If the heart overpowers the head, the realm of art is entered: poetry, music, song, painting, sculpture. But if head and heart are united, you enter into Omkar.

A religious person stands above the greatest scientist; he looks down on the greatest artist, because his search contains the essentials of both. Science and art are dualities; religion is the synthesis.

Nanak says: "Ek Omkar Satnam."

He is one, he is Omkar, the supreme truth.
He is the creator ...

To take them literally limits your understanding of Nanak's words. It will be a mistake.

One difficulty of the sage lies in the need to use words in general usage. He has to talk to you and so he must speak your language, but what he means to say is beyond words. Your language cannot contain it; it is very limited, whereas truth is very vast. It is just as if someone were trying to compress all the sky into his house, or to gather all the light within his palm. Yet he has to use your language.

It is because of words, because of language, that there are so many sects. For instance, Buddha was born two thousand years before Nanak and used the language of his time. Krishna was born yet another two thousand years before Buddha. His was quite a different kind of language because he belonged to a different country, a different climate, a different culture, and so it was with Mahavira and Jesus. The difference is one of language alone, and languages differed because of people; otherwise there is no real point of difference between the enlightened ones. Nanak made use of the language prevailing during his lifetime.

Nanak says, "He is the creator." But at once the thought arises: "If He is the creator, and we are the created, that establishes a difference between the two," but Nanak has denied duality in the very beginning, saying that "God is one." It is language that is responsible for all the obstacles, and these will increase as we proceed further into Nanak's words.

The first words uttered by Nanak after samadhi were: "Ek Omkar Satnam."

Now the fact is that the entire Sikh religion is contained in those three words. Everything else is merely an effort to teach you, to help you understand. Nanak's message was complete in these three words. Because it was not possible for ordinary people to understand the message directly, an effort had to be made to expand on it. Explanations are given out of your inability to understand; otherwise Nanak had said all he wanted to convey:

"Ek Omkar Satnam." The mantra was complete. But for you it has no meaning yet. These three words alone cannot solve the mystery for you; then language must be used.

God is the creator. But realize that He does not stand apart from his creation. He is absorbed and one with all that He has created. This is why Nanak never separated the sannyasin from the householder. If the creator was separate from his creation, then you would drop all worldly activities in order to seek Him, abandoning the shop, the office, the marketplace. Nanak did not give up his worldly duties till the very end. As soon as he returned from his travels he would go to work in the fields. All his life he ploughed the fields. He named the village in which he settled, Kartarpur, which means the village of the creator.

God is the creator, but do not think He is separated from His creation. When man sculpts an idol and the idol is completed, the sculptor and the sculpture are no longer one; they are separate. And the sculpture will remain long after the sculptor is dead. If the image fractures, the sculptor is not also broken, because the two are separate. But there is no such distance between God and His creation.

What kind of relationship exists between God and His creation? It is like a dancer with his dance. When man dances can you separate him from his dance? Can he return home leaving the dance behind? If the dancer dies, the dance dies with him. When the dance stops, he is no longer the dancer. They are united. This is why since ancient times, Hindus have looked upon God as the dancer, "Nataraj." In this symbol the dancer and the dance are one.

The poet is no longer related to his poem, once it is finished. The sculptor is separated from his sculpture as soon as it is completed. A mother gives birth to a child, and they are separate; the father is always distinct from the child. But God is not distinct from His creation; He is contained in it. It would be more accurate to say: the creator is the creation, or the creator is nothing but creativity.

Discarding all idea of separateness Nanak says there is no need to renounce or run away from the world. Wherever you are, He is. Nanak has given birth to a unique religion in which householder and sannyasin are one. He alone is entitled to call himself a Sikh who, being a householder is yet a sannyasin; who, being a sannyasin is still a householder.

You cannot become a Sikh merely by growing your hair or wearing a turban. It is difficult to be a Sikh. It is easy to be a householder or to be a sannyasin, but to be a Sikh you have to be both. You have to remain in the house—but as if you are not there, as if you are in the Himalayas. Keep running the shop, but maintain the remembrance of His name ever throbbing within; you can count your cash but take His name along with it.

Before attaining samadhi, Nanak had many small glimpses of God—what we call *satori*. The first occurred when Nanak was working in a grain shop where his job was to weigh wheat and other grains for the customers. One day as he measured, "One, two, three... " he reached the number thirteen. Now the number thirteen is *tera* in the Punjabi language. "Tera" also means "yours." When Nanak reached thirteen, tera, he lost all consciousness of the outside world because he was reminded of his beloved lord.

He would fill a measure and repeat "Tera, Thine, Thou." Again and again he filled it... "Tera"—as if all numbers ended at tera. Tera became his mantra. The destination was reached; everything ended at tera for Nanak. People thought him mad and tried to stop him, but Nanak was in a different world altogether: "Tera! Tera! Tera!" He could not move past tera. There was nothing beyond it.

There are really only two halting places; one is I and the other is you. You start with I and finish at you.

Nanak is not against the mundane world. In fact he is in love with it, because to him the world and its creator are one. Love the world and through the world, love God; see Him through His own creation.

When Nanak came of age, his parents told him to get married. Nanak did not refuse, though people feared he would because his ways were so different from others' since his childhood. His father was very much troubled on his account. He could never understand Nanak—all these devotional songs and always in the company of holy men.

Once he sent him on a business trip to the adjoining village with twenty rupees to buy some goods for resale at a profit. Since the way of business is to buy cheaply and sell at a higher price, his father told him to buy something which would be profitable. Nanak made a few purchases. On the way back he came across a band of holy men who had not eaten for five days. Nanak pleaded with them to come to his village instead of sitting there expecting food to come to them.

"But that is the vow we have taken," they replied. "God will provide when He pleases. We are happy to abide by His will. Hunger is no problem to us."

Now Nanak thought to himself, "What can be more profitable and worthwhile than feeding these great holy men? I should distribute among them my food I have bought. Didn't my father say to do something profitable and worthwhile?"

So he gave away to the sadhus whatever he had brought from the village, though his companion, Bala, tried to stop him, and said, "Are you mad that you do that?"

Nanak insisted: "I am doing something worthwhile, as my father wished," and returned home very pleased with himself.

His ways were strange and his father was very angry. "What a fool you are. Is this how you make a profit? You will ruin me!"

Nanak answered, "What could be more profitable than this?"

But nobody else could see the profit either, much less Kalu Mehta, Nanak's father. He could not see any good in this act. He was certain the boy had gone astray in the company of these holy men and lost his senses. He hoped marriage would make him more reasonable. People generally think that since the sannyasin renounces women and runs away, the way to keep a man in the world is to tie him to a woman. This trick did not work on him because Nanak was not against anything.

When his father told him to get married Nanak readily agreed. He married and had children, but this did not change his ways at all. There was no way to spoil this man, because he saw no difference between God and the world. How can such a person be defiled? If a man leaves wealth behind to become a sannyasin, you can tempt him just by giving him riches. If another has left a wife behind, give him a woman and in no time he falls. But how can you spoil a man who has left nothing? There is no way to bring about his downfall. Nanak cannot be corrupted.

My view of the sannyasin is similar to Nanak's, because he is a formidable sannyasin who cannot be corrupted. <u>He who sits right in your world and yet is not</u> <u>of it can in no way be tempted</u>.

This God Nanak refers to as the creator, the fearless, because fear is when the other is. An expression of Jean Paul Sartre has become famous: "The other is hell." It describes your experience. How often do you want to escape from the other, as if he is the source of all your trouble? When the other is closer to you, the turbulence is less than when the other is more remote, stranger. But the other is always troublesome.

What is fear? Fear always involves the other: if someone can take something away from you it destroys your security. Then there is death and there is illness—both are the other. Hell is being surrounded by the other; hell *is* the other.

But how can you escape the other? Should you run away to the Himalayas you will still not be alone. Sit under a tree; a crow's dropping falls on your head, and you are filled with anger towards the crow. There are the rains and the sun—irritations everywhere. How will you escape the other who is present everywhere? The only way to escape the other is to seek the one; then no other remains. Then all fear fades away. There is no death, no illness; there are no inconveniences, because there is no other. Finally you are alone. Fear persists as long as the other remains the other for you.

"Ek Omkar Satnam." Once this mantra has penetrated your being, where is fear? God has no fear. Whom should He fear? He is the only one, there is no one besides him.

He is the creator, beyond fear, beyond rancor.
His is the timeless form.
Never born ...

Understand that time means change. If nothing chan-ges you will not be aware of time. You cannot tell the time if the hands of the clock do not move. Things are changing constantly: the sun comes out and it is morning; then it is afternoon, then evening. First there is the infant, then the youth, then the old man. A healthy man becomes ill, an ill person becomes healthy; a rich man becomes a pauper, a pauper becomes a king. There is constant change. The river is forever flowing. Change is time.

Time means the distance between two changes.

Just imagine getting up one morning and no events occurring till evening. There are no changes: the sun stands still, the hands of the clock do not move, the leaves do not wither, you do not grow older—everything is at a standstill. Then how will you know the time? There will be no time.

You are aware of time because you are surrounded by change. For God there is no time because He is eternal, perpetual, immortal. He is forever. For Him nothing is changing; everything is static. Change is the experience of sightless eyes that do not see things in their full perspective. If we could see things from the furthest vantage point all change drops away, and then time stops; it ceases to exist. For God all things are as they are; nothing changes, everything is static.

His is the timeless form.
Never born, self-creating.

He is not born of someone. God has no father, no mother. All who are begotten by the process of procreation enter the world of change. You have to find within your own self the unborn one. This body is born, it will die. It is born by the conjunction of two bodies; it will disintegrate some day. When the bodies that gave birth to it have perished, how can something remain which is a component of the two?

But within this, there is also that which was never born but has nevertheless come with the embryo. It was there even before the formation of the foetus, and without it the body will one day return to no more than clay. The timeless has penetrated within this body; the body is no more than a piece of clothing to the timeless. That which is beyond time dwells within the time-bound. Only when you attain the timeless being within your own self will you be able to understand Nanak's words. You have to seek within yourself that which never changes, that which is changeless.

If you practice just sitting with your eyes closed, you will be unable to make out within yourself what age you are. You would feel yourself the same inside at the age of fifty as you felt at the age of five—as if time has not passed for the world within you. Close your eyes and you will discover that nothing has changed inside.

What is changeless within is not born through the womb. You have come through your parents, but they are only the path for your coming; they do not bestow life on you. You have passed through them because the requirements of your body were nourished by them, but what has entered into your body has come from beyond. The day you attain the unborn within you, you will know that God has no origin, no source, because God is the entirety; He is the aggregate of all things. God means the totality. How can the totality be born to a particular someone? There is nothing beyond totality for there to be a mother and father, so He is "Never born, self-creating."

The meaning of self-creating is that He exists by Himself and has no support except His own; He is self-begotten and has no origin. The day you glimpse, however briefly, this fact within yourself, you will be rid of all anxieties and worries. Why do you worry? Your worry always arises out of your dependence on things, because any support can be snatched away from you at any moment. Today you have wealth? It may be gone tomorrow. What will you do then if you consider you are rich because of your wealth, not because of yourself?

A sannyasin is rich by his own right; he is rich because of himself so you cannot rob him of his riches. What will you steal from Buddha or from Nanak? You cannot make them poorer by taking anything from them; you cannot add to their wealth nor subtract from it. Whatever Nanak is derives from being one with the supreme support. You have nothing to lean on.

The supreme being is not a separate entity. God is without support. The day you too are prepared to be without support, your union with God will take place.

This definition of God is not the philosopher's interpretation, but is valid for the seeker so that he may know the characteristics of God. If you want to attain God, you will have to make these characteristics your religious practice. You have to try to be God in a small way. As you gradually begin to become like Him, you will find a rhythm establishing itself and a resonance struck between you and God.

Never born, self-creating.
He is attained by the guru's grace.

Why does Nanak say "by the guru's grace"? Is not man's own labor enough? It is necessary to understand this very subtle point, because Nanak stresses the guru a great deal. Later Nanak says that without the guru God cannot be attained. What is the reason for this? If God is omnipresent why can't I meet Him directly? What is the need to bring in the guru?

Krishnamurti says there is no need of a guru at all. This idea appeals to the intellect and to reasoning. What need to introduce the guru since I am born of God, as is the guru? Mind does not approve of the guru; so a congregation of egoists revolve around Krishnamurti. What he says is perfectly correct, that there is no need of a guru—provided you are capable of annihilating your ego yourself.

But it is as difficult to drop the ego yourself as it is to lift oneself up by your bootstraps. It is just like a dog trying to catch his tail. The quicker he turns, the further his trail swishes away. If, however, a person is competent enough, then Krishnamurti is absolutely right that no guru is necessary.

But here lie all the complications. No sooner have you somehow conquered your ego than you will say, "I have dropped my ego," and there you introduce a new form of ego even more dangerous than the old. The guru is needed so that this new ego is not born. Even as you say, "By the grace of the guru," you can convey by your behavior: "See how humble I am! No one can be more humble!" And now these new paths are etched out by the ego. Till yesterday you were proud of your wealth; today you are proud of its renunciation and your humility. The rope is burned but the twists remain. How is this arrogance to be destroyed? —hence Nanak's emphasis on the guru.

There is no difficulty in attaining God directly, because He is present right in front of you. Wherever you go, there He is. But the one difficulty is that *you* stand within yourself, and how will you remove this interfering you? Hence, "the guru's grace." The seeker may labor but the attainment will always be by the guru's grace. This concept of the guru's grace will not allow your ego to form. It will destroy the old ego and prevent the new from forming; otherwise, you rid yourself of one ailment and contract another.

A very funny situation has arisen. A crowd of egoists have collected around Krishnamurti, people who do not wish to bow before anyone. They are completely at ease since they don't have to touch anyone's feet; they bow to no one. They firmly believe that the guru is not required, they will arrive by themselves. And this itself is the difficulty.

If there were a person like Nanak or Ramakrishna around Krishnamurti then his message would have been effective, but the crowd around him consists of those very people who are unable to drop their egos—the ones in most urgent need of a guru. This is the ultimate irony: all those around Krishnamurti *need* a guru. Those who surrounded Nanak were people who could have done without a guru.

Now, you might say this is all a riddle, but it is a fact that those around Nanak would have arrived even without a guru, because they were people ready and eager to accept the guru's gift; they were ready to renounce their own selves. The attainment comes without the guru, but the idea of the guru is effective in destroying the ego so that you are not filled with arrogance for whatever you accomplish. Otherwise you will boast, "I can stand on my head for three hours, and I meditate every morning!"

The wife of a Sikh gentleman once complained to me: "Things are getting out of control. My husband comes to see you, so please advise him."

"What is the matter?" I asked.

"He gets up at two in the morning and begins to recite the Japuji. It is impossible for the rest of the family to sleep. If I complain he tells us that we should all get up and chant too! What should we do?"

I called the husband to me. "When do you recite the Japuji?" I asked him.

"Early every morning, about two," he replied proudly.

"That is proving to be quite a nuisance to others," I said.

"That is their fault," he said. "They are lazy and indolent!—they should all get up at that time. Besides, I'm doing them a service by reciting aloud so that the holy words can fall not only on the family's ears but the neighbour's as well."

"Take it easier with your practices," I advised him. "You can get up at four in the future." You have to bring down such a person by degrees, or else it is impossible to bring him down at all.

"Never!" he replied. "I never expected to hear such words from you. Do you want to rob me of my religion?" He couldn't believe his ears.

Now this was his arrogance—that no one could recite the Japuji like him. This alone is his obstacle. You may repeat the Japuji all life long, but the real need is to destroy your arrogance.

Therefore Nanak says time and again, "Nothing can be attained by whatever you do, unless you eradicate your own self." This concept of the guru is a priceless alchemical device to annihilate the ego, because whatever you do, you just say, "It is all the grace of the guru." "I am doing" is the difficulty. If you can eradicate your I without any help, you do not need a guru. But it is one in a million who can do this; he is the exception for whom we need not make any rules or regulations.

It happens sometimes that some person drops his ego without the help of a guru, but it requires a very deep and profound understanding which you do not have. The understanding should be so deep that you can order your ego to stand before your eyes—and by your mere looking, the ego *must* drop. Your eyes must be like the eyes of Shiva, through whose very glance the god of love turned to ashes. You should have such awareness. A Buddha, a Krishnamurti, surveys the ego with such intensity that it melts into nothingness. No other feeling then arises in its place; and they are not even aware of having done something, it just happens.

But you are not they. Whatever you do, a voice within constantly repeats: "I have done this, I have done that...." If you sing hymns, you are conscious that *you* are singing the hymns. If you meditate, the feeling within is: "*I* am meditating." With your prayer or your worship your ego is replenished and recreated every moment.

Let us leave these one-in-a-million exceptions aside, because they are bound to attain. For the millions of others there is only one way: whatever they do, whatever practice or ritual or repetition, the feeling should be that whatever results is due to the guru's grace.

He was truth before the ages began and as time ran its course.
Nanak says, Now is He truth eternal, and forever will He be.

There is a very old saying in India that during the Sat Yuga, the age of truth, the guru was not needed much, but in Kali Yuga, the age of darkness, the guru will be a necessity. What is the reason? The Sat Yuga was the period when people were very alert, full of awareness. In the Kali Yuga people are insensitive, slumbering, almost unconscious.

Therefore the religions of Buddha or Mahavira born in the Sat Yuga, are not of as much use in today's world as the religion of Nanak. Nanak's religion is the newest, though it too is now five hundred years old. We need another new religion, because those who heard Mahavira and Buddha were relatively more alert than us; they were also wiser, simpler and more artless. And even further back, the people who listened to Krishna were even more aware and alert.

As we move backward we find more innocence...just as when a person recounts his life backwards, he arrives at the period of his childhood. In infancy he is simple and innocent; in youth he begins to become complicated. It is difficult to conquer an old man filled with wisdom. He knows nothing and yet he feels he knows everything. He has been thrown about by life. Through his suffering he feels he is very experienced; he has gathered trash and he thinks he has collected diamonds.

The child is simple, innocent; he is the symbol of Sat Yuga. The old man is highly complicated, and his insensitivity increases day by day as death is drawing near—he is symbolic of Kali Yuga. The child's consciousness is very fresh because the fountain of life is very close to him. He is like a wave just arisen from God. The old man is dirty, weighted down by dust, and about to fall back into God. The child is a fresh bud; the old man is a withered flower whose life breath is just about spent.

Kali Yuga means that period where the end is near. Life is now old. In Kali Yuga you cannot, under any circumstances, do without the guru because you will be constantly filled with ego. When each little thing that you do fills you with ego, how will you not be filled with arrogance when you do your spiritual practice? If you build a small house and pride yourself on it, fill your treasure chest and your conceit will know no bounds; and when you start on the quest for the supreme treasure your self-importance and vanity will be unfathomable.

Notice the contemptuous look of the man who goes to the temple or to the mosque towards those who do not. His eyes tell you: "You sinners will rot and burn in hellfire! Look at me! I pray every day and I am saved." He recites, "Ram, Ram," and thinks the gates of heaven are open for him and all others will go to hell.

The greater your insensitivity, the more somnolent you are, the greater your need for a guru. Understand that. If you are fast asleep, how can you awaken yourself? Someone else will have to shake you. Even then the chances are that you will roll over and fall back asleep again.

He was truth before the ages
and as time ran its course.
Nanak says, Now is He truth eternal,
and forever will He be.

This is the definition of satya, truth, and asatya, untruth. "Satya" is that which never was, which now is, but again will fade into nothingness. It means that which is nonexistent at both ends and exists only in the middle. Take dreams for example: during the night as you slept, dreams existed; in the morning when you awake the dream is lost, and then you say that dreams are untrue.

Once in the past your body did not exist, and one day again it will cease to be. Thus body is a falsity. Anger comes; a moment before it was not there, and after a while it shall again not be there. Anger is like a dream because it is not truth. Only that is true which is forever. If you can only grasp this thought and allow it to penetrate you deeply, your life will undergo a transformation. Don't be taken by things that are not. Seek only what is unchanging and unmoving.

Who it is within you who never changes, look only for him. All changes occur around him like the shaft of the wheel: it never moves but the wheel revolves around it and because of it. If you remove the shaft the wheel falls. All changes that take place occur around the eternal; the hub of the soul is static, while the wheel of the body revolves around it. No sooner does the hub disintegrate than the wheel falls apart.

Nanak says that God alone is the truth, that one alone, because He was beyond all beginning of things. He still is; He always will be; He is forever. All else is a dream. Let these words penetrate deep within you.

When anger comes or hatred or greed, repeat these words to yourself. Let it remind you of what is real, what is true. Remember, what wasn't before but which now is , can only be a dream and will fade away. There is no need to become too involved in it, but maintain the attitude of the witness.

Gradually, all that was useless will fall away from you on its own because your connection with it has broken; and that which is useful, meaningful, will begin to take root within you. The eternal has begun to arise, the world has begun to fade away.

We cannot comprehend Him though we think a million times;
Nor quiet the mind by silence, however long we sit;
Nor a mountain of bread appease the hunger of the soul;
Nor one hundred thousand feats of mind achieve unity with Him.
How can truth be attained and the veil of falsehood torn?
Nanak says, By submission to the divine order which is preordained.

This is a very valuable sutra. It is the quintessence of Nanak's teachings. With all our thinking we cannot think of God. We think a million times yet we cannot think about Him. Nobody has ever arrived at Him by thought; in fact we have lost Him through excessive thinking. The more we think, the more we lose ourselves in thought.

God is not a concept, not a thought. He is not the settlement of an argument, not an outcome of the mind. God is truth. Thinking isn't relevant—you have to *see*. By thinking you will only wander. You have to open your eyes, but if they are filled with thoughts and concepts, they will remain sightless. Only eyes without thoughts enable you to see.

It requires what Zen masters call no-mind, which Kabir names the *unmani* state, the state of no-mind. Buddha refers to it as the dissolution of the mind and Patanjali named it *nirvilkalpa samadhi*, the samadhi without thoughts. They are all describing the same state in which all doubts and debates end. This is what Nanak is referring to.

We cannot think of God even with infinite thoughts, although we think a million times. By keeping quiet we cannot attain this silence, although we can remain in continuous meditation.

Why is it that with all our thoughts we are not able to conceive of Him? Why is it that we cannot attain silence by effort?

You will find that the harder you try, the more impossible it is to become silent. Certain things cannot be attained by effort. Sleep cannot be brought about by effort; the harder you try, the more difficult it becomes. The essence of sleep is the absence of all effort; then only does sleep come. Effort keeps you awake, but stretch out on the bed completely relaxed with all activities suspended and sleep comes. Similarly, how can you make yourself silent? You may force yourself to remain seated in a buddha–like posture while the mind keeps boiling within.

Nanak was a guest of a Mohammedan nabob. For Nanak there were no Hindus and no Mohammendans; the sage observes no secretarian boundaries. The nabob said to Nanak, "If you really mean what you say—that there is no Hindu, no Mohammedan—then come along with us to the mosque. Since today is Friday, let us pray together."

Nanak readily agreed, but he insisted, "I shall offer prayers only if you also pray." The nabob replied, "What a strange condition to set! That is exactly why I am going."

The news spread like wildfire through the village. Everyone gathered at the mosque. The Hindus were greatly upset, and the members of Nanak's family were particularly abusive; everyone thought Nanak was becoming a Mohammedan. In such a way do people burden others with their own fears.

Nanak reached the mosque and the prayers were begun. The nabob was very annoyed with Nanak, because, whenever he turned around to look, he found Nanak still erect, neither bowing nor offering prayers, but just standing like a statue. The nabob raced through his prayers as quickly as possible, because how can a person pray when he is angry? Finally he turned to Nanak and said, "You are a fraud. You are neither saint nor seeker! You promised to pray but you never did."

Nanak said, "I did promise, but have you forgotten the conditions? I said I would pray provided you also prayed. But you didn't, so how could I pray?"

"What are you saying? Are you in your right senses? There are so many witnesses here; everyone saw me offering prayers!"

"I can't believe these other witnesses because I was looking within you all the time. You were buying horses in Kabul."

The nabob was taken aback because that was exactly what he was doing. His favorite horse had died just that morning and he was still strongly affected by the loss of such a fine animal. His mind was preoccupied with how to reach Kabul as early as possible to buy another thoroughbred. To him a horse was a symbol of status and honor.

"And the priest who led the prayers," continued Nanak, "was busy gathering the harvest in his fields." The priest admitted that he was worried about his harvest that was ready to be reaped. "Now please tell me, did you offer your prayers so that I could offer mine?"

You force yourself to pray, you force yourself to worship, to meditate—it is all meaningless. By bending the body into certain postures you cannot force the mind to follow suit. The cacophony of the mind continues, and in fact it becomes louder and more intense. When the body was engaged in some activity the energy was divided. Now when the body sits absolutely inactive, all the energy flows to the mind and the thoughts spin at even greater speed!

This is why when people sit to meditate, the mind becomes more and more active ... a real avalanche of thoughts cascading one upon the other! You sit to worship, but the marketplace still grips your thoughts. You go to the temple and ring the bells, but the mind races in other directions. Normally the mind is not so restless. You go to see a film and the mind is quiet and you feel at peace, but no sooner do you enter the temple or mosque or church, it becomes its most restive. What is the reason? The theater is linked to your desires. In the movies all the things that you are filled with are brought out, all the rubbish, all the trash. It strikes a chord within you. In the temple what you hear touches nothing within, and hence the confusion.

Nanak is saying that by enforcing silence you will gain nothing, because you cannot attain *that* silence. Even if you remain in constant meditation, nothing is going to happen. The hunger cannot be appeased even by a mountain of bread, because this is not a hunger that can be appeased by bread. The hunger for meditation, the hunger for God, is not an ordinary hunger. Nothing of the world can appease it. This thirst is unique. It can only be quenched if God Himself descends on the seeker.

How can we become authentic, true? How can the veil of falsehood be destroyed? The answer, says Nanak, is to follow when God orders, according to His wish alone. Everything should be left in His hands; everything should be left to His will, to His design, and that alone will help.

How can truth be attained and the veil of falsehood torn?
Nanak says, By submission to the divine order which is preordained.

Nothing will happen by your doing. Whatever you do, it will be your doing. Even when you tell a truth, because it arises out of your false personality, it will be a falsehood. From where can you utter truth when you are absolutely false?

Nanak was a guest of Lalu, a poor carpenter. The rich landlord of the village was performing a religious sacrifice to which he had invited the whole village. He sent a special invitation to Nanak. When Nanak did not appear the landlord himself came to bring him along.

He said, "How can you refuse to come to my mansion and partake in such a feast? Everything is of the best and purest ingredients, and it is specially prepared by brahmins who have first bathed and performed their rituals. Can you refuse this food cooked with the water of the Ganges and prefer the meager meal of this lowly carpenter who is not even a brahmin?"

Nanak said, "If you insist, I will go with you," but he asked Lalu to follow him and bring his food.

It is said—and this is a symbolic story—that Nanak took Lalu's dry bread and squeezed. A stream of milk poured forth. With the other hand he squeezed the landlord's bread and a stream of blood came out.

Nanak said to the landlord, "You cannot hide your impurity. Whether you have your food cooked by brahmins, whether you clean each grain with the Ganges water, it makes no difference. Your whole life is one long tale of exploitation, deceit, theft and lies. Blood is hidden in every bite of your bread."

Whether blood actually came out of the bread or not is inconsequential, but the story deals with truth. Only if you are true in your very being, can you be truth. Otherwise who can remedy it?

Nanak says nothing will happen by your doing. You are dishonest, so dishonesty will creep into your truth also. Your truths will somehow be made to serve your dishonesty, and in such a way that it harms others. You will look for such truths that will pierce another person's heart. Before you harmed the world with your lies, now you harm the world with your truths. Whatever you do will be wrong if you are wrong.

What is the cure? Nanak says the only remedy is to leave everything to God: His will be done. Await His pleasure. Live the way He wants you to. Be whatever He wants you to. Go wherever He takes you. Let His command be your one and only spiritual practice. Brush aside hopes and desires, and fill yourself with wonder and gratitude. If He has brought you sorrow there must be a reason behind it, some meaning, some mystery. Do not complain but be filled with gratitude. "Come joy, come sorrow, keep me as Your will!" If He has kept you poor, welcome poverty; if He has made you rich, be grateful. In happiness or in sorrow let one tune play incessantly within you: "I am happy the way You keep me. Your command is my life."

Suddenly you will find yourself tranquil. What did not happen through a thousand meditations begins merely by leaving all to His will; and it is bound to happen, because now there is no cause to worry.

What do you mean by "worry"? Worry arises whenever things are not happening as you wished them. Your son lies dying; that should not happen, is your worry. You have done bankrupt; this should not be, is the anxiety. You are trying to impose your will on existence. Things should not have happened as they have happened, and things should not be happening as they are happening: this is your anxiety, and then you suffer because of it.

With all these troubles plaguing you, you sit down to meditate. What can you do but go on reaping your harvest or buying a horse in Kabul! Your anxieties infiltrate and take over your meditation. Then how can you possibly become tranquil? There is only one formula for this: *Accept whatever is.* If you grasp it, you have understood the entire quest of the East from Lao Tzu to Nanak.

The ancient name for this is fate or destiny. The words have been spoiled as all words are through long usage, because the wrong kind of people use them and hence attribute wrong meanings. Now to insult someone as irresponsible or old-fashioned you accuse him of believing in fate. Nanak says: *By submission to the divine order which is preordained.* Everything should be left in His hands; everything should be left to His will, to His design, and that alone will help.

Think, take a chance, experiment a little; live as He wishes you to. Haven't you tried hard enough? Are you any better off than you were? You are perhaps more deformed, but certainly no better than what He made you. You have not even preserved the innocence and simplicity that were yours in infancy. You have filled to capacity the book of your life with your scribbling. It stands spoiled, defiled, and what have you gained besides suffering, pain, tension and remorse?

Try to listen to Nanak's words and act on them for a few days. "Leave all unto Him," Nanak says—no prayers, no mantra, no penance, no meditation, no resolutions. There is only one spiritual practice—His wish. As soon as the thought is nourished deeply within you that all happens at His command, an intense peace, a gentle shower inside washes away all tension, all anxiety.

The West is filled with anxiety and tension. It is much more prevalent than in the East in spite of the East's backwardness, its poor and its diseased; there is not enough to eat or to cover the body, nor even a roof over everyone's head. The West has everything, and yet it is filled with such tension and anxiety that large numbers of people are on the verge of breaking down or require tranquilizers.

What is the reason? It is clear. The West has tried to force its own will on existence. The West has tried to have its own way. Western man has faith only in himself; we shall do everything for ourselves. There is no God! And he *has* done a great deal, but the man is almost lost as he is turning schizophrenic. He has performed wonders outside, but within himself everything has become sick and diseased.

If this verse penetrates you, nothing remains to be done. Just let things happen by themselves. Do not swim, float. Do not fight with the river because it is not your enemy but your friend. Float! By fighting, you create enmity; when you swim against the current, the river opposes you. It is not the river but you who introduces the struggle. The river flows along its course; it is not even aware of you. Of your own will you begin swimming against the tide. You are asserting your will by going in the opposite direction, and that means you are nourishing and strengthening your ego.

His wish...and you become one with the current. Now wherever the river takes you is the destination. Wherever it takes you is the shore. It if drowns you, that is your destination. Then where is the anxiety, then where is the pain? You have cut off the very roots of suffering. What Nanak says is invaluable—that all be left to God's will and command. Only by following the path he has etched out for you can everything happen.

Nanak has closed all doors on the ego: first, by emphasizing the guru's grace—that whatever you attain through your effort is attained only by the guru's grace—and then, that whatever happens, wherever the current of life takes you, is by His command. Then nothing remains to be done. Then it will not be long before you realize that:

We cannot comprehend Him though we think a million times;
Nor quiet the mind by silence, however long we sit;
Nor a mountain of bread appease the hunger of the soul;
Nor one hundred thousand feats of mind achieve unity with Him.
How can truth be attained and the veil of falsehood torn?
Nanak says, By submission to the divine order, which is preordained.

Chapter 2

The Weight of a Flower

By divine order all form was created,
But His order cannot be described.
Divine order has created all life,
And by it all greatness bestowed;
By divine order are some high and some low,
And pain and pleasure granted;
By His order do some attain salvation,
Or endlessly wander through cycles of death and birth.
All are subject to His order; none is beyond His reach.
Nanak says, He who understands His order becomes freed from his self.

Those who know power will sing of His might.
Knowing charity, some sing of His bounty as the sign.
Some sing of His virtues and His greatness.
Some sing of His knowledge, when scholarship is their bent.
Some sing that He creates the body and turns it back to dust.
Some sing that the life He takes will again be reborn.
Some sing that He is far, far away.
Some sing that He sees all and is everywhere.
There is no end to His attributes,
Though a million describe Him in a million ways.
The giver gives eternally, though the receiver tires of receiving;

Since the beginning of time have they subsisted on His endless bounty.
He is the ordainer and by His order does the universe turn.
Says Nanak, He is without a care, endlessly blissful.

THERE ARE TWO ways of living. One is the way of conflict, the other is the way of surrender. In conflict you feel that your will is different from the will of the whole. In surrender you feel that you are a part of the whole, with no question of your will being different or apart. If you are aloof and apart, conflict is natural and inevitable. If you are one with the whole, surrender is natural. Conflict brings tension, restlessness, worry, and anxiety. Surrender brings emptiness, peace, joy and finally the supreme knowledge.

The ego thrives on conflict and is destroyed in surrender. The worldly man is always in conflict; the religious man has given up all struggles and surrendered himself. Religion has nothing to do with your going to a church or a mosque or a Sikh temple. If your tendency is to fight, if you are struggling even with God, if you are trying to enforce your own will—albeit through prayer or worship—you are irreligious.

When you have no desire of your own, then His wish is your wish; if you have no separate goal of your own, wherever He takes you is your destination. When you are ready to move as He pleases, when you have no expectations of your own, when you make no decisions, then you cease swimming and begin to float.

Have you watched a hawk soaring high in the sky? When it has flown to a sufficient height, it stretches its wings wide and floats in the air. When your mind reaches that stage it is in a state of surrender. You need no longer flap your wings, you merely float, weightless in His atmosphere. For all weight is caused by conflict; it is born through resistance. The more you fight the lower you fall.

The more you abandon the fight, the lighter you become; and the lighter you are, the higher you soar. If you leave all conflict completely, you reach God's heights, which signifies being free of all burden, weightless. Ego is like a stone tied round your neck; the more you fight, the heavier it becomes.

Once Nanak happened to camp by the side of a well outside a village inhabited by Sufi fakirs. Early the next morning when the head of the Sufis came to know of Nanak's arrival, he sent Nanak a cup of milk filled to the brim. It was so full that not a drop could be added. Nanak broke a flower from a nearby shrub, put it in the cup and sent it back to the Sufi guru. The flower floated on the milk, because what weight has a flower? Nanak's disciple, Mardana, was puzzled and asked Nanak what all this meant.

Nanak explained: "The Sufi's message said there was no room, that the village is so full of sages that it can accommodate no more. My reply let him know that I shall ask for no extra space, because I am as light as the flower and shall float at the top!"

He who is unburdened is a sage. He who has weight is still ignorant and his weight can harm others until he is completely free of all burdens. Nonviolence occurs on its own. Love flowers on its own. No one can bring about love or implant compassion; if you become free of all burdens, it all happens on its own. As a shadow follows a man, so hatred, anger, malice and violence follow the man weighted down with anxiety. Love, compassion, pity, prayer follow in the wake of a weightless person. So the primary issue is to annihilate the ego within.

There is only one way to annihilate the ego. The Vedas have referred to it as *Rit*; Lao Tzu calls it *Tao*; Buddha has called it *Dhamma*; Mahavira's word is *Dharma*;

Nanak refers to it as *Hukum*—divine order. He who conducts himself according to His command without making a single movement on his own, with no desires or feelings of his own, or need to introduce his own self, is alone the religious man.

And he who puts himself under His command attains all; there is nothing left to be attained. To obey His command is the gateway to His heart. To believe in oneself is to turn your back on God; obey His will and you face Him again. You may lead your life with your back to the sun and you will never be able to shake off the darkness; no sooner do you turn your face towards the sun than the darkness of innumerable lives vanishes. The only way to stand before God is to leave your own will. To float is enough. There is no need to swim and carry a load unnecessarily. All defeats and all victories are diseases of your own ego.

Your condition is like that of the fly who sat on the hub of a huge chariot wheel which raised an immense cloud of dust as it moved. The fly looked around and saw nothing but dust. It said to itself, "I am raising so much dust that I must be very big myself!" Whether you are successful or suffer defeat, it is all because of this dust. You are nothing more than the fly on the chariot wheel, so don't bring in your puny self by thinking it is you who is raising the dust. The dust is of His chariot, as is the journey.

You must have heard the story of the lizard. Once his friends invited him for a walk in the jungle. "I am sorry, I can't go," he answered, "because if I were to leave, who will support the ceiling of the king's palace? If the ceiling falls, the responsibility will be mine." The poor thing thinks so much depends on it! And if it is possible for a lizard to think so....

Then there was the old lady who owned a rooster that crowed every morning as the sun came out. The old woman became haughty and arrogant. She told the villagers to be careful of their manners towards her because if she went away to another place with her rooster, the sun would rise no more for them.

Now it was a fact that every day when the cock crowed the sun came out, but the villagers laughed and made fun of her. They told her she was out of her senses. Finally in anger the old woman left and went to another village. There also the cock crowed and the sun came out. She thought, "Now they will beat their breasts and cry. The rooster is no longer there to make the sun rise!"

Your arguments and the old woman's logic are very similar. It has never happened that the cock has crowed and the sun did not come out, yet you have it all backwards. But who can explain this to the old woman and make you understand too? When the old woman saw the sun come out in the new village she was certain that if it had risen there, it could be nowhere else.

Your intelligence and capacity to think is also so limited. God is not because of you; you are because of Him. Your breath flows from Him, not because of you. It is not you who prays; it is He who prays through you.

If this feeling penetrates your understanding, Nanak's priceless words will become clear. Each word is a jewel.

> By divine order all form was created,
> But His order cannot be described.
> Divine order has created all life,
> And by it all greatness bestowed.

Nanak uses the word hukum, which means the divine order or the cosmic law which governs all of existence. All life is born out of the divine order, and it is hukum that gives you greatness.

When you are successful, do not consider yourself the victor. Then you will not consider defeat as your defeat. It is He who is victorious, it is He who is defeated. All is His play. In fact the Hindus look upon the whole world as play. This signifies that it is He who wins and He who loses. He wins with one hand and loses with the other; however, the apparent winners and the losers, who are no more than a means, an implement, mistakenly consider themselves doers.

Krishna says to Arjuna in the Gita, "Don't bring yourself into things. It is He who does, and He who gets things done. It is He who has brought this battle about. He will kill those He wants to kill, He will save those He wants to save. Do not imagine that you are the killer or the savior." What Krishna has expressed in the whole Gita, Nanak has said in this sutra: It is He who has created the great and the small.

Let us ponder over this: if it is He who has created all things great and small, then no one is big, no one is small, because all are His creations. You make a small idol, you make a big idol, but you are the sculptor of both. When there is but one maker, what issue can there be which is big or small? Our trouble throughout life is that we think in terms of great and small. No matter how hard we try, we cannot become great enough to satisfy our ego.

As soon as you begin to see the hand of the formless within yourself, you immediately become great. The maker is one. He who makes the lowliest flower also creates the majestic pine tree that seems to touch the skies! If the hand behind both is one and the same, who is great and who is small? The victory is His, the defeat is His. We are just pawns in the chess game.

You must have heard many a devotee saying: All that is good in me is Yours; all that is bad is mine. On the surface the devotee attributes all his virtues to God while holding himself responsible for all his shortcomings. This apparent humility is not genuine, because if all the goodness is His, how can all the badness be yours? Genuine egolessness would give way completely at the feet of the Lord, keeping nothing for itself—not even the bad. It is the ego in the garb of humility that holds back this little support for itself. However much you may insist, how can success be His and failure yours, goodness be His and evil yours? This talk is hollow; it holds no substance. Either both are His or both are yours.

There is a difference between true humility and false humility. False humility says: I am only dust at your feet. When a person says that to you, look into his eyes and you will see that he expects you to say, "Oh, no! How can you say that? It is I who am dust at *your* feet." If however you accept his statement and say, "Yes, you are quite right. That is exactly what I think," then you have earned an enemy for life. He will never forgive you.

All praise is His, all blame His. We have no part in it. We are but the bamboo flute; let Him play on it as He will. It is still arrogance that says: If there is any fault it is mine—because then the ego is still preserved. The I is such a disease: guard even a speck of it and the whole is saved. Either you let go of it completely or it remains completely, hidden safely within you.

Nanak says: All forms have arisen out of the divine order. It cannot be expressed in words. All that is most significant in life cannot be put into words. Divine order is the most significant. There is nothing beyond it. Words are adequate only for the purpose they ordinarily serve, to carry on our day-to-day life. But there is no way of expressing the extraordinary in words. There are many reasons for this.

Knowledge of the supernatural occurs only in silence. And what is experienced in silence, how can that be expressed in speech? Silence and speech are antithetical. When He is experienced within there are no words, only complete silence. How can you find in words what you have known in emptiness? The medium has changed. Emptiness is a different medium altogether—the formless—whereas words have shape and form. How can you give form to what is formless? This has been a problem for all who have known. How can it be expressed? Imagine hearing a beautiful song and trying to explain it to a deaf person.

There is an old Sufi story: A deaf shepherd was grazing his sheep near a mountain. It was afternoon, long past the usual hour his wife brought his lunch and he was very hungry. As she had never been late before he began to worry whether she was taken ill or had met with an accident. The shepherd looked around and saw a woodcutter perched high on a tree. He reached up to him and said, "Brother, would you keep an eye on my lambs? I would like to run home and get my food."

Now, as it happened, the woodcutter also was deaf. He said, "On your way! I have no time to waste in idle gossip." The shepherd understood from his gestures that he had agreed to his request. He ran home as fast as he could and returned with his food. He counted his sheep and all was in order. He thought it would be nice to offer a gift to the woodcutter as a gesture of his gratitude and good will. Having a lame sheep which he would have to kill some day, he took it with him to where the woodcutter was.

Now when the woodcutter saw the shepherd with the lame lamb, he cried out in anger, "What? Do you mean to say I made her lame?"

The more the shepherd offered the lamb to him, the louder shouted the woodcutter. Now it happened that a horseback rider who had lost his way came upon the two. He meant to ask them the way but immediately the two of them caught hold of him. As luck would have it, the rider, who also was stone-deaf, had just stolen the horse and was riding away with it. When these two caught hold of him he thought they must be the owners of the horse. Meanwhile the shepherd asked him earnestly to explain to the woodcutter that he was presenting the lamb as a gift to him.

The woodcutter said, "Please tell this man I did not so much as look at his sheep, much less make this one lame!"

The horseman said, "You may take back the horse. I admit my guilt, please forgive me."

While all this confusion was going on a Sufi fakir happened to pass by. All three rushed at him, caught hold of his clothing and begged him to clear things up for them. The fakir had taken a lifelong vow of silence, and although he understood each of their problems, what was he to do? He looked deep and long into the eyes of the rider, who began to get restless. He thought this man was hypnotizing him. He became so frightened that he jumped on the horse and rode away.

Now the fakir turned and looked piercingly at the shepherd who also felt he was losing consciousness. He quickly gathered his sheep and went on his way. When the fakir turned to the third man, he was equally frightened.

The fakir's eyes were very powerful. Those who observe prolonged silence develop a unique luster in their eyes. All the energy accumulates and the eyes become the channel for expression. When the fakir looked at him deeply, he quickly tied his bundle of sticks and went off. The Sufi laughed and continued on his way. He had solved their problem without saying a word.

This is the difficulty that holy men experience, and there are not only three who are deaf; there are three billion deaf in this world! And each one makes his point but nobody listens; nobody hears anybody else. There is no dialogue in life, only debates and disputes. What is the saint to do then? He has developed the art of silence so there is no way to speak. Besides, however much he speaks, as in the case of the Sufi fakir, deaf men are never able to follow. He would only have added to the confusion. So he merely looked deep into their eyes.

The saint has always tried to solve your problems by looking deep into your eyes. He tries to pour into your eyes what is contained within himself. Therefore Nanak talks a great deal of the company of saints. He says: Associate with holy men if you want to know what they have known. Keep the company of saints, because mere hearing and talking will not take you far. You will be told one thing, you will interpret it in another way—people are deaf. You will be shown something and you will see something else—people are blind. You will draw your own conclusions, give different meanings to the saints' words.

Nanak says the divine order cannot be expressed, yet hints can be given. These hints are not mere words, because the divine order cannot be contained in the words. These words are like milestones telling you that you are on the right path, that the destination lies ahead. Many cling to the milestones and go no further.

You can also do this. If you get up each morning and merely repeat the Japuji you will know the Japuji by heart and no more. You will be clinging to the milestone! Instead, travel the way the Japuji directs you to go. Understand it; don't cling to it. Travel you must, because religion is a journey, but to hold on to Japuji or the Koran or the Bible or the Gita is clinging to the milestones. Understand them, go forward and the mystery will unravel itself !

> *By divine order all form was created,*
> *But His order cannot be described.*
> *Divine order has created all life,*
> *And by it all greatness bestowed.*
> *By divine order are some high and some low,*
> *And pain and pleasure granted.*

Think a little: when you are unhappy, you hold the other responsible for your sufferings. If you must do this, hold the divine order responsible. When the husband is unhappy he blames his wife, when the wife is unhappy she lays the blame on her husband. The father holds the son responsible, the son rebukes the father. If you must hold someone responsible, let it be the divine order. You cannot settle for less.

It is most ironic that when you are in trouble you blame another, but when you are happy you take the credit entirely for yourself. What logic is this?—happiness is on your own account, but your unhappiness you put on another's account! This is why you can neither overcome your sufferings nor unravel the secret of happiness, because you are wrong on both counts: neither is the other responsible for your sufferings nor are you responsible for your happiness. God alone is responsible for both. And if joy and sorrow come to you from the same hand, why make a difference between the two?

There was a Mohammedan king. He was very fond of a particular slave, and the slave worshipped his master. One day as they were going through a forest the king saw one lone fruit hanging from a tree. The king picked it and as was his habit, he gave some of it to the slave. When the slave tasted it he said, "Master, give me a little more."

The slave asked for more and more till there was hardly any left for the king. Yet he kept insisting and even tried to snatch what remained from the kings hands. The king quickly put the remaining bit in his mouth but spat it out immediately.

"Have you gone mad?" he shouted at the slave. "This fruit is poisonous and you stand there smiling at me! Why didn't you tell me?"

The slave fell at his master's feet as he said, "The hands that gave me the sweetest of fruits—should I complain against those hands if they gave me but one bitter fruit?" Notice that he ignored the fruits, but only took account of the hands.

The day this wisdom dawns on you, that it is through His hands alone that sorrow comes to you, then would you still look upon it as pain? You only know suffering as suffering because you do not see His hand behind it. The day you realize that both joy and sorrow are given by Him, they lose their impact. Then happiness will no longer raise you up nor sorrow produce pain. When joy and sorrow become equal to you, bliss appears to take their place. When the duality of joy and sorrow ceases, the indivisible descends and you are filled with bliss!

Do not hold anyone around you to blame—neither husband nor wife, neither son nor daughter, neither friend nor foe. Let God be the owner of all responsibility. When joy comes or success, don't fill your ego. He is master of all success, the owner of any rewards, of all sweet fruits! If you leave everything to Him, joy and sorrow disappear and only bliss will remain.

By divine order are some high and some low,
And pain and pleasure granted.

By His order do some attain salvation,
Or endlessly wander through cycles of death and birth.
All are subject to His order; none is beyond His reach.
Nanak says, He who understands His order becomes freed from his self.

Once you understand the essential, that all is His, what remains of the I? There is no one left to say I. Understand that you desire to get rid of the ego when it causes you pain; yet the trouble is, it is the same ego through which you can experience happiness. That ego gives you pain is well known: when a person abuses you, your ego feels hurt and you want to be free of it.

People come and ask me how they can be freed from sorrow. They also say they know that it is the ego that is the cause of all suffering. Then they ask how to get rid of the ego. I tell them: How is not the question. If you really felt that the ego was the cause of all your ills, you would have abandoned it long ago. There is no need then to ask!

But it is not so simple; you want to rid yourself of the ego half of the time; you want a fifty-fifty arrangement. The same you that is hurt by accusation and wants to get rid of the ego is delighted when praise comes and the ego feels nourished. Make a mistake and you suffer, perform well and you are delighted; when people abuse you it hurts, when they sing your praises you are all smiles. Both alternatives take place on the plane of the ego.

The trouble is that if you let go of the ego your joys will end along with your sorrows. You want to preserve your happiness and be rid of unhappiness. This has never happened, nor can it ever happen. If they stay, they remain together; if they go, they depart together. They are the two sides of the same coin. You want to throw away one side and keep the other. Since that is impossible, you alternate: one minute you throw the coin aside and the next you pick it up again. You can't keep—or abandon—one side without the other.

Understand the plight of the ego: if you leave both sorrow and joy to God, who is the authentic source of all life, your ego has no place to stand. Then how will you say, "I am"? I is nothing but a collection of all your actions. It is not an object, and has no independent existence. If you let go of the doership and say, "You are the doer, I am only an instrument," then where is the ego? Then whatever He directs, you do; whatever He does not direct, you do not do. If He makes you a sinner, you are a sinner; if He makes you a saint, you are a saint.

Try to understand the uniqueness of Nanak's statement. He says that only through divine order does a person attain knowledge, and it is through divine order alone that a man wanders through countless cycles of life and death. What Nanak means to convey is that if you are a sinner do not brand yourself a sinner. Rather, say His will.

You might think there is the danger of a person gaily committing crimes blaming His will. The crux of the matter is that once a person knows it is all His will, whatever he does is a worthy deed. As long as you do not know, there is a continuous conflict between you and Him, which by definition, gives rise to sin. Sin is the result of the struggle between you and God. This conflict brings about the state of inflicting suffering on oneself as well as on others. The day you leave everything to Him, all sins flee.

Nanak says that too is happening through Him. If you are a sinner, it is He; if you are a saint, it is He. Don't think it is you who has done the good deed nor that it is you who has committed the sin. The very concept "I have done" is an error, a mistake.

There is only one ignorance; it lies in the belief that I have done.... There is only one knowledge; it consists in recognizing the ultimate creator. The creator does everything; I am only the means, the instrument. There is no one and nothing outside of the divine order. Everything resides within it.

Those who know power will sing of His might.
Knowing charity, some sing of His bounty as the sign.
Some sing of His virtues and His greatness,
Some sing of His knowledge, when scholarship is their bent.
Some sing that He creates the body and turns it back to dust.
Some sing that the life he takes will again be reborn.
Some sing that He is far, far away.
Some sing that He sees all and is everywhere.
There is no end to His attributes,
Though a million describe Him in a million ways.
The giver gives eternally, though the receiver tires of receiving;

Since the beginning of time have they subsisted on His endless bounty.
He is the ordainer and by His order does the universe turn.
Says Nanak, He is without a care, endlessly blissful.

His definitions are countless, and still incomplete. How can man who is himself incomplete define the complete? Whatever he says will be incomplete. How can the part bear witness to the whole? Whatever the part utters will relate only to itself. Can the atom know the absolute? Whatever it understands cannot transcend itself.

So those who can sing, sing of His attributes, and yet the unknown remains unknown. The Upanishads sang His praises till they were tired, as did the Gita, the Koran, the Bible. He is indescribable, undefinable—He is made that way. It has been impossible to define Him completely. All scriptures are incomplete and they are bound to be, because they are limited to man's effort to manifest the infinite.

The sun comes out, and the artist paints a picture of it. However well he paints, the picture will give off no light. You cannot keep the painting in a dark room and expect the room to be lit by it. If a poet witnesses the sunrise and writes a beautiful song about it, no matter how earnest and profound the feelings he conveys, his song cannot light the darkened room.

All songs sung in praise of God, all pictures representing His attributes, are incomplete. No song can tell of Him completely, because we cannot bring His being down into them. Words are hollow and must remain hollow. If you are thirsty, the word water will not quench your thirst. If you are hungry, the word fire is not going to cook your food. And if the desire for God has arisen within you, the word god is not enough. It is enough only for those with no desire.

Understand well: if you are not thirsty, the word water or H_2O is enough to name it. But if you are thirsty, the difficulty begins. Then neither the word water nor the symbol H_2O works. You may gather together all the words for water—there may be three thousand languages in the world—and tie them round your neck, they will not yield a single drop of water. If you are not thirsty, you may play with the words.

Philosophy is a game for people who are not thirsty. Religion is the journey of those who are thirsty. Therefore philosophy plays with words; not so religion. Religion takes cognizance of the hints the words give and follows them. When the quest is for the lake, what can the word lake do? When the search is for life, the word life alone sounds hollow.

Let us understand a little about a profound question facing the philosopher. A tourist comes to India and he is given a map of India. What is the relationship between

India and the map? If the map is the same as India then it must be as vast. If it is exactly like India, it would be useless, because you couldn't carry it in your car, much less put it in your pocket. If it is not like India, how can it still be useful?

The map is a symbol. It is not like India and yet by means of its lines, it conveys useful information about India. You may roam the whole of India without ever seeing a map of India. Wherever you go you will find India; the map is nowhere to be seen. But if you have the map with you and understand it and use it, the journey will be made easier. By either keeping the map in your pocket, or by looking at the map and never leaving your room, you will not learn a great deal. Both together make for the fullest understanding of the experience.

Religious people the world over hold the maps to their chests as if the maps were the actuality, the totality. Scriptures, holy books, images, temples, all contain hidden pointers that keep the maps from being just a burden. The Hindu is carrying his load of maps, the Mohammedan his, the Christian his. The maps have become so numerous that the journey is now almost impossible, so weighted down are you by maps. The maps should be short, abridged, and they are not to be worshipped in themselves, but to be utilized on the journey.

Nanak drew his essentials from both the Hindu and the Mohammedan religions. He cannot be called Hindu nor Mohammedan; he is both or neither. It was very difficult for people to understand Nanak. There was a saying: Baba Nanak is the king of the fakirs. He is the guru of the Hindus and the saint of the Mohammedans.

He is both. Of his two special disciples, Mardana and Bala, one was Hindu and the other a Mohammedan. Yet Nanak has no place in the Hindu temple or in the Mohammedan mosque. Both doubt his position and do not know where to place him. Nanak is the confluence of the two rivers, of Hinduism and Islam. He harvested the essence from both. Therefore the Sikh is neither Hindu nor Mohammedan; they must be both or none since their religion arises out of their junction.

Now it is difficult to understand this confluence; when there is a river on the map it is clear-cut, but here two rivers have become one. Some words relate to Islam while others reflect Hinduism, and together they become hazy, but gradually the fog clears when you enter into the experience. If you keep Nanak's words on your chest as you do other scriptures, it becomes like any other holy book—and we do find the Sikh worshipping his words as if they were the guru. Is it not astonishing how we repeat our mistakes?

Nanak went to Mecca. The priests there told him to be careful not to point his feet toward Kaaba while he slept. As the story goes, Nanak's reply was that they should turn his feet where God was not, and, it is said, the holy stone of Mecca turned wherever they turned his feet. The symbolism means only this: wherever you turn your feet, there God is. Where will you put your feet if He is omnipresent?

I was invited to the Golden Temple at Amritsar. When I went they stopped me at the entrance saying I must cover my head before entering the place of God. I reminded them of the incident with Nanak at Kaaba and asked them, "Does it mean that right here where I stand with my head uncovered, there is no God, no temple? We keep on repeating our mistakes!" I further asked, "Then please show me a place where I can be without a headcovering. And don't you remove your turbans while bathing, and while sleeping? Then isn't that also an affront to the Lord?"

Man's foolishness is the same everywhere. Whatever Buddha says, his followers paint with their own brush to suit them. And so also with Nanak. The same web is woven once a master has pronounced his words, because man's foolishness has not changed, nor has his deafness improved. He hears, but he draws his own individual conclusions which he then follows accordingly, never putting into practice what he actually hears.

Nanak says, no matter how many songs are sung about the lord, nobody has covere it completely. Different people sing different songs because there are many paths to reach Him. However antithetical their songs may seem there is no contradiction anywhere because they all contain the same message. The Vedas say exactly what the Koran says, but the method by which Mohammed reached is different from Patanjali's approach. Buddha also says the same thing but his method is entirely different.

Infinite are the gates to His abode. Whichever way you go leads to His gate. Once arrived you can begin to define the gate through which you entered, and describe the path you have trodden. Another person will likewise describe his own door and his road. Besides, it is not only the path that differs, but your understanding, your perception, your emotional attitude all play a significant part.

When a poet enters a garden, he sings in ecstasy; an artist would paint a picture; if a flower-merchant comes along, he will think in terms of sale and profit; a scientist will analyze the flowers or soil to find out their chemical composition and why they grow; a drunk will be oblivious to the beauty around him, he will not even know that he went through a garden. Whatever you see passes through the windows of your own eyes which impose their own color on everything.

Says Nanak: Some sing the praise of His power—He is all powerful, omnipotent. Some sing of His benefaction and munificence—He is the supreme giver. Some sing of the glory of His attributes, His beauty—He is the most beautiful. Some call Him truth, some call Him Shiva, some call Him the beautiful.

Rabindranath has written: I found Him in beauty. This says nothing of God; rather, it tells of Rabindranath. Gandhi says: For me, He is truth—truth is God. This speaks of Gandhi rather than of God. Rabindranath is a poet; for a poet God resides in beauty, supreme beauty. Gandhi was no poet, he is practical, and it is natural that such a mind sees God as truth. From the point of a lover—He is the beloved.

How we see Him reflects our insight. He is everything simultaneously and also—none of these. In this context Mahavira's reflection is wonderful. He says: Unless and until your sense of vision drops, you cannot know Him. For whatever you will know, you will know through your own seeing; it will be your view of knowing. Mahavira calls his method no-view. Seeing only occurs when all vision drops.

But then you will lapse into silence, because how will you speak without a viewpoint? When you are freed of your vision, you will become like Him; because you will be so extensive, so comprehensive, you will be one with the open skies. How will you speak? You will no longer be separate unto yourself, but one with the absolute. A viewpoint means that you stand apart from what you see; to have a viewpoint means that you are separate from Him.

Therefore Nanak says that all the viewpoints are correct but none is complete; when the partial is proclaimed as complete and perfect, the illusions begin. Any sect or organization claims one particular incomplete vision as

कोई इन्हें वापिस "

perfect. One sect stands against another, whereas all sects are different aspects of religion, and no one sect is a religion. If we were to amalgamate all possible sects that have been, that are and that will be, then religion would be born. No sect on its own can be called religion.

The word for sect in Hindi, *sampradaya,* also means the path, that which takes you to the goal; whereas religion, dharma, means the destination. The destination is one, the paths, many.

> Those who know power will sing of His might.
> Knowing charity, some sing of His bounty as the sign.
> Some sing of His virtues and His greatness.
> Some sing of His knowledge, when scholarship is their bent.
> Some sing that he creates the body and turns it back to dust.
> Some sing that the life he takes will again be reborn.
> Some sing that He is far, far away.
> Some sing that He sees all and is everywhere.
> There is no end to His attributes,
> Though a million describe Him in a million ways.
> The giver gives eternally, though the receiver tires of receiving.

In spite of saying it millions of times, there is much more left unsung. The benefactor gives and gives and gives, while the receiver drops with exhaustion.

These are very significant words. It is He who gives life. It is He who breathes your breath. It is He who pulsates in every heartbeat. He keeps on giving...giving. There is no end to His giving, and He asks for nothing in return.

As a result you mistakenly feel life to be a cheap commodity and other things appear expensive. You are always ready to abandon life and aliveness but not wealth; because wealth is acquired with great difficulty and life is given you without any effort on your part—it comes free! Whatever He has given you, He has given freely and you have given nothing in return.

When this begins to occur to you, you begin to question your own worthiness for all that you have received: Would it have mattered one bit if I were not? The life potential, the flowering of consciousness that has bloomed within you—if it had not, to whom would you have complained? And what is your worth that makes you eligible for life? How have you earned it?

For every small thing in life you need proof of worthiness. To be a clerk in an office or a schoolteacher, you have to be qualified for the post; you have to earn your place in life. How have you earned your life itself? It is a gift freely given and not because of some special qualification of yours. The day you begin to realize this, prayer will arise within you. You will say, "What shall I do to express my gratitude? How shall I repay Thee?"

Prayer is not begging but an expression of gratitude for what is already received. Prayer of another kind, when you go to the temple to ask for something, is false prayer.

Nanak also goes to the temple, but only to express his thanks and gratitude: I cannot believe all that You have given me! I see no reason why You should cover me with so many gifts, because I am not worthy. If You do not give I have no complaints, but You are such that You give and give...and give.

And we? It would be difficult to find more thankless people than us. We offer no thanks, show no gratitude. His gifts are unending and our ungratefulness knows no bounds! We cannot so much as thank Him; we find it so difficult our throats seem to choke.

You are ready to say thank you if you drop your handkerchief and someone picks it up for you, but you have no word of thanks for the one who has given you life. If you ever go to pray, it is always a complaint. You tell

Him of all the wrong He is doing: "My son is ill, my wife does not treat me well, my business is failing." And you exaggerate your complaints so! You manage to convey: "You aren't there. And if You are, why don't You satisfy all my desires ?"

Atheism means that your complaints have reached such a pitch that you can no longer believe there is a God. Your complaints kill God.

And what is the meaning of theism? You are so filled with gratitude and thanksgiving that you see Him all around you. Everywhere you see His hand, everywhere His reflection; everywhere you feel His presence. Theism is the peak of thanksgiving; atheism, the nadir of complaints.

> *The giver gives eternally, though the receiver tires of receiving;*
> *Since the beginning of time have they subsisted on His endless bounty.*

Enjoy Him as much as you will, you cannot exhaust Him. To empty an ocean with a teaspoon is more possible, because whereas the scope of the spoon is limited, so also is the ocean limited. But you can never drain God because He is boundless. For aeons upon aeons you have been enjoying His bounty but never has a word of thankfulness risen from your heart to proclaim how grateful you are that all He has given is boundless. Whenever you have spoken, it has always been to express your dissatisfaction, emphasizing your worthiness and minimizing what you received.

A high official came to visit me from Delhi. The higher the post the greater is the number of complaints. He felt he was treated very unjustly and should have become a minister, preferably prime minister. He said, "Show me how to bear up under this injustice I have suffered."

Every person lives with this pain that he has not been awarded what he deserved. He who was worthy of becoming a vice-chancellor, lands up an ordinary schoolmaster; another feels he should be the master, but becomes a peon. And it goes on and on. Even the prime minister aims at becoming an international figure, having attained the highest position in his own country. You cannot satisfy an Alexander the Great—and everyone is an Alexander in his own right—big or small.

Desires always go ahead of you, as you think yourself worthy of more and more. These are the characteristics of an irreligious person. A religious person believes: Whatever I am given is beyond my worth.

Think it over for yourself. Whatever life has given you—is it more or less than what you deserve? It is always more—much more. For we have done nothing to earn this vast existence that we have attained unasked and undeserved, and yet there is no sign of gratefulness within us!

Nanak says we cannot exhaust Him even by partaking of Him for infinite ages. The divine order shows the way through His command.

Here is a very deep clue, a critical part of Nanak's thoughts: He governs the world through His commands and is forever ordering you. Had you the slightest ability to listen, you could understand His command and flow accordingly. But you never listen!

You go to steal. He tells you inside, "Don't, don't!" twice, a thousand times. But you do as you please. The voice gradually becomes weaker and weaker until you become deaf towards it. Then you don't hear Him at all though He keeps calling.

There is not a single sinner who has lost his internal voice, the voice of the divine order. You cannot find the most evil person whom He has stopped calling. He never tires of you; He is never disappointed; He never considers you beyond redemption. However deep your illness, He has a cure. God has infinite hope, infinite potential. He is never disappointed in you.

There was a Sufi fakir by the name of Bayazid. His neighbor was a total rogue, a cheat, a criminal. He had committed every sin under the sun and the whole village was terrified of him. One day Bayazid prayed to God, "Oh Lord, I have never asked anything from You. But this man is now going beyond all limits. Please remove him from our midst."

At once the inner voice spoke to Bayazid: "I am not as yet tired of him, then why are you? And if I still have faith in him, why don't you?"

You cannot make Him tired of you, no matter how much you sin for unnumbered lives. You cannot outlive Him. He keeps on calling. He never gives up on you.

And if you become silent for a moment and listen, you will surely hear His voice within you. Whatever you do, the internal voice ordains how you should do it.

He is the ordainer and by His order does the universe turn.

This is why Nanak calls Him the ordainer—for it is His order that comes. The consciousness that is within your heart is the instrument that brings His voice to you. He speaks through your consciousness. Before doing anything, close your eyes and listen to Him. If you obey His command, bliss will shower on your existence. To go against it is to create your own hell, by your own hands. Turn your back to the voice, and you are taking a dangerous step. Before deciding on anything, before taking any step, close your eyes and ask Him. This is the thread in all meditation, that first we shall ask—seek the voice, then proceed. We should not take a single step without His permission. We should close our eyes and hear His voice, and follow His voice, not ours.

Once you acquire this key, it will open infinite doors for you. The key is within you; each child is born with it. We develop the child's intellect but do nothing to develop its consciousness. It remains undeveloped, incomplete. We heap so many layers of thoughts over the voice, it gets hidden so deep that we no longer can hear it, though it calls all the same.

That art of hearing the inner voice is called meditation. It is imperative to know His command. We must know what He wishes, what is His will.

He is the ordainer and by His order does the universe turn.
Says Nanak, He is without a care, endlessly blissful.

He keeps on giving but expects nothing in return—not even an answer. He keeps calling out to you whether you hear or not. He does not care, He does not worry that you do not listen. He never feels He should stop since you have turned a deaf ear to Him, much less would He cast you aside as a lost cause.

You cannot make God anxious. And for this very reason, a man who has begun to see the reflection of God within himself has no anxiety. He will be simultaneously concerned and unconcerned. He will care for you and at the same time he will be carefree. You cannot make him anxious or worried.

Here I am! God knows how many people I am concerned about and yet I am carefree. You come to me with your woes and though I am concerned you do not cause me worry or anxiety. I do not become sad with your sorrow or

I would not be able to help you. Though I need to sympathize with your troubles and find ways and means to
lighten your distress, I cannot be so concerned that your
worry grips me too.

And I should not be displeased with you if you come
the next day without acting on my advice—which will
surely happen. I dont feel: I took so much trouble and you
disregarded my advice. I still care, and through it all I
remain carefree.

God is concerned about the whole world. He is forever
ready to raise you up but He is not in a hurry. And if you
wish to wander a little longer in fleeting pleasures, you
are welcome to do so, by all means, but then He is
carefree.

His concern is boundless and unaffected by you. He is
always full of bliss—or you can imagine what state He
would have been in by now! He would surely have gone
mad with all the people there like you, and what trouble
they are creating all around. God is one—and you are so
many. You would have pushed Him into madness long
ago; but existence is carefree, which is why it is saved
from going berserk.

Carefree does not mean indifferent. Note the subtlety.
His endeavors for you remain unchanged—His desire to
raise you, to change you, to transform you. But His desire
is nonaggressive. He will wait. Every morning the sun
and his beams knock at your door and your door is closed.
The sun will not force his way in. He will wait. It never
happens that he will be angry and turn back. Whenever
the door opens, he will come in.

God is concerned about you; existence cares about you.
This is bound to be true for existence creates you, has
developed you; it has great expectations of you. Existence

is endeavoring to become conscious within you, to attain buddhahood from within you. God is endeavoring to bring forth flowers within you. But if you delay, He will not be troubled, He will not be anxious; He remains unaffected if you do not listen to Him, or refuse to heed Him. If you can understand both these things together, then you will understand why existence is filled with bliss. God is bliss.

Nanak says: He gives commands, and shows the way, and yet He has not a care! He keeps evolving in supreme bliss. His flower keeps blooming—always and always.

For us there are only two possibilities: either we care and that gives rise to worry, or we are unconcerned and there is no anxiety. This is why tradition has separated the sannyasin from the everyday world. If you stay at home you are bound to be involved with the family, then how could you be unconcerned and carefree? If your wife is ill you will worry; if your child has some disorder you will worry about his treatment and be filled with pain if he does not improve. But if wife and children are not before our eyes, we shall forget them—out of sight, out of mind! So we run away to the mountains and turn our backs to the world, so that by and by we shall forget.

We see only two alternatives: if we stay in the world we cannot remain unconcerned, and if we are concerned we are bound to worry, then there is no way of being blissful. The other choice is to run away and become carefree and unconcerned, so without worry the prospects of bliss increase.

But this is not the way of God. Therefore Nanak remained a householder as well as a sannyasin. He was concerned and also unconcerned. And this is the art, the spiritual course—to be concerned and yet free from anxiety. Outwardly you do everything required of you, but nothing attaches to you inside. You educate your son and take great care of his upbringing; but if he turns out useless, or does not study, or fails in life, you are not worried.

Until you combine the two, and be a sannyasin within the household, you cannot reach God, because that is God's way. He is in the world and yet not of it. His way should be yours, on a lesser scale, in order to reach Him.

If the child is ill, take care of him with all the medical care he requires, but what is the need to be worried? What value is there in disturbing or destroying your internal carefreeness?

Outwardly be in the world, inwardly be in God. Let the outer physical boundary be in contact with the world but let the center remain untouched. This is the essence.

And this is what troubled people about Nanak—that he was a householder but he wore the robes of a sannyasin. People could not categorize him. The Hindus would ask: "Are you a householder or are you a sannyasin? You talk like a sannyasin, your way and manners are those of a sannyasin and yet...this wife and child? If you plow the fields and look after your family, what sort of a sannyasin can you be?"

The Mohammedans questioned him in the same manner. They would say, "You dress like a fakir: then why haven't you left your house and family?" At many places many gurus told him to leave everything and become their disciple. But Nanak did not budge from his path. He was constantly practicing the art of remaining outside of everything while remaining within everything, and that alone is the way of God; and that alone should be the way of the seeker.

People ask me: What are you doing giving sannyasins' robes to householders? But that is the way of God; He is in the world and yet not of it. And this should be your path too.

> *He is the ordainer and by His order does the universe turn.*
> *Says Nanak, He is without a care, endlessly blissful.*

He is cheerful, filled with bliss, blooming like a flower and yet He has not a care! He is concerned about you—but He does not worry.

Put this experiment into practice in your life: work, mind your shop, but let there be a distance between your work and your being. Let your work be a play, a leela, and do not be the doer, that is all. Be an actor, let the art of acting become your life's thread, because that is the way of God and that should be your way, your practice.

Chapter 3

Solving the Riddle

The Lord is truth. Truth is His name.
His praises are sung in endless ways.
Even while praising they ask for more and more,
And the Lord keeps on giving.
Then what offering can we make to gain a glimpse of His court?
And what language shall we speak to endear us to Him?
Nanak says, Remember the true name and meditate on its glory in the ambrosial hour.
Through your actions you receive this body,
And by His grace the door to salvation opens.
Nanak says, Know then His truth, because He alone is everything.

He cannot be installed in any temple, nor fashioned by any skill.
The faultless one exists unto Himself.
Those who serve Him attain the glory.
Nanak says, Sing His praises, Lord of all attributes.
Sing and hear only of Him; engrave Him in your heart.
So banish sorrow and suffering, and make bliss your abode. (આનંદ નિકેત)
The guru's word is the sound of sounds, and the Vedas too.
The Lord abides in his words.
The guru is Shiva, the destroyer; the guru is Vishnu, the sustainer;
The guru is Brahma, the creator; he is the trio of goddesses, Parvati, Laxmi and Saraswati.
However well I know Him, He cannot be described.

He cannot be expressed by words.
The guru is the secret that solves the riddle.
He is the benefactor of all. Let me never forget Him.

SAHIB, THE LORD, is the name given by Nanak to God. We can write about God in two ways. The way of the philosophers is to talk about God, but their words are dry and without love. Their words are intellectual and lack emotion completely.

The other is the way of the devotee. His words are juicy; he looks upon God not as a doctrine, but as a relationship. Unless there is a relationship the heart is not influenced. We can call God truth but what the word *sahib* conveys can never be conveyed by truth. How can we establish a relationship with truth? What would be the bridge that would connect truth to our heart?

The Lord is a loving relationship. The Lord immediately becomes the beloved and now we can be related; the way is open. The devotee longs for something that he can touch, something he can dance around, sing around. The devotee wants a place to lay his head. Sahib is such a beautiful, lovable name. It means: the master, the owner. Thus the relationship can be of many kinds.

The Sufis look upon God as the beloved, so the seeker becomes a lover. The Hindus, the Jews and the Christians have spoken of God as the father, so the seeker becomes a child. Nanak saw God as the lord and master so the seeker becomes a servant.

It needs to be understood that for each relationship the path is different. With the beloved we stand as equals: neither is higher, nor lower. The relationship between a father and son is a relationship of circumstances: because we are born in a particular household, so the relationship.

Since, given the opportunity, we ourselves would like to be the master and make God the servant, the role of servant best serves to obliterate the ego. The ego does not disappear either in the father-son relationship or the lover-beloved relationship; it can only drop away in the master-servant relationship.

And this is the most difficult relationship, because it is the state which is exactly the opposite of ego. Ego believes: I am the master, all existence is my slave. The devotee says: All existence is my master, I am the slave. And this is the authentic yoga headstand, not literally standing on one's head: you must let the ego touch the ground, because the ego is the actual head. Therefore it is the servant the devotee who practices the real headstand. He turns upside down. As you have observed the world through the eyes of a master, it is different from the world you see when you develop the servant attitude.

When a beggar begs from you, is there a chord struck within you which builds a relationship between you? No, just the opposite is the case. As soon as he asks, you shrink within; then even if you give, it is done unwillingly. You make a mental note not to pass that place again. When someone asks something of you, you pull back and want to withhold; when a person does not ask, you feel more like giving.

Try to understand yourself a little and the way towards God will become clear. When someone asks, you do not want to give because his asking seems like an act of aggression. All demands are aggressive. But when nobody makes demands on you, you become lighter and you give more easily.

Buddha had told his monks that when they went to the village to obtain alms, they were not to beg. They could only go and stand at a door; if there was no response they should move on.

This is the difference between a begging monk and a beggar. We have honored certain begging monks as we have never honored our kings; whereas beggars remain last in our minds. We barely hold them worthy of insult and try to avoid them. The monks asked, "How will people give if we do not ask?" Buddha replied, "Things are easily obtained in this world merely by not asking. As soon as you ask, you constrict the other and create difficulty for yourself. When you do not ask you make others eager to give."

You will find this story hidden in all life's relationships. Your wife asks for something, and giving becomes difficult. If you do get it for her, it is halfheartedly, only to ward off a quarrel. It arises not out of a bond of love, but as a way to maintain peace in the household. If the wife never makes demands you feel like giving her something. Giving is possible when not asked.

You are separated from God by your demands. All your prayers consist of: Give me! Give me! You want God to serve you. You wish to use Him as a servant. You say, "My foot hurts. Take away the pain.... My financial condition is bad, improve it." You say, "The wife is ill, make her well," or "I have lost my job, give me another." You always stand a beggar at His door. Your very asking shows you consider yourself the master whom God is to serve. Are your needs so important that you press even God into your service?

If God is the master and you are the slave then what is left of the demands? The most amazing thing was that you kept asking, and He kept on giving. It is not that you are refused when you ask—you keep on getting, but the more you get this way, as you keep on asking for more and more, the further away from Him you become.

A demand can never be a prayer. A desire can never be a prayer. A longing can never be worship. The essence of prayer is to offer thanksgiving and not ask for hand-outs. He has already given enough—more than necessary, more than we deserve. The cup is full to the brim and already overflowing.

The genuine devotee offers thanks, his prayer is full of gratitude, saying: You have given me so much, I am not fit to receive it all. And at the other extreme, there you stand: See the injustice, I deserve more. I want more!

Nanak says people keep on asking, and He keeps on giving. Yet there is no end to their asking. He keeps giving, and the beggars keep asking. If you are constantly asking, when will you pray? When will your worship begin? If you fulfill one desire ten others take its place. For how many births have you thus been asking? And you are still not full!

You can never be satisfied, because it is not the mind's nature to be full; its essential quality is to be unsatisfied. Only when one is rid of the mind, does satisfaction appear. You will never find a man who can say that his mind is satisfied. If you ever happen to hear someone say that, look deep into him because he is sure not to have a mind.

What is the mind but a collection of all your demands: Give, give and give more.... There is no greater beggar than the mind, caring not how much we receive. Even Alexander the Great was a beggar, no better than any beggar soliciting by the side of the road. It is necessary to understand the nature of the mind.

How can the mind pray, for prayer is a state of no-mind? The whole viewpoint is changed as soon as you put the mind aside. It means you have come for thanksgiving and not begging. Reintroduce the mind and you feel you don't have enough, you need more. Mind keeps its eyes on the absence of things. Abolish the mind and you begin to see existence.

It is like this: take a man who sees only thorns to a rosebush. He begins counting the thorns and does not even look at the flower. Try your utmost, he will not notice the flower. Where there are so many thorns, what worth is a simple flower? And be very careful. Don't touch the flower. It might be thorns in disguise!

Who can refute his argument? If his heart has been pricked by a thousand thorns, he is naturally afraid of them, and he is bound not to trust in flowers either. He will take them to be an illusion, a trick to deceive him, a dream. Who could see the flower amongst such a plethora of thorns?

Now if you take into account only the flowers, lost among them and filled with their touch and their scent, another state is born in you. Then you think: Where there **are** such lovely flowers how can there be thorns? And the few there are, are only there to protect the flowers and help them to bloom. And it is God's will that they should exist too. Perhaps the flowers could not be without thorns; they are the protectors to save the flowers from all harm.

And as your attention to the flower increases, you will realize that the same sap flows in the thorns as in the flowers. Therefore how could there be conflict between the two? The mind tends to concentrate on the thorns; it turns its attention to what is not, to where the fault is, the complaint, the failing. It has an eye for dissatisfaction, nonfulfillment. What is left but to make demands? So a man filled with the mind goes to a temple to ask; he is a beggar.

If you set the mind aside a little, you begin to see more and more flowers; you attain to the power and the joy of life. So much have you received from the very beginning, what source is there for complaint? And if He who has given so much has kept something back, there must be a reason for it. Perhaps you are not yet prepared to receive it, or lack the worthiness.

Anything that comes before its time brings suffering rather than joy. Everything has its own time to ripen. When you have ripened God will give. Infinite are His ways of giving; thousands are His hands, spread in all directions, raining bounty on one and all!

The Hindu concept of God is a thousand-armed being. This concept is full of love. They say: He gives with a thousand hands, not just two! You will not be able to hold His gifts because you have only two. He gives with a thousand hands, but at the right time, so wait for the moment without complaint and His grace begins to rain in torrents.

Nanak says even when they sing the Lord's praise they do not fail to ask, and the Lord keeps on giving. But these blind people see not, and still clamor for more. While His grace pours down on them, they wail endlessly that they are thirsty, as if they have fallen in love with their suffering!

Then what offering can we make
To gain a glimpse of His court?

This is very significant. Nanak says God has given so much, there is nothing left to be asked for. When complaints fall away and you are filled with gratitude, you wonder what you should take as a love-offering to His feet. What shall we offer at His court? What shall we place before His feet when we express our thanksgiving? How shall we worship, how shall we adore Him? You take flowers, pluck them from bushes—His bushes. They were better off on the plant, still living. You plucked them and killed them. You kill His flowers and offer them at His feet, and you are not ashamed? What can you give Him— everything is His!

When you spend your money to build a church or mosque, what are you doing? You are returning to Him His own things, and yet you are filled with pride. You say, "I built the temple. I fed so many poor. I distributed so many clothes." You give so little, yet you become arrogant.

What does this show but that you have not understood? Returning a little bit of the infinite gifts you receive from above is not a matter of pride. Yet you go to offer the gift and you are not even ashamed!

"What will you put before Him?" Nanak asks. How shall we approach, with what, so that we can see His courts, and can come near Him? What shall we put before Him—rice dipped in saffron, flowers from the market, wealth, treasures—what?

No! No gift will serve the purpose. To understand that everything is His, is enough. The gift is accepted! As long as you feel something belongs to you, you think of offering something. As long as you consider yourself the master you may give if you like, but you err. Anything you may offer, your whole kingdom, is nothing. For everything is His, even you are His! Whatever you have earned, whatever you have gathered, is all His play.

Nanak says, "What shall we do to stand in Your court, to stand in Your presence? To look into each other's eyes?" When you come to understand that everything is already His, there is no need to take anything. The flowers on the tree are already an offering to Him; everything stands

offered at His lotus feet, even the sun and the moon and
the stars. What will your miserable lamps do before the
orb of the sun? Open your eyes and see that all of existence stands offered at His feet. This exactly is the meaning of the word master. He is the master of all, everything
stands as an offering to Him.

So Nanak says, "What are we to give?" This is Nanak's
question: What language shall we speak, hearing which
He may love us? What shall we say to Him? What words
shall we use? How should we entertain Him? How shall
we please Him? What shall we do so that His love pours
on us?

Nanak does not seem to give any answer. He raises
the question and leaves it unanswered. And that is the
art, because he says that whatever we say, it is He who
speaks through us. What is so exceptional in offering His
own words to Him? Only in ignorance can it be done.
Wisdom recognizes that: Nothing is left to offer Him because I too am an offering at His feet. No words can
become a prayer, because all words are His. It is He who
speaks; it is He who throbs within the heart; it is He who
is the breath of breaths. Then what is the wise one to do?

Nanak says: Remember *satnam*, the true name, and
its glories in the ambrosial hour. There is nothing else to
be done. What is the wise one, the sensible person to do?

> Remember the true name
> And meditate on its glory in the ambrosial hour. (ਅੰਮ੍ਰਿਤ ਵੇਲਾ)

The Hindus call it *sandhya*, which literally means
evening; it is used to designate the hour of prayer at
twilight and at dawn. Nanak calls it *amrit vela*, which
means nectar or ambrosia time. It is an even more ap-
propriate name. The Hindus have been working on this
path for thousands of years. In search of the reality of

existence and exploring consciousness, they have found paths in almost all directions; almost nothing is left undiscovered. They have gradually determined that in the twenty-four hours of the day there are two short periods of sandhya.

In the night when you retire to bed, there is a short period when you are neither asleep nor awake. At this particular moment your consciousness, so to speak, changes gears. In changing the gears of the car, you have to move through the neutral gear before going to the second gear. So for a moment, the car is in no gear.

Sleep and wakefulness are two very different states. When awake you may be filled with misery; in sleep you become an emperor! You do not even wonder that the one who is a beggar in the day can be a king at night. You are in an altogether different gear. You are on a plane of consciousness that is entirely different from your ordinary daytime consciousness; and these two levels have nothing to do with each other; otherwise you would have remembered for an instant that you are a beggar and why have you become a king? But when you dream you are entirely identified with the dream. You experience the waking hours of the day as a different existence altogether from the world of sleep. You enter an entirely different world.

In the day you are a saint, at night you are a sinner and do you even wonder at it? Have you ever doubted your dreams while dreaming? Once you do the dream will break apart, for doubting is part of wakefulness; it is a part of waking consciousness. In dreams you are not conscious of the fact that you are dreaming.

There are many orders of seekers where the spiritual exercise is taught that when they prepare to sleep at night, they should keep one thought in mind: This is a dream...this is a dream. It takes three years for this remembrance to become strong enough for the seeker to recognize the dream as a dream, at which point it breaks. From then on, there are no dreams for him, because now the gears are not separate. The two planes of consciousness merge into one: now he is awake even when sleeping. This is what Krishna means when he says the yogi is awake when others sleep. The wall between the compartments has fallen and now it is one big room.

Both in the night when you are about to fall asleep and in the morning just as sleep departs and you are about to awake, these are the two moments when consciousness, in its process of changing gears, drops for a moment into neutral, when you are drifting between sleeping and waking consciousness. This is the time that Hindus call sandhya and Nanak calls amrit vela. Sandhya kal is a scientific term. *Kal* means hour, and sandhya refers to middle, neither here nor there, neither belonging to this world nor to that. At the moment of sandhya kal you are nearest to God; therefore the Hindus have made use of this time for prayer. Amrit vela, nectar time, is sweeter the moment you are nearest to ambrosia.

It all happens in this temporal body: with one mechanism of the body you sleep, with another you awake. All dreams pertain to the body. All waking and sleeping happens to the body. Behind this body is hidden a you who never sleeps, never awakens. How can he who never sleeps, awaken? There is a you who never dreams, because that requires sleep, and that never sleeps. Behind the various states of this body hides the ambrosia, the nectar that is never born, never dies. If you succeed in locating the sandhya kal, you will come to know of the bodiless within the body; you will know the master hidden behind the slave. You are both. If you look at the body alone, you are the slave; if you look at the master within,' you become the master.

So, says Nanak, there is only one thing worth doing and that is to meditate on the glory of satnam, the true name, in amrit vela. You will gain nothing by going to temples making various demands. Nothing will result from worship and sacrifices, by offering leaves and flowers, because what sense is there in offering Him what is already His? There is only one thing worth doing: pray ✳ ✳ ✳ in the ambrosial hour.

Sandhya kal lasts but a moment, but your mind is never in the present, therefore you always miss it. Every day it comes; once in every twelve hours you are nearest to God, but you miss Him, because your eyes are not alert enough to the present, to catch this subtle moment.

As you sit here now, are you here or have you gone to your office and started your daily work? Are you involved in what I say or are your thoughts engaged in thinking about what I say? If so, you will miss the present.

If you want to catch the ambrosial moment, you must become conscious of the present at every moment! When you eat, let only eating be; no other thought should fill your mind. When you bathe, bathe only; no other thought should be in the mind. When you are in your office, let your thoughts be only of the work, not thinking of home. When you go home, forget about the office. Be completely, wholly, within each moment and not here, there and everywhere. This way the subtle sight will develop gradually and you will be able to see the present moment.

It is only after this that you can meditate in the nectar hour, because that is a very subtle moment. It passes by in a flash. You may be thinking of something else and the moment has come and gone!

Before falling asleep, lie in bed completely relaxed. Still the mind in every way, don't let any thoughts drag you here and there, or else you will miss the moment. Let the mind become like the cloudless sky: not a trace of a cloud, that's how empty the mind should be. Keep watching, be alert, because when the mind becomes empty there is the danger of your falling asleep. Keep watch within. If you succeed in remaining awake, soon you will hear a sound, the changing of gear, but it is a very, very subtle sound. If thoughts are rambling within, you will never hear it. Then you will be able to witness the day turn into night, waking turn into slumber, and also sleep turning into awakening. You stand apart, witnessing the various processes.

The one who is witnessing, the seer, is the nectar. Then you will easily observe waking consciousness fading out and sleep coming in; and in the morning you will see slumber depart and consciousness dawning. When you become capable of seeing both sleep and awaking, you will stand apart from both. You become the seer. This is the nectar moment. Nanak says, "At this moment, the amrit vela, let your experience be of His glories."

And this feeling should be: He is truth, His name is truth. Do not say the words, keep only the feeling within. If you begin reciting the Japuji you will miss it; no words, no thoughts, only feelings. If in that moment you begin reciting His attributes: You are great, You are boundless, You are such...you will miss it. The moment is so very subtle.

Remember the experience of falling in love. Did you need to express your feelings over and over? Do you need to sing the beauty of your beloved every time you meet? Words make everything hollow and superficial. The truth is, as soon as you begin to express it, the glory of love is gone! You cannot express love in words.

When you sit with your beloved in silence a feeling of the glory of love resounds within the heart. You are thrilled, you are in bliss, you are happy and cheerful without any reason. You feel filled to the brim for no reason. All emptiness is gone; you are replete with love. The lover feels the stream of love overflowing, like a river so full that it pours over its banks! You will always find lovers silent, while husband and wife are always talking. They are afraid to be silent. In silence there would be no connection between them, because their relationship is one of conversation and words. If the husband is quiet the wife is worried; if the wife is quiet the husband feels something has gone wrong. Only when they quarrel are they quiet. The silence you now use for quarrels should be used for the highest love.

When two people are intensely in love they are so overwhelmed with feeling that there is no room for words. In this state they may hold hands or embrace, but speech is completely lost. Lovers become dumb; talking seems trivial, it seems an obstruction, for speech would destroy the profound silence, speech would snap the strings of the heart, speech would disturb the surface of the ocean and waves would begin to form. Therefore lovers become silent.

In that moment of nectar you are not to allow a single thought, or form any words. You have to preserve the mood, the feeling of His supreme glory, of loving gratitude for all He has given. You are full, overfull; you want nothing. Let thankfulness, gratitude flow from you.

What language shall we speak to endear Him to us?

There is nothing to say, what can we say to Him? All words are useless. Meditate on satnam. Be filled with the true name and you will feel you have established a rhythm with the amrit vela. Be alert and you will be shocked! You will feel you have become a flame of light without beginning or end, which always is, true and eternal. It is in this flame that the doors of existence open and the hidden truth is revealed.

Nanak says: Through your actions this body is achieved. In that intense moment you will know that the body is a result of actions, of karma, and it is His benevolent, all-compassionate eyes that open the door of salvation. The body is the fruit of your actions.

A few things need to be clarified here. First: only certain things can be attained by actions, only what is petty and trivial. The vast absolute cannot be attained through actions. Kabir has said: All happens by nondoing. You have to be in the state of nondoing in order to attain the absolute.

Whatever I do cannot be greater than myself. How could it be otherwise? The action can never be greater than its doer. The sculpture is never greater than the sculptor, the poem never transcends the poet. It is just not possible. Whatever comes out of you is invariably less than you, or at the most it can be equal to you, but never greater. How will you attain God? Your actions will achieve nothing; the more you try through action the more you will wander.

In a vain attempt to hide this wandering you have carved images in temples. There is no way to fashion God, because God fashions us. You make idols, you make temples; these bear the imprint of your hands and therefore are insignificant. How can the absolute that is so vast come out of your hands? But it is also possible that your creation may bear the stamp of God when you leave yourself completely to Him; then it is He who acts, and you are only the implement.

A wealthy Indian industrialist has constructed many temples bearing his name. No trace of God will ever be found there. What has it to do with God? You will not find Him in the temple, nor in the church, nor in the mosque, nor even in the gurudwara, because these bear the stamp of Hindu, Christian, Mohammedan and Sikh.

There can be no name to God's temple. He is without name; therefore His temple also has to be nameless. Whatever you make, however beautiful, however loaded with precious stones, it will bear the stamp of man. Your temple may be bigger than other temples, it cannot be bigger than you. And He can only manifest in your temple when you become completely nonmanifest; there should not be a trace of you anywhere.

Until now we have been unable to construct a temple where there is no stamp of man. All temples belong to someone or other. The builder of the temple is very much in the atmosphere of the temple. No temple is truly His. The truth in fact is, there is no need to build a temple to Him because the whole of existence is His temple. It is He twittering in the birds; it is He blooming within the flowers; it is He wafting in the breeze; it is He gurgling in the rivers and brooks. The whole wide sky is His expanse and you are a wave that has arisen in Him. His temple is so vast, how can you contain Him in your small places of worship?

Man can do a great deal through his performance. The West is an example of this. They have attained a great deal through actions. They have succeeded in building good houses, good roads. They have made scientific discoveries, made the hydrogen bomb. They have made great preparation for death and destruction. But they are completely bereft of God.

The more they attained in the physical field, the more they lost all those things that are born of the nondoer state. The very first thing they lost was God. Nietzsche said a hundred years ago: God is dead, and for the West God was really dead. When they are filled with actions and deeds, all connection with Him is broken; then He is as good as dead for them. And since God was almost lost to them, all prayers became hollow and superficial. Meditation was completely lost. There was no point in meditating. For if everything is to be attained by action, what is left to inaction? And meditation *is* inaction.

Therefore the occidental mind takes the Easterner to be lethargic and indolent. Nanak's father thought the same of Nanak, that he was lazy, indolent. What was he doing just sitting all day? The father had a business mind and this son posed a problem for him by doing no work and showing no inclination to follow any trade. Whenever he went to work he was thrown out. He did not study, because he would invariably get into an argument with the teacher. For he would tell him, "The last word is already spoken. What more is there to know? And have you attained Him in spite of all your learning?" When the teacher had to reply in the negative, Nanak said, "Then I shall seek a way to know Him myself," and the teacher regretfully took him home, acknowledging his inability to teach him.

Kabir says: All the world has learned books upon books, and never has even one become a learned man. He who learns the four letters of l-o-v-e, becomes a wise man.

Nanak set out to learn these four letters of love in order to attain knowledge. Why should he endure the business of all this knowledge which has such a different goal altogether?

Mulla Nasruddin was a school teacher. Every day for many years he rode his donkey to school. At last the attitude of learning caught hold of the ass too, and one day he turned to the rider on his back and asked, "Mulla, why do you go to school every day?"

The Mulla was quite taken aback. Was he hearing right? Did the donkey really speak? He had heard many donkeys speak, but never a four-legged one! However, if those others can talk, why not this one? The Mulla thought, "It must be that all this going to school has had an effect on him and he has just begun to speak. It was my own fault bringing him to school every day."

"Why do you want to know?" asked the Mulla.

"I am curious, that's all. Why do you come to school every day?" said the donkey.

"I come to teach the children."

"Why?"

"So the children can learn."

"What happens by learning?"

"A person gains intelligence and wisdom."

"What use is intelligence?" persisted the ass.

"What use you say? It is because of my intelligence that I am riding you!" said the Mulla.

"Teach me also, Mulla. Give me intelligence!" said the donkey.

"Oh, no," said the Mulla, "I am not that foolish. Then you will be riding me!"

All that we learn in this world serves as a means of getting the better of one another. It is a plan for your conflicts in life. You will be able to fight better and win if you have more degrees. The universities are a reflection of your aggression; armed with its weapons you can compete and exploit others more efficiently. You can harass them more systematically, and commit crimes lawfully. With the right rules and methods you can do effectively all that you otherwise could not do, and which you *should* not do. Education teaches dishonesty and deceit. As a result you may win out over others, but you will never be wise. Rather, people are becoming more and more unwise, ignorant. Our universities are not centers of learning, because no wisdom is contained there.

So Nanak's teacher himself took him home and acknowledged to his father that he was unable to teach him.

When Nanak reached the age of twelve, he was about to be initiated into the Hindu religion and receive the sacred thread. It was an important ceremony. Many people were invited and a band was arranged. When the priest had finished his incantations and was about to place the sacred thread on him, Nanak said, "Wait! What will happen by wearing this thread?"

The pundit said, "You will become a *dwija*," which is a member of the Hindu faith, literally a twice-born.

Nanak asked, "Will the old really die and the new be born? If that is so, I am ready." The pundit was concerned because he knew to the contrary, that nothing would happen, that it was only an empty ceremony. Nanak asked, "What if this thread were to break?"

"You can always buy a new one from the market and throw away the old," said the pundit.

"Then let this one go now," said Nanak. "How can any anything that breaks by itself and is sold in the marketplace for a trifling amount, help me to find God?" How can man's creation help to find God? For man's performances are always petty and inferior.

His father, Kalu Mehta, was convinced the boy was a total good-for-nothing. He had done his best to bring him round to doing something, but had failed. When there was no other way, there was a last resort that came in handy in the villages: he was sent to graze the cattle. Nanak went quite happily to the pasture and was soon lost in meditation while the cattle destroyed the adjacent fields. The next day he had to be removed from this, too. His father was now doubly convinced that the boy could do nothing and would amount to nothing.

Now it is an interesting fact that those people who have done the most for the world are denied this world completely; those who are the just claimants of the other world are almost unable to do anything in this world. It is not that they are not capable, but their whole quality of being and doing is different. They become only a means, a medium through which many things can happen.

What would Nanak have attained by grazing cattle? Many people can do it. What would Nanak have attained by running a shop well? Many do, and yet the world remains as before. This person has removed himself from the world of action and is drowned in the world of glory.

Glory means: Thou art the doer. What can I perform? No sooner do you begin to feel your worthlessness, expressed as, "What can I do?" than your ego begins to fall away, drop by drop. The day you feel this in totality, that you are unqualified, incapable, nothing happens because of you, you are helpless, the doors of liberation open for you.

Through your actions you receive this body,
And by His grace the door to salvation opens.
Nanak says, Know then His truth because He alone is everything.
He cannot be installed in any temple, nor fashioned by any skill.
The faultless one exists unto Himself.
Those who serve Him attain the glory.
Nanak says, Sing His praises, Lord of all attributes.

God cannot be installed in any place; therefore, how can you make temples? How will you consecrate His idols? He is complete in Himself, so you have no need to create Him. He was when you were not, and He will be still when you are no longer. Do not bother yourselves with the worthless task of creating His images. Rituals, temples, idols—these will lead you nowhere.

Then what will lead you to the goal? Those who have served Him, those who have revered and worshipped Him, have attained His presence. If He is everything, service is prayer; if He is everything, service is worship. The more you get absorbed in service, the nearer you will come to Him. If the tree is thirsty, water it; if the cow is hungry, feed it. You are thereby quenching His thirst and feeding Him.

You need sensitivity in order to serve. Temples, big or small, serve no purpose. They are just devices to escape prayer. His temple is enormous, and equally great should be your attitude of service, because that alone is He, the whole wide universe and all that it contains!

When Jesus was about to be crucified, his followers asked him, "What shall we do now?"

Jesus said: "Do not worry. If you quench the thirst of the thirsty, the water will soothe my throat. If you serve the poor and needy, you will find me hidden within them. If you have been angry or abused someone, there is no point in coming to the temple. If while you kneel in prayer, you realize your mistake, get up first and beg pardon of the person. For till then how can you pray? It is He who is spread everywhere." Therefore Nanak says, "Those who have served Him have attained His glory."

What kind of worship? Service! This word is very significant, so allow it to go deep inside you. Remember to keep in mind that whoever you serve is God.

You can serve people in another sense also, wn. very different. When you serve people knowing that they are poor, miserable or needy, it is out of pity; then you are above him and he is below. When you are being kind, taking pity, you are not serving. Then it is an ordinary social service and this service is not worship. You are a mere social worker, a member of the Lions Club or a Rotarian flaunting the motto: We serve. You are filled with arrogance. You build a small hospital but your publicity is enormous. Social service is not worship; you are throwing crumbs to the hungry, you are doing great kindness, obliging others. You are at the top, serving those who are way down at your feet and who should be grateful. This is not worship.

Service becomes worship when the one you serve is God. He is master, you the slave. It is not He who is indebted; rather you, that He gave you the opportunity. You have given a poor man bread and also thanked him.

There is an old Hindu custom of giving alms to the brahmin as well as a love offering, a gift as a token of gratitude for his having accepted the alms, that he accepted your service. Feeling indebted to the one you serve converts your service into worship; it is not social service but a religious act.

Understand well the difference: to be proud of what you do as a welfare worker, is not Nanak's idea of service. Service makes you humble. Service sees God in the lowly. Service makes you a servant. He who is last becomes the first. And you will stand the very last. Service also presumes that you are indebted to him who gives you an opportunity to serve.

The faultless one exists unto Himself.
Those who serve Him attain the glory.

This glory is not of your ego because it is only realized when the ego is no more. Then these servants of the Lord became famous and buddhahood shone through them. Then the darkness of their house was banished and the lamp within shone full and bright.

Nanak says, Sing His praises, Lord of all attributes.
Sing and hear only of Him; engrave Him in your heart.
So banish sorrow and suffering, and make bliss your abode.

And this can only happen if you dedicate all your actions to Him. When you sit in your shop and a customer comes in, see not the customer but God within him. Deal with him as if God himself has entered your shop. If you wish to be drowned in Him all day long there is no other way than this. While eating feel it is He entering you in the form of food. Therefore the Hindus say food is Brahma. Do not eat thoughtlessly. Remember, it is He who bloomed in the plants; it is He who has become the grain. Accept Him most gratefully. When you accept food as Brahma, when drinking water you feel it is He come to quench your thirst in the form of water; only then can you absorb Him all the twenty-four hours. What other way is there for you?

You go to the gurudwara or church and pray or chant, or sing hymns for an hour or so while your mind runs here and there. Even for this short period, you check your watch to see whether it is getting late, whether it is time to go to work. How can you worship Him in bits and pieces? You try to pray a little in the morning and a little while in the evening while you remain your ordinary old self the rest of the day.

To be religious is a twenty-four-hour undertaking; the religious spirit should pervade you all day long. Religion doesn't exist in odd moments; there is no religious day or religious hour. All life in its totality is His. All moments are His. Religion is a very different way of living in which everything you do is in some way or other connected with God.

Nanak says: Sing in praise of the Lord of all attributes. Sing only of Him, listen only to Him, let only Him reside in your heart.

As you sit listening to me you can hear in two ways: either as if someone is talking, or as if it is God's voice coming to you. In the latter case you will feel a change coming over you. Keep Him in mind always. Thus you will be rid of suffering and carry home the bounty of bliss. Thus after a full day's labors you will reach home carrying not sorrow but joy. Now coming home you carry nothing but the pain of some customer who tricked you, or someone who picked your pocket, or whatever you ate that was not good; there is always cause for complaint. Your day is a collection of sorrows.

But if you begin to see God all around you in whatever you do, you will reap a rich harvest of joy, says Nanak. Not only will you live in happiness in your everyday home, but at the hour of death when you prepare to leave for your real home, you will be overflowing, filled to the brim, saturated with joy. Then you will depart dancing, not crying. If death does not become a dance, know that life has gone to waste. If death is not an occasion of joy and celebration, know that your life was ill-spent, because you are returning home; and if going home is not a matter of celebration, then your whole life adds up only to sorrow.

So banish sorrow and suffering, and make bliss your abode.

Your suffering exists only because you are trying to steer your life without God. Having set Him aside, you have trusted yourself too much and taken yourself to be too clever; there is no other reason for your unhappiness.

And the reason for your happiness is equally simple: you have set your cleverness and intellect aside, giving no credence to your abilities but experiencing Him in everything; you have begun to live more in Him and less in yourself. Ultimately you may dwell entirely in Him.

Why should you see your wife as wife, and not as God? Why should you see your son in your son, and not God as your son? As your perception changes, happiness joins you. If your son dies you will be unhappy because your perception was wrong. You thought: *My* son. Had you realized beforehand that he is God's son, you would have thought: When He wished, He sent him to me; when He wished, He called him back. All is His command. And you would have accepted all conditions, knowing it was His son sent to you, and feeling grateful for the days He let you have him.

To whom to complain, and about what? He gave when He pleased, He took away when He pleased. You have no hand in it. All is His, everything! Then, where are the tears? Where the anxiety, the sorrow and distress? If He gives, you are happy; if He does not give, you are happy. His ways are unique. Sometimes He gives and thus creates you. Sometimes He takes away and in so doing you evolve further! Sometimes suffering is necessary, because sorrow wakes you up, makes you conscious. In happiness you are lost and asleep! In suffering you awaken.

There was a Sufi fakir by the name of Hassan. One day as they were getting in a boat his disciple said, "That there is joy I can understand, because God is our Father, and it is but natural that He should give joy to His children; but why sorrow, why unhappiness?"

Hassan gave no reply but began to row the boat with only one oar. The boat began to turn in circles. "What are you doing?" the disciple called out. "If you row with one oar we shall never reach the other shore. We shall keep going round and round in this one spot. Has the other oar broken or is your arm paining? Let me row the boat!"

Hassan replied, "You seem to be a much more intelligent fellow than I thought!"

If there is joy alone, the boat will go only in circles and arrive nowhere. For it to work, the opposite is also needed. A boat moves with two oars, a man walks with two feet, and two hands are needed to work. In life you need night and day, joy and sorrow, birth and death, or else the boat keeps going round and round, reaching nowhere.

When a person begins to perceive correctly, knowing that He is in everything, he is filled with thanksgiving; even when sorrow comes he accepts it cheerfully. Then you accept His joy and you accept His sorrow equally. Then joy is no longer joy, sorrow is no longer sorrow; the dividing line is lost. When you begin to look upon them impartially, your attachment to joy and rejection of suffering are both broken and you stand apart, free from both, having arrived at the attitude of a witness. Then you shall be rid of sorrow and carry home joy.

Sing and hear only of Him; engrave Him in your heart.
So banish sorrow and suffering, and make bliss your abode.
The guru's word is the sound of sounds, and the Vedas too.
The Lord abides in his words.
The guru is Shiva, the destroyer; the guru is Vishnu, the sustainer;
The guru is Brahma, the creator; he is the trio of goddesses, Parvati,
Laxmi and Saraswati.
However well I know Him, He cannot be described.
He cannot be expressed by words.
The guru is the secret that solves the riddle.
He is the benefactor of all. Let me never forget Him.

Understand that Nanak has glorified the guru to a great extent. All saints have sung the glory of the guru, placing him above the scriptures. If the guru says something that is not found in the Vedas, forget the Vedas, because the guru is the living scripture. There is a reason why saints have extolled and treasured the guru's words so. First of all, the Vedas are also expressions of gurus; but these gurus are not present today. And the words have lost the purity they had when they were first uttered, because those who collected them, of necessity, combined and mixed them with their own thoughts. This they could not help. Though it was not done on purpose, it is certain that it happened.

If I tell you something with instructions to repeat it to your neighbor, you are bound to lose something and add something to what I said. The mode of speaking will change. Even if you use exactly the words I used, your preferences and your emphasis will be different from mine. When you speak, your experience, your knowledge, your understanding will creep into the words.

I give you a flower, and you take it in your hand to give to someone from me, but the flower will have caught some of your smell. Just as the flower's scent remains in your hands, the flower also picks up your scent. The flower is no longer the flower I gave you. And if the flower has passed through a thousand hands, it will carry the scent of all those hands. And if the flower were to come back to me, I would never be able to recognize it as the same flower. The essence of the flower I knew would be lost by the touch of a thousand hands. It will not look the same as when I gave it, but will have fallen into pieces, its petals scattered here and there. People will have to stick on other petals to complete the flower before they bring it back to me.

The Vedas are the utterances of gurus. Those who have known have spoken. But now it is thousands and thousands of years since these words were spoken. Much has been deleted, much added. Therefore it is great good fortune to come across a living guru when the book has turned stale.

Another very interesting thing is: when you read a book, you interpret the words in your own way. It is you who reads and you who interprets, and your interpretation cannot be more than you; it cannot transcend your own understanding. You will attach your own meanings to the words.

So the book cannot become your guru; you become guru to the book! You have not learned the scriptures, rather you begin to teach the scriptures; thus you find thousands of interpretations. Look at the Gita, how many commentaries there are! Whoever reads it takes his own meanings from it. Krishna is no longer here to censor by saying, "Brother, this is not what I meant!" When Krishna spoke, he was definite about what he meant, but who is to say now what his intention was? Even Arjuna could not say, though he was the one to hear it, because whatever he says will have been changed by him.

The whole Gita has been written by Sanjay, who was no more than a news reporter of his day. It was his job to report on the battle being fought over one hundred miles away to Dhritrashtra, the blind king. He must have seen the whole thing on television! The deaf are listening and reporting to the blind! So the truth lies even further away. What Krishna said, even Arjuna could not have reported correctly, but only in the light of his own understanding. He could repeat only what he understood and not what Krishna actually said. And now we introduce Sanjay who is collecting the news. He is the reporter, the third person!

Then thousands of years elapse while we have all the commentators, each claiming to elucidate it out of his own understanding. By then each word acquires infinite meanings, and the Gita becomes meaningless. Whatever you put in has become a new edition.

Therefore Nanak and Kabir and others have stressed one point: seek a living guru. The scriptures had all become stale and secondhand, thirdhand, even at the time of these saints.

> *The guru's word is the sound of sounds, and the Vedas too.*
> *The Lord abides in his words.*
> *The guru is Shiva, the destroyer; the guru is Vishnu, the sustainer;*
> *The guru is Brahma, the creator; he is the trio of goddesses, Parvati, Laxmi and Saraswati.*
> *However well I know Him, He cannot be described.*
> *He cannot be expressed by words.*

Those who have seen Him with their own eyes, cannot describe Him completely. He cannot be expressed through words. And you go looking for God in books?—the Gita, the Bible, the Koran or Guru Granth! Even a living guru cannot explain Him thoroughly. About himself Nanak says: Even if I had known completely, I would not have been able to give a complete description, because He cannot be expressed through words.

What cannot be expressed through words you are trying to understand through explanations and the printed word, but you can only get news of Him through a living guru. And it is not that you will understand all that the guru says; you will understand what the guru *is*. The guru's presence will make you understand His very being. To be with him, to breathe the air around him, is to be in a different climate altogether! At least for that much time you are lost to the world; you reside in a different world, and your consciousness has assumed another form. Be

ready and willing to look through the guru's window.
There is no other way besides this.

> *The guru is the secret that solves the riddle.*
> *He is the benefactor of all. Let me never forget Him.*

Gur means technique, method; he who gives the
method is the guru. And the secret method, the technique
according to Nanak is:

> *He is the benefactor of all. Let me never forget Him.*

He is the one creator of all, the maker. May I always
remember this truth: that He is hidden behind all. He is
the hand of all hands; He is the eye of all eyes. It is He who
throbs; it is He who is life.

> *Let me never forget Him.*

May this remembrance remain every moment. By
grasping this secret, you will gradually see beyond the
beads of the mala and be able to grasp the thread that
goes through them all. That thread is God and you are the
beads. The stream of life that flows through you is God;
He is the thread on which turns the bead of your body,
and this thread is the same in me as in you. It is the same
that runs within the trees, the birds, the animals, the
mountains, the plains. It is He living in the various forms,
swelling in every wave, so catch hold of the constant
remembrance of this thread and never forget it, and you
have the secret at hand. All riddles will then be solved by
themselves.

So what will you do? How will you guard this remembrance all day long? You will need fierce courage, for there
are many difficulties to be faced. Had it not been for these
obstacles the world would have become religious long ago.
Pains and difficulties there are and will continue to be,
because any attainment without trouble is almost useless. Without traveling you can never reach your destina-

tion; you are bound to wander. You will only appreciate and care for that which you acquire with difficulty. Besides, if you are out to attain the ultimate truth you will have to make some sacrifice!

Religion is to lose on one side and gain on the other, and so problems arise. If you begin to see God in the customer, how will you cheat him? It will be difficult. If you are a pickpocket, seeing God in your victim, your hand will be paralyzed. How can you do evil? How will you be angry? How will you make enemies?

If you see Him in everything the structure of your life will begin to crumble from all sides. The house you have built stands against all He signifies, because you built it when you had forgotten Him. If now you begin to remember Him the house cannot remain. One thing however is certain: though you cannot see it today, you will get a bigger house.

Therefore we need gamblers on the path, people with the courage to leave whatever is at hand in order to realize something about which they cannot be absolutely certain. Therefore I always say, religion is not for the businessman, it is for the gambler! The gambler stakes his all with the hope of attaining twice as much. Whether he will or not, is never certain. He does not know which way the dice will fall; no one knows. It is that kind of gambler's courage that you need if you wish to walk along with Nanak.

All religions have become feeble because we have not the courage of the gambler, but stick to the mathematics of the businessman. Then it becomes very difficult to remember this sutra, which aims to change your life from its very roots; you will not be the same from even such a small sutra. It will start such a raging fire in your life that this life will disappear.

Kabir says: Only he who is prepared to burn his house need walk with me. Which house is Kabir talking of? The edifice you have created round yourself, the house of lies, deceit, anger, enmity, malice, jealousy and hatred; this is what your house is.

Remember this sutra, only this:

He is the benefactor of all. Let me never forget Him.

That within, the master of all, is one. For your life to change, you need nothing more. You do not need to do Patanjali's yoga asanas, nor have you to worry about the ten commandments of the Jews, nor concern yourself with the Gita or the Koran.

A small secret, such a tiny secret, to change your entire life! Through this secret Nanak attained and you can also.

But remember Kabir: Only he who is prepared to burn his house, he alone need walk with me.

Chapter 4

Some Other Ganges

If I have succeeded in attaining His pleasure,
I have bathed in all the holy rivers.
And if I fail to please Him, why should I bathe and adorn myself?
In this whole created universe, nothing is attained without actions;
But he who listens to but one teaching of the guru,
His understanding becomes like a precious jewel.
He is the benefactor of all.
Let me never forget Him.
Were you to live through four ages, or even ten times more,
Were you known on all nine continents,
and were you to gain universal following,
Were you to earn fame and praise from all of mankind,
If you have not His grace, nothing will save you.
You are like the lowliest worm;
even the worst of sinners may point the finger at you.
Says Nanak, He makes the worthless worthy,
And showers the gifted with more gifts.
None but God can bestow such excellence.

S UDDENLY ONE NIGHT Nanak left his house and disappeared. Nobody knew where he had gone. They searched all the temples and dwellings of sadhus where he was likely to be, but he was nowhere to be found. Someone said he had been seen going towards the cremation ground, but nobody could believe it. No one ever goes to the burial ground of his own will. Even the dead man does not want to be there, so the question of a living person going voluntarily seemed impossible. But when Nanak was nowhere to be found, as a last resort they had to look for him there. They found him sitting before a fire deep in meditation.

His people shook him and said, "Are you out of your mind sitting here at this hour, leaving your wife and children behind? Don't you know where you are? This is the cremation ground."

Nanak replied, "He who comes here has already died; death is no longer ahead. What you call your house is where you will die in due course. Then which one is to be feared? Is it where people die or where people never die? Besides, if some day you have to come here, it is most unseemly to come riding on four people's shoulders; therefore I came myself."

This incident is very significant. Nanak has no quarrel with what has to be. He accepts all that is. Death is to be; death is welcome. Why trouble others? It is better to come on one's own. But we are always opposed to what will be. Our desire is for it to be different, but Nanak has no such desire. All is His wish! If He wills that Nanak should die, he accepts His wish.

That night, however, people persuaded him to come home. After he returned Nanak was never the same again; something within him had died and something new had been born. It is only by dying completely within that the new birth takes place. In the process of birth you have to go through the burning grounds, and he who passes through the burning ghats knowingly, voluntarily, attains a new birth. This is not the birth of a new body; it is the unfolding of a new consciousness.

You are full of fear, and where there is fear there can be no connection with God. All your prayers and worship are because you are afraid—not out of love for God. You visit the holy places, bathe in the holy rivers, perform sacred rites and worship—all out of fear. Your religion is the medicine of your fear; it is not a celebration of joy. You do all this to protect yourself. These are the precautions you take for your wellbeing. Just as you amass wealth, build a house, have a bank balance, take out an insurance policy, in the same manner God is also your insurance policy.

And who has ever arrived through fear? Fear is a way of separating; love is a way of integrating. Fear creates distance; love brings closeness. Fear and love never meet. When fear is completely gone, only then does love arise. As long as fear prevails you can only hate. Though you may cover and decorate your hatred you cannot love.

How can you love one whom you fear? You fight the one you fear; you can never surrender to him. And even if you surrender, it will only be a new device for battle; futilely you hope to be rid of fear this way.

If I have succeeded in attaining His pleasure,
I have bathed in all the holy rivers.
And if I fail to please Him,
why should I bathe and adorn myself?

People go to holy places and bathe in the holy waters, not as an act of joy but in the desire to be rid of sins. It is believed that by bathing in the Ganges all sins are carried away by the waters of the river. Now why should the Ganges wash your sins? How is it involved in your evil deeds? Besides, your sins come not from the body but from the mind. How can the Ganges wash your mind? At most it can clean your body and remove its dust and dirt; it cannot cleanse the dirt of your mind.

The Ganges is all right for washing your body, but not as a means of washing your soul. You will have to look for some other Ganges. There is an old story which says: One Ganges flows on earth, one flows in heaven. You will have to find the Ganges of heaven. The earthly Ganges can only touch the body, which is also of the earth. The Ganges of heaven will touch your soul and wash it. How is one to find the heavenly Ganges? Where is one to look for it?

These sutras direct you to the Ganges of heaven:

If I have succeeded in attaining His pleasure,
I have bathed in all the holy rivers.

That He should be pleased with you is as good as bathing in the heavenly Ganges. Attaining His pleasure is a very deep and profound saying. Try to understand it. You will gain His pleasure only when you do not stand against Him. You will gain His pleasure only when you have completely dissolved yourself in Him, when your sense of being the doer is completely annihilated. He is the doer, you are only a means; and that is enough to please Him!

Right now however, there is a constant strain within you: I am the doer...I am the doer.... When praying it is *you* who prays; while bathing in the holy waters it is *you* who bathes; when you do charity, again it is you. Everything goes to waste: your bath, your charity, your worship. All is in vain, and all because of your sense of yourself as the doer. Until now you have been thinking only in terms of myself, mine.

There is only one difference between a religious person and a nonreligious person: for a religious person He is the doer; for a nonreligious person I am the doer. Everything happens through Him—this attitude endears you to Him, because this attitude is religion. You stand with your back towards Him by your own will. It is your sense of doing that turns you away from God. The moment you give up this attitude you will stand face to face with Him, and all opposition ceases.

What are your performances that you are so proud of? Neither birth nor death nor life itself is the outcome of your actions. Everything is done by Him, but somehow you acquire this attitude of the doer. And with your sense of doing, when you commit sin it is sin; and even when you perform good deeds they too become sin. Remember! You are in the wrong. It is the sense of being the doer that is sinful! And nondoing is virtue! All good deeds become sinful if the sense of the doer persists. Then whether you build temples, perform worship, observe vows, observe fasts, go to holy places—to Mecca or Kashi—all goes to waste.

The more you say "I have done," the more you add to your sins. So sin relates not to the act but to the attitude. Any act performed in the attitude of nondoing cannot be sinful. But if your attitude is that of doing, all acts are sins.

In the Gita this is exactly what Krishna exhorts Arjuna to do. He tells him to abandon all sense of being the doer, to do only what God is doing through you. Let His will be done; don't put yourself in between. Make no decisions by yourself. Do not think: What is right? What is wrong? How can you know what is right or wrong? What is the scope of your vision? What is the strength of your understanding? What is your experience? How much consciousness do you have? Don't try to see with your small lamp of consciousness when it cannot see more than four feet ahead—whereas life spreads into infinite space.

Do what He makes you do; be a medium only. Just as the flute allows the flute player to play his tune, give way to Him to act through you.

He who becomes His implement becomes His beloved. He who remains a doer becomes His foe; however, His love flows all the same, because it is unconditional. It makes no difference who you are, His love pours on everyone all the time. It is you who are unable to accept His love. Similarly, an upright pot gets filled with rain water, but if it is kept upside-down it will not fill. The rain pours all the same, because it is unconditional. It does not say: If you do this, or be like this, then only shall I rain on you.

This is important to understand, since, hearing Nanak's words, many people thought that "If I become this way He will love me." No, this is wrong! His love and benediction pour forever. If it were not so, what is the difference between temporal love and divine love? The very bane of human love is: If you do this I shall love you. If you become like this I shall love you. I shall love you only if you fulfill my conditions. This is what the father says to the son, the wife to the husband, the friend to a friend.

Nanak refers to an experience beyond worldly love. His love rains forever. If you fulfill the conditions you will be filled like the upright pot. Filled to the brim, you will overflow with His love and everyone around will receive the overflow.

The guru is one whose vessel is so filled with God's love that he can contain no more. As he begins to overflow other vessels are filled through him. The guru means one whose wants are all fulfilled, since all desires have died and longing is silenced. His vessel is so full that now he is capable of giving. And what can he do but give? When the cloud is saturated it must rain. Then only can it become light. The flower saturated with fragrance must give it up to the winds.

In the same way, when your vessel is filled with His love, it will shower all around you. There is no end to His grace. Once you know that you will be filled merely by keeping your vessel upright, the grace from above never ceases to pour. Then no matter how much you give out your vessel is always brimming.

So remember, Nanak is addressing *you* when he says he has succeeded in winning His love by bathing in all the holy rivers. Know that He lives! Otherwise how could you exist? Had He not wanted you to be even for a moment, you would have disappeared long ago. He resides in every one of your breaths. It is He throbbing within your heart. Existence has loved you, desired you, made you. It does not matter what you are like; it is still giving you life. You are already the loved one. But you turn your back to Him, afraid of His love. You run away and hide just when He wishes to fill your being. When Nanak speaks of winning His love he means to become upright, stand facing Him, and shed all fear.

It is only out of fear that you overturned your vessel, fear that it may be filled with something unwanted or wrong. It is out of fear you have closed all doors: for fear of thieves, for fear of enemies. Out of fear you have closed your heart on all sides. When you close your doors thieves cannot get in, but then the beloved cannot enter! <u>For the door is only one, either for the thief or the lover</u>. Avoiding the thief, remember, you have shut the door to the beloved too! And what is this life without the beloved?

You are so afraid of something entering that you have covered the opening and then cry that you are empty. You complain that no visitor ever comes to your house, no one ever knocks at our door, but it's your house; no one ever knocks at your door, but it's your fear that has turned you away from your God.

It is interesting that your religions are only an expansion of your fears. Your so-called gods are concepts born of your own fears, and out of fear you have accepted them. You are afraid of doubting and so you raise no question, but real faith is not within you. If you are a believer out of fear, then faith is only superficial and doubt lurks within. How then can you meet the most mysterious, the most profound?

Mulla Nasruddin stood for election. He got only three votes: one his own, the second from his wife and a third from a stranger. When his wife heard this she cornered him: "So who is she?"

What lies hidden within surges up on the slightest pretext; it does not take long for superficial faith and love to break down. Any slight happening and doubt raises its head; a thorn pricks and you begin to doubt Him, your head aches and your faith is gone; you lose your job and your love for God flies out of the window.

When the hidden doubt bursts out it is like an ulcerated boil; a slight knock and pus begins to flow. You may try to cover it with the ointment and plaster of faith, but it serves no purpose. Who is there to cheat? You can't even fool yourself, because you know very well that your faith is because of your fear, and you are filled with internal doubts.

You may bathe in the holy places or pray in the temple, church or gurudwara, but to no avail; unless the note of faith and trust arises within, you have not really called Him. Also, when you go out of fear, you are bound to ask for something; fear always begs. If you get what you ask for you are satisfied; if not, the doubt becomes more intense. You are forever asking. Faith is only a form of thanks: "Already You have given too much. Your grace, Your compassion is so great." Faith is always filled with gratitude; and gratitude dispels all sign of doubt. Where there are demands, doubt is lurking. The demands are a form of test.

There is a story in the life of Jesus. After he performed the excruciating forty-day ordeal, Satan appeared to him and said, "Since it is said in the scriptures that when a prophet is born God always protects him, if you are really the Son of God jump from this mountain and He will save you!"

Jesus said, "That is correct, but the scriptures also say that only those who doubt test Him. I have no doubts. I am sure that the angels are standing there to protect me. I am thoroughly convinced. Had I the slightest doubt that perhaps they are not there, or that perhaps I am not the Son of God, then I would have tested Him."

As soon as there is doubt, the question of trial and investigation comes in and you make your demands. Your conditions are: "Fulfill my desire if you exist. If it is fulfilled then You are; if not, You are not." The faithful one makes no demands, makes no tests. Being always filled with gratitude, he never asks favors. The day you stop your demands, your fear will cease. As you are filled with gratitude, the demands will lessen and you will feel your face turning Godward, straightening your vessel. And as your vessel becomes upright, drops of His grace will begin to fall in it and fear will vanish. Then you will find He is always pouring and you were unnecessarily frightened. Then you will open your doors wide because you know that even in the form of the thief, it is only He; in the form of the cheat, it is He. And until you begin to see Him in all, you will not be able to see Him at all.

And if I fail to please Him why should I bathe and adorn myself?

If He does not like me, my bathing and adorning will only strengthen my ego. Have you ever seen a man returning from a pilgrimage to Mecca? He becomes the picture of arrogance. Had he really gone on a pilgrimage he would have returned a more humble person, a changed man, who left his ego behind. But the reverse happens— he expects a loud welcome with great applause, and wants people to touch his feet and praise his action.

Even when you perform good deeds, you only want to fulfill your ego. You fast so that you may be feted. You secretly desire that bands should be playing and far and wide it should be known how much you have fasted. And as the ego gets stronger, you turn further and further away from Him.

The more you are, the more you stand with your back to Him. Understand that equation: the less you are, the more you are turned in His direction. And when you are completely not, He stands before you. Then the thief who enters is also Him and all fears vanish, because He is everywhere.

> *If I have succeeded in attaining His pleasure,*
> *I have bathed in all the holy rivers.*
> *And if I fail to please Him, why should I bathe and adorn myself?*
> *In this whole created universe, nothing is attained without actions....*

Whatever He has created and whatever is visible, nothing is attained without actions. Nothing is attained in this world without actions. This causes the illusion that we have to labor, to strive, in order to attain to God. Understand that although everything in *this* world is attained through labor, love is not attained thus—nor is prayer, nor worship, nor faith nor proximity to God.

Why? Because actions make the ego stronger. If you want to gain wealth, you will have to work hard. If you want to be known in this world you cannot afford to sit doing nothing. You will have to run about, plot and plan for or against others; you will have to carry many anxieties. Since effort, labor and work are the only ways to achieve anything in this temporal world, it is but natural for us to think it must require even more effort to reach the all-embracing, vast existence! And this is where we go wrong. The rules of that realm are entirely opposite to the rules of this world. To attain anything of this world, we need to have our backs towards God.

Understand that the more we ignore His support the more effort we have to make, because then we have to do what normally He would have done for us. We have to substitute our labor for His. To go out into this world is to turn your back towards Him. His help is less, the flow of nectar is no more; although it keeps flowing, we do not receive it because our doors are closed in our desire to be self-reliant, to be in charge.

Thus, Nanak says again and again: He is the Master; I am the slave. The very endeavor to be self-reliant is because of the ego. The more we feel, "*I* shall do it," the more we deny the support of His power. It is like a man trying to row his boat against the wind. Nanak has given us the secret. Why use the oars at all? Go wherever the winds take you.

And Ramakrishna said the same: Why do you row the boat? Why do you not float along with the current? Open your sails and relax! The winds will themselves take you to the shore. You have to keep an eye on the right moment and the right direction—that is all. Do not go against the wind. If the wind is blowing towards the other shore, then too, open your sails. Do not labor unnecessarily.

If you go against the wind or the flow of the river, you will have to struggle, and what will be the outcome? You will never arrive, you will only get tired. Observe the face of a wordly man after a whole life's labor—nothing but signs of fatigue. People are dead long before they die, so that at life's end they hanker for rest—at any cost ! Why do you tire yourself so?

When man gets old he becomes ugly. The animals of the jungle do not become ugly but remain as beautiful as when young. So also the trees; there is not a grain of difference in their beauty. With each year they grow a little more, and more and more people can rest under their shade. Their beauty increases with every year, and the pleasure of sitting under an old spreading tree is so much more than under a younger tree which has had so much less experience.

God knows how many seasons the old tree has seen, how many monsoons, how many springs, how many summers and winters; how many people rested under its shade; how much life passed under it and the winds and the clouds that passed overhead; and how many sunrises and moonrises it must have witnessed, and how many dark, moonless nights. All is contained within it. To sit next to an old tree is to sit next to history. A profound tradition has flowed through it.

The Buddhists are still trying to save the tree under which Buddha attained enlightenment. the unique event that took place under its branches is still contained within its experience. It still throbs with its vibrations; the rays of the light of the supreme knowledge that Buddha attained are still contained in its memory. To sit under it is to feel a peace you have never felt before. Having known infinite peace, it allows you to share in its experience.

Old trees become more beautiful. Old lions become yet more majestic, because in the young there is still a kind of excitement, impatience, and longing that have become quiescent in the old. Man becomes ugly because he gets tired. The trees do not fight existence; they keep their sails wide open, and they are happy where er the wind takes them. You are fighting existence; therefore you break. You become old and decrepit because your life is one long struggle.

All that is achieved in the object-world is attained through hard labor and toil, but you need no action to attain God. You need no worship, no prayer, nor yoga, nor austerities, nor the repetition of some mantra. He cannot be attained by deeds—but only through love! The direction of love and the direction of deeds are very different from each other.

Love is an emotion. Love is the only thing in life that never gets tired, because love is no work, no deed. The more you love, the more proficient you become at loving. As your experience of love deepens, you find your capacity to love also increases. Love keeps expanding. In the flood of love it is always high tide, never low. Love always ascends higher and higher; there is no descent.

But love is a divine gift—not the fruit of your labor. In the right perspective love is your resting place; therefore, you always find yourself fresh when in love. You are calm, composed and relaxed. This is also true in what we ordinarily know as love. When you are in love with someone, beside him, all fatigue leaves you; you feel light and fresh. You are filled with cheer; all the dust of toil is shaken off.

Now imagine the condition of divine love! The day His love is born within you, what effort, what fatigue remains? God is attained not by labor but through His grace. Nanak speaks of the guru's gift. You cannot have a direct relationship with Him, your eyes are not ready as yet. In order to look at the sun you have to start with a lamp. Concentrating on the flame of the lamp, you go on to a bigger flame, then to a yet more powerful light. Only gradually do you concentrate on the sun itself; or else, with your ordinary sight, the sun will make you blind.

The vessel has to be kept straight. First, it should be turned towards the guru, who is the preparation. When you are ready to be filled with the guru, when you become thrilled and happy and all your fears have left you, only then can you open towards God. A direct opening towards God can be dangerous, because you may not be able to contain Him. To bring the goddess Ganges down from Heaven you need a Bhagiratha, the king who achieved it through his penance. You will not be able to hold her up, since a small puddle is enough to drown you—as you are now.

Nanak lays so much stress on the guru, and this is solely because the guru prepares you. As you become more and more capable of learning directly what flows from the guru, you will become a Bhagiratha. Then you too will be capable of supporting the heavenly Ganges.

If God is attained but not through actions, then how is He attained? Nanak answers:

But he who listens to but one teaching of the guru,
His understanding becomes like a precious jewel.

It is very difficult to listen to even one teaching of the guru since you cannot hear anything with your present being. It requires a complete transformation of your life. For the guru's teachings you have to be eager and look up towards him, you have to learn the art of being quiet and serene in his presence. You must learn to leave your head behind at home, because if you bring it along with you, you will not be able to hear. Even if the guru teaches, your head will draw different meanings. You will be told one thing, you will hear another. Having come empty-handed, you will leave empty-handed.

The guru's teachings cannot be learned through the head, but heard through the heart. He has to be listened to with total faith. When the guru teaches, if you are thinking he is right or he is wrong, you are still sitting in the classroom and not yet in a gathering of seekers.

Coming to the guru means: I am tired of judging right and wrong. Now I can judge no more. It means: I am tired of thinking, I can think no more. It means: I am sick and tired of myself and I want to give myself up. In short, this is what is called faith.

You come to the guru only when you are completely tired of yourself. If you still think yourself to be very intelligent, there is no point in coming to the guru because you are still your own guru. You still need to wander a bit more, bear more hardships, incur more pain through doubts and indecisions. It is no use coming when you are still raw. More pain and suffering are needed to ripen you. The day that you are completely fed up with yourself, then go to the guru.

People often go to the guru when they are not yet ready; they still believe in their own selves. Thus whatever the guru says they sit and weigh his words, judging the right and wrong. What suits them they will believe; what does not they will not believe. In that case, you are obeying your own self and not the guru.

You cannot look upon this as faith, or call it surrender because you have changed nothing. There is only one secret in going to the guru: leave your self behind and go.

Then whatever the guru says is right; there is nothing for you to decide. Only then can you hear his teachings with the entire heart—then only can you learn. He who has heard the guru's teachings becomes a Sikh.

The word *sikh* is a beautiful word, coined from the Sanskrit word for student. He who is ready to learn is a Sikh. He who is ready to listen to the teachings is a Sikh. He who is ready to listen to the teachings is a Sikh. But he who is still full of ego and not prepared to listen is not a Sikh. To put on the turban and adopt all the outward signs of a Sikh does not make you a Sikh, because to become a Sikh is an emotional happening.

Nanak says:

But he who listens to but one teaching of the guru.
His understanding becomes like a precious jewel.

By hearing a thousand things, nothing happens; by hearing just one, everything happens. And no matter how much *you* hear, nothing whatsoever happens. And no matter how much *you* have read, it brings no change within you—and the reason is clear: you have not heard from where you should have heard.

There are two ways to listen, with the intellect or with the heart. When the intellect listens, there is always a dichotomy: it thinks in terms of right/wrong, correct/incorrect, believable/unbelievable. The intellect never goes beyond the ego. It looks upon the heart as insane and never trusts it. The heart has almost been smothered because it cannot be trusted. You never know when it might make you do things you'd have to pay for later.

You are going along a street, you see a hungry man, and the heart says: "Give him something." The mind says: "Wait. First find out if he is a genuine case. He might be a fake out to deceive you. Besides, he seems fit enough to work, so why doesn't he?" The intellect will tell you a thousand things, but if even one emotion arises in the heart the intellect suppresses it.

If love arises in the heart, the mind says, "That's a dangerous path. Love is blind and has ruined many. Open your eyes and gather your wits about you. The path of love is a footpath wandering into forests and glens: the path of intellect is like the royal path, wide and clear. Where are you going? Don't lose the main road. Go along with the crowd, because it is always better to go where others are and dangerous to go on one's own."

Love is the path that has to be trod alone; it needs privacy, seclusion, solitude. Love says: "Give!" The intellect says: "Wait! Make inquiries before you give." But then you never will give. Love says: "Surrender! Rest your head on someone's feet and forget about yourself." The mind asks: "How can that be? The world is full of deceit. God knows how many have taken advantage of gullible people!"

But what have you that anyone can take away from you? What is it that you will lose by giving? There is nothing but misery and miserliness inside you, yet you protect and preserve it with all your might.

If you live according to the dictates of your mind, your heart will gradually contract and break. There is such a distance created between you and your heart that no news of the heart reaches you. When the mind stands in between, then even if you love, you love with your mind.

Have you noticed that your love also comes from the head? Even if you say you love with all your heart, these words are but inventions of your mind. If you search your heart there is not the slightest stir there; there is no thrill, no dance, no song within you.

The guru's teachings can only be heard with the heart. When Kabir said, "If you can cut off your head and put it on the ground, come with me," which head was he talking about?

Bodhidharma, the Buddhist master, went to China. He sat facing a wall and said, "I will only turn my face when the true disciple comes. Why should I talk to anyone else? It is as useless as talking to the walls!"

And one day a man came by the name of Hui Neng. He stood silently behind Bodhidharma for twenty-four hours. Finally he said, "Bodhidharma, please turn this way," but Bodhidharma did not move. Hui Neng cut off his right arm and placed it before Bodhidharma, saying, "If you still persist, I shall cut off my head and put it before you."

Bodhidharma said, "Of what use would that be? Are you really prepared to cut off your head?"

Hui Neng said, "Yes, I am prepared for whatever you wish."

That was the first time Bodhidharma turned his face towards somebody; Hui Neng received this honor. When Bodhidharma had asked if he was ready to lay down his head, he was not talking of the head on his shoulders; he was talking of the ego. As long as there is an "I am," or *I* am the judge, you cannot be the disciple; you cannot hear the guru's words.

> But he who listens to but one teaching of the guru,
> His understanding becomes like a precious jewel.

His mind attains to such a cleanliness, such a transparency that he begins to see through things. Thoughts vanish, because they are not of the heart. As intellect is pushed away and its fog clears, what remains is a purity that is crystal clear, a freshness. It is this cleansing that is referred to as "bathing in the Ganges."

When Nanak speaks of bathing in the sacred rivers, it is an internal bath where the understanding becomes clear, where you think no longer, where the head is put aside. The head is a borrowed affair given to you by this world. When you were born the heart already was, but there were no thoughts—only innocence. One by one you were given words and society began conditioning your thinking to prepare you for what is necessary in the world. It gave you your mind. It had to crush anything that endangered the society. A dichotomy was created within; the heart and the mind were broken apart.

The heart was your own. But unfortunately, that which was truly yours was taken away and became not your own; and that which was created by society was made your own. What was implanted from above became your center, and you have completely forgotten the heart—the authentic center.

Only by removing the head can you hear the guru's teaching. And one teaching is enough; there is no need for a thousand. One lesson, one secret is more than enough, and what is that secret?

He is the benefactor of all.
Let me never forget Him.

There are two states that require understanding: *smarana* means remembrance and *vismarana* means forgetfulness. The remembrance, smarana, is always flowing inside whatever you may be doing—walking, talking, sleeping, working.

A pregnant woman does all her daily chores—she cooks, she sweeps, she makes the beds—but all along she is extremely aware of the child she holds within her. A new life has struck root within her, a tiny heart has begun to throb. This awareness of the life she holds and has to protect is always with her; it results in a particular way of walking, so that from her walk you can tell she is pregnant.

Remembrance does not require a separate effort, because then you will keep forgetting. A thousand times in the day such a remembrance would be lost—while cooking, marketing or in the office. Similarly, it is not the remembrance of repeating a mantra. If you say, "Ram, Ram, Ram," all day, this is not smarana. Should you continue this, you could meet with an accident if you don't hear the car honking behind you. Any remembrance that is brought about by effort, rattling only in the mind, is not smarana.

That which permeates each hair of your body is what Nanak calls the unremembered remembrance. This remembrance has not to be repeated outwardly, because such a remembrance is superficial. Rather it saturates every pore of the body, every bit of you; whatever you do as His remembrance should reverberate like a soft melody within. Such remembrance Kabir called ṣurati; therefore we have his "Surati Yoga." Surati also means remembrance.

Then there is the other state, vismarana: you remember everything—except one thing—you have completely forgotten who you are. And he who has no remembrance of his own self, what can he know of existence?

In this century Gurdjieff has put great emphasis on self-remembering. His method consisted mainly of one thing: to remember all twenty-four hours of the day that *I am*. By constant knocking, this remembrance becomes stronger and stronger. A crystallization takes place—a new flowing element forms within.

But there is a great danger in this method, as also in the method of Mahavira and in Patanjali's yoga. And that danger is that you connect this new element to your ego, because they are very close together. Gurdjieff calls this element the crystallized self, and there is every possibility that you will be superimposing the ego over it. You might become filled with arrogance. You may begin to say: I alone am. There is the real hazard that you might deny God. Then, having almost arrived, you will not arrive. Then you will almost have reached the other shore and turned back.

The same hazard lies in Mahavira's method, because there too you have to intensify the feeling of I am. This leaves no place for God. Mahavira says when the feeling of I am becomes total, through it alone will God reveal Himself; the total I-amness becomes God. It is true and that is how it happened for Mahavira. However, the followers of Mahavira could not experience this; therefore, the flow of his method was stopped. The danger also exists in this method that the ego may begin to proclaim itself in the name of the *atman*.

This explains why we find no monks as egoistic as the Jaina *muni*. A Jaina monk cannot even fold his hands in *namaskara*, in greeting; he does not fold his hands at all. Again, the method is correct but hazardous. While every method has its hazard, there is no such risk in Nanak's method, because Nanak does not tell you to remember *yourself*. He says: There is one benefactor of all living creatures—may I never forget Him! The One resides in all; the One is hidden in the many—Ek Omkar Satnam. It is He that trembles in every leaf; it is He who wafts in every gust of the wind; it is He in the clouds, the moon, the stars, in every grain of sand. It is He! It is He! It is He! May I never forget Him! May His remembrance within me become crystallized and solid.

It is difficult to find a sage more humble than Nanak, because if He resides in everyone, it is easy to fold your hands and bow to another. It is easy to touch the feet of another because He is in all.

If there is no risk of egoism in Nanak's method, there is another type of hazard: in the constant remembrance that He is in all, you may forget your own self. You may forget that *you also are* and fall into a deep slumber, and begin to live as if in a trance. You will see Him all around you, except in your own self. All four directions will be filled with Him. You will sing his praises. You will tell of His glory but you will remain untouched by His glory.

This danger is less than that of egoism, because he who is asleep can be awakened but he who is filled with the ego is in deep sleep, in a coma that is very difficult to break. The sleep of the devotee can be broken. Yogis have given this sleep the name of *yoga tandra*, which is not actually sleep; if you are in tandra and someone claps his hands the tandra breaks.

Nanak's path is easier than Mahavira's, but each method carries some risk of going astray and falling from the path. The path of Mahavira got lost in renunciation; the path of Nanak went astray in wordly pleasures.

Mahavira said to renounce the world completely, and to not allow an iota of enjoyment, but become the supreme sannyasin. As a result Mahavira's sannyasins lived as enemies of the world. But to develop enmity with someone is to become tied to the very foe. While Mahavira's renunciate is constantly fighting with the mundane world, the very struggle keeps the remembrance of the object-world always fresh within and the remembrance of soul pushed to one corner. He worries about where to sleep, what he will eat, his clothes, his food. So deeply involved is he in mundane things that he has gone astray.

Nanak has said just the opposite: Everything is He. Since He is present in all things there is no need to leave the world, so his followers went astray *within* the world. The Punjabis, the Sikhs, the Sindis—all followers of Nanak—center their lives in eating, drinking, clothes; they take the mundane world to be everything. This was not Nanak's intent. When he said there was no need to leave the world, he did not mean that the world alone is enough. We have to seek Him in the world. The world need not be renounced nor is it everything.

Since there is a risk in every method, if you are not conscious and aware of it, ninety-nine times out of one hundred you are bound to fall into the hazard. For your intellect never follows a straight course but is like a donkey walking: he never walks straight, but either sticks to the wall or goes to the other extreme. While a dull fellow can be called a stupid ass, intellect is true donkeyishness. Intellect never walks a straight line but is either at one extreme or the other; the wise person is always in the middle.

Most of the secrets of Nanak's path were lost. The Sikhs still exist, but they are not truly Nanak's Sikhs—those who have heard the teachings, those who have set aside their heads, those whose hearts are filled with faith and those who have remembered but one thing, one secret method that solves everything: that there is but one benefactor of all beings—*Let me never forget Him!*

This knowledge should remain within constantly. If every act fills your very being with remembrance, then being in the world, you transcend the world—living in the middle of the world, you can reach *there*. There is no need to go to the temple, since the house itself becomes a temple. If the most ordinary task is filled with His special dignity, no work of yours will be ordinary; it will be extraordinary. Wherever you bathe, there will be the Ganges.

Whatever the hazard, it is all right. It makes no difference what you do; the real question is your own self. When *you* are different, the most ordinary stream becomes the Ganges; but if *you* are no different from the ordinary, then even the holy waters of the Ganges become ordinary. So it is a question of your being ordinary or nonordinary. And what is ordinariness but to live without His remembrance? Extraordinariness is priceless. It is to live with His remembrance. Accept losing everything but not His remembrance.

> But he who listens to but one teaching of the guru,
> His understanding becomes like a precious jewel.

Why talk of jewels? You will leave everything if need be, but not a jewel. If the need arises and you have money and a ruby in your pocket, you will part with the money, but not give up the ruby, because it has the most value. Remembrance is the precious jewel; let anything else in life drop away, because you know it is not worth a penny.

> Were you to live through four ages, or even ten times more,
> Were you known on all nine continents, and were to gain universal following,
> Were you to earn fame and praise from all of mankind,
> If you have not His grace, nothing will save you.

Nanak says you may have a life of four *yugas*, extending from the Sat Yuga to Kali Yuga. Your life may become the life of creation—and ten times more.

All the people in the world and in creation may know you and go along with you, great may be your name and fame, yet if He is not pleased by you, all this is useless, worthless.

What is the reason? Have you ever come across a person who is satisfied? Even after attaining wealth is the millionaire ever contented? After achieving fame, were Alexander the Great or Hitler satisfied? Instead of an atmosphere of wellbeing and fulfillment around the so-called successful man of the world, the reverse is the case. The nearer you approach these people, the more you sense their wretchedness. Their begging bowl has become bigger—they ask for more, and yet more! The nine continents of the world are not enough; life—four yugas long—is not enough. Infinite are their demands; they can never be filled because the more they receive the more they desire.

Desires always precede you. Wherever you may go, whatever you have, there is no sense of satisfaction and the ego won't let you retrace your steps.

Two beggars were resting under a tree when one of them began to complain. When even kings are unsatisfied, imagine the complaints of a poor beggar! "What a life! Is this living? Today we are in this village, tomorrow another. When they discover us traveling without a ticket they throw us off the train. Everyone preaches at us; if we ask for bread we get a sermon. They are always telling us we are fit enough to go to work. Nothing but insult and injury! Everywhere we are driven away. Every policeman is after us. Wherever we sleep they awaken us. It's impossible to get a good night's sleep."

The other beggar said, "Then why don't you quit this work?"

"What?" said the first beggar. "And admit I failed?"

If a beggar refuses to accept failure, how can a millionaire? How can a politician who is always proving himself accept his defeat? No one has yet been able to prove that he has accomplished anything real in worldly matters; if anyone had, Mahavira, Buddha, Nanak would all be fools.

But the ego refuses to turn back; it forever goads a person forward. Maybe the goal is still ahead. Who knows? Perhaps just a few steps more and we may reach. The ego spreads its net of hopes before you, drawing you further and further on, preventing you from turning back. You have come so far without acknowledging that you are on the wrong path, how can you do it now? So you cover your weakness and hide your faults and go on, as if some day you are sure to succeed.

All your so-called successful men hide the tears within and don't allow them to show. Their public faces are different from their private faces. They are all smiling and laughing, but alone in their own rooms they cry.

Nanak says: After attaining all there is no satisfaction. You can be satisfied only if He is pleased with you. Even a naked fakir sometimes attains satisfaction, whereas a man having everything remains unhappy. This means that satisfaction has nothing to do with what you have. It has everything to do with your connections with the supreme law—not your worldly attainments but your relationship with God. If you have established a relationship with Him, if you have succeeded in turning your face towards Him, having His grace, that decides whether you are fulfilled or not.

This is the meaning of attaining favor in His eyes. If He is not pleased with you, why did He give birth to you? He loves you, but alas, you stand with your back to Him! To find favor in His eyes means to stand facing Him, to have His grace. When you see His face in every face and feel His presence everywhere, then you find Him throbbing even in a stone; and when you begin to see Him everywhere, then you have found favor with Him.

Nanak says: If I have attained His pleasure, I have bathed in all the holy rivers. Now the heavenly Ganges has truly descended on you, not by bathing in the Ganges that descends from the Himalayas and flows through Prayag and Kashi. His Ganges descends from on high, when you find favor with Him.

Any worldly attainment is less than worthless; it is a loss in a deeper sense. All your fortunes are no more than misfortunes, since the only fortune worth attaining is to find favor in His eyes. When this becomes your only quest you become a sannyasin in the world. Then, whatever you do, your eye is on Him. You keep busy in works great or small, but never for a moment is He out of your mind. He is always present within you. This smarana, this surati, this remembrance which is the unrepeated repetition, gradually carves a place for you within His heart. Finding favor in His eyes, receiving His grace, your life is filled with dance and celebration is everywhere. Then you have nothing—and you have everything.

You are like the lowliest worm; even the worst of sinners may point the finger at you.

Nanak says that he who is bereft of God, even if he amasses all fortunes, is rated the lowest of worms, and even the worst of sinners heaps abuse on him.

Says Nanak, He makes the worthless worthy,
And showers the gifted with more gifts.
None but God can bestow such excellence.

None but God can bestow you with good qualities. To miss Him is to miss all. Remember, He is the target, the bull's eye, the only attainment. If the arrow of your life does not reach Him, no matter where it falls, you have failed.

Imagine how it feels to fall in love. The beloved accepts you, takes you to his heart, and your life thrills with the magic of love. Your feet hardly seem to touch the ground; you seem to fly in the air, as if you have developed wings. Unknown bells begin to ring in your life; you have never heard such a melody before. Your face lights up with a strange charm, your eyes convey something not of this world!

Therefore it is difficult to hide love. Everything else you can hide. If you are in love it will show in your face—in the way you walk, the way you talk—your eyes and everything about you will give news of it. Every pore of your body will be saturated with love, because love is a remembrance. If the love and acceptance of an ordinary person fills your life with such thrill, then when the whole existence accepts you, what will it be like? When the whole existence loves you, embraces you; when you are tied in the bond of love with existence...!

This is what Meera means when she says, "Krishna, when will you come to the nuptial bed? I have adorned it with flowers. When will you come? When will you accept me?"

The devotee is always thirsting for the lord, as the beloved is for the lover. When the partridge thirsts for the morning dew he calls out. Even a single drop satisfies; one drop becomes a pearl. When a person is so thirsty, the longing is so great, then ordinary water turns into pearls. When your longing is so great, a single teaching of the guru becomes a jewel. One drop is enough; one teaching of the guru can become the ocean. And what is the teaching? It is such a small sutra. If you understand it, grasp it—it is small; if you do not, you may take infinite lives more to understand!

So Nanak says one small secret formula quenches all your thirst, that is all: *He is the benefactor of all. Let me never forget Him.* Such a small maxim—and it quenches all thirst, destroys all desires! And Nanak says: *He makes the worthless worthy* and fills you with qualities. When you face Him you become worthy of all attributes. You always were worthy. You were always empty and as you turned towards Him, Lo! You were filled. His glory has stirred you. The *veena* was always ready within. When you entrusted it to His hands, when His fingers have touched the strings...lo! music is born—the music that lay dormant all this time, awaiting His touch. It can only happen if you put your veena in His hands.

This entrusting itself is *shraddha*, disciplehood—to surrender, to be a Sikh. To entrust the veena is the meaning of sannyas. Then you say: Thy will be done. Your wish is now my life. All that is mine is to remember You; all else is Yours. The only need in life is that He should fill your vessel for you not to remain a lonely wanderer in life, that He should be your friend and companion, or else you may seek Him in many places but find Him in none.

Some look to wealth to bring a comrade. Some look to a wife, a husband; but all these quests are imperfect. Until you seek Him directly you will not attain Him. All disqualifications and shortcomings vanish as soon as He is attained.

Nanak does not suggest that you get rid of your defects one by one, because they are infinite. Avoid stealing, killing, anger, sex, greed, attachments, envy and what else? Nanak does not advise this. He says turn your face Godwards. Remember Him! As soon as His gaze falls on you everything will change. When you have been accepted and have won His favor, then wrath will vanish and greed will fall all on its own.

Once He is attained, for what are you greedy? What is left for your wrath? Where is the sex? Where is the desire when the ultimate coupling has already taken place—the union with existence? After the ultimate nuptial there is no more search for the beloved. Kabir says: I am Rama's bride. When you are in love with Rama, when you become His bride, what sexual desire remains?

In our lust we were really searching for Him. We sought Him in dirty gutters and were never satisfied, because the filth of sex could not satiate. It is like forcing the swan to drink from the gutter when it is used to the crystal-clear waters of Lake Mansarovar. The swan within asks also for Mansarovar. Nothing less than God can quench your thirst.

Wander where you will, no one besides him can satisfy you. You are wandering for lives on end without Him, yet you have not come to your senses. You still hope to reach without Him. Your ego stands guard behind, telling you not to let a full life's toil go in vain.

It is just as if a man builds a house on shaky foundations, perhaps on sand. When the house is nearing completion another man comes and tells him not to enter the house, because it is sure to fall and he may die. Then the mind says, "You have spent so much money, taken so many pains, gone through so much difficulty. Can you let so many years' toil go in vain? And who knows? It might not fall ! Perhaps the expert is wrong. Besides, right now it is standing. Who can be sure it will fall?"

Such is your case too, like a man who has lost his way and has been told that he left the road far behind.

In reading the memoirs of a poet, I particularly liked one incident. He writes that he lost his way in the valleys of the Himalayas. He stopped his car before a hut. When a woman opened the door he asked, "Am I on the right path to Manali?"

The woman looked at him keenly and said, "But I don't know which way you are heading."

The poet thought she was a mountain girl and perhaps not too intelligent, so he said, "Tell me, is the light of my car pointing in the direction of the road to Manali?"

"There is a light," she said, "red in color."

When you have travelled a number of miles in mountainous terrain and someone says your light points in the wrong direction, you feel a terrible blow. It means you have to retrace your steps and go back all the way you came. Your ego protests and says, "Go a little further; don't give up. Who knows, this woman may be wrong! She may be stupid, or mad, or lying, or trying to mislead you!"

To turn back is a blow to the ego. You wonder, "Could I have been wrong all this time?" Therefore it is easier to teach children than to teach older people. If they have already walked sixty or seventy miles, can they admit to being wrong all that time? The child never resists, because the child has yet not walked. He will go wherever you take him. An old man never will. He will insist that the path he has followed is correct—because his ego depends on it.

You are all old! God knows how many lives you have been walking, and that is the difficulty. You haven't the courage to abandon the wrong path, because it involves so much effort through infinite lives...rather than to admit that all is in vain, that for lives on end you have been ignorant. Therefore, when you go to a sage you prepare a thousand devices to save your old self, lest His grace pour on you and your cloak of knowledge and experience come off !

Remember! You will have to turn back, because you have left the road way behind...far, far away. It is in this light that Jesus said: Become like children once again. He is telling you to turn back, to be once again innocent as children. Once you move your intellect out of the way all attributes will shower on you. They always have!

Nanak was not a highly educated person, nor did he come from a rich family. He was born in an ordinary household. On the very first day he started school, schooling was seen to be useless, and yet the divine showers poured on him.

It it rained on Nanak, if it rained on Kabir, why not on you? The only obstacle is that you stand with your back to Him.

One secret formula solves everything: *He is the benefactor of all* living creatures. *Let me never forget Him.*

Chapter 5

The Art of Listening

Through listening occult powers and saintliness are gained,
Heaven and earth are made stable,
And the world and lower worlds revolve.
Through listening death does not touch.
Nanak says, Through listening devotees attain bliss,
And sin and sorrow are destroyed.

Through listening Vishnu, Brahma and Indra came into being,
The most sinful will sing His praises,
And the secrets of yoga and mysteries of the body are revealed.
Through listening all the scriptures and teachings are known.
Nanak says, Through listening devotees attain bliss,
And sin and sorrow are destroyed.

Through listening all truth and contentment are attained,
And the virtue of bathing at the sixty-eight holy places is gained,
And through listening again and again honor is earned.
Through listening spontaneous meditation happens.
Nanak says, Through listening devotees attain bliss,
And sin and sorrow are destroyed.

Through listening the highest virtues are acquired,
Sage, saint and king come into being,
And the blind find the path.

Through listening the fathomless is fathomed.
Nanak says, Through listening devotees attain bliss,
And sin and sorrow are destroyed.

M AHAVIRA HAS DESCRIBED four starting places from which you can reach the other shore. Of these, two can be understood: that of a *sadhu* and that of a *sadhvi*, a holy man and a holy woman. The other two seem more difficult: that of a *shravaka* and *shravika*. Shravaka means one who has learned the art of listening; he knows how to listen and understands what listening means. And shravika is used for the female.

Mahavira says that there are some who must keep on performing *sadhanas* in order to arrive. This is necessary for those who are not adept at hearing because if you can listen—totally—there is nothing more to be done to reach the other shore.

These sutras of Nanak depict the glory of shravana, listening, although on the face of it, it seems an exaggeration that everything can be attained merely by listening. We have been listening for infinite births and nothing has happened. It is our experience that no matter how much we hear, we remain the same. Our vessel is greasy; words fall on it but they slide off, leaving us untouched.

If our experience is correct, Nanak is exaggerating. But it is not true; our experience is incorrect, because we have never listened. We have many tricks and devices not to listen. Let us understand them first.

The first trick is: we hear only that which we want to and not what is being said. With great cleverness we hear what lets us remain as we are; nothing goes in which may cause a change in us. This is not only the observation of the sages; scientists who have carried out research on the human mind say that ninety-eight percent of what we hear we do not take in. We only hear the two percent that fits into our understanding; that which doesn't, cannot bypass the many obstructions.

Anything that synchronizes with your understanding cannot change you. It can only help to reinforce that understanding. Rather than transform you it gives yet more stones and cement to strengthen your foundations.

The Hindu hears only what strengthens his Hindu mind; the Muslim hears only what strengthens the Muslim mind; so also the Sikh, the Christian, the Buddhist. If you listen only to strengthen your own preconceptions, to strengthen your own house, then you will miss hearing completely, for truth has no connection with Hindu or Muslim or Sikh. It has nothing to do with the conditioning of your mind.

Only when you set aside your entire way of thinking will you be able to understand what Nanak means; however, this is a very difficult thing to do, because our concepts are invisible. They are microscopic, or as transparent as a wall of glass; they cannot be seen. Unless you knock against them you are not conscious of their existence. You think that there is wide open space ahead, and the sun, moon, and the stars. You are not aware of the transparent wall in between.

Hearing a speaker you tell yourself that he is correct when what he says is consistent with your thoughts. To other things you say that it is not so because it disagrees with your thoughts. So you are not truly listening but only lend your ear to what agrees with you and strengthens your opinion. The rest, that you don't care about, you ignore and forget. Even if you do happen to hear something that is contrary to your understanding, you tear it to bits with your reasoning, because one thing you are sure of: whatever matches your thoughts is correct, what doesn't is incorrect, false.

If you have attained truth there is no further need to listen, but you have not attained truth so it is incumbent on you to listen. How can you still be searching for the truth if you have the idea that you have already attained it? Instead, you have to stand before truth absolutely bare, empty, void, naked. If your scriptures, your beliefs, your doctrines stand in the way you will never be able to listen; whatever falls on your ears will be nothing but the echo of your own concepts and you will hear only your own thoughts throbbing within you. Then Nanak's words will seem a preposterous exaggeration.

Another way to escape listening is to fall asleep when something significant is being said. This is a trick the mind uses to save itself; it is a very deep process by which, when something is about to touch you, you fall asleep.

I was a guest at the house of a very learned pundit. He was well-versed in the Shastras and there was no one to equal him in reading the Ramayana. Thousands of people came to hear him. We were staying in the same room and as we put off the lights to prepare to sleep, J heard his wife come in. She spoke in a low tone but I could still hear. "Please say something to Munna. He won't go to sleep."

"How will my talking help?" asked the pundit.

"I have seen a number of people falling asleep when you speak at your meetings, so how could a small child resist your words! Come, say a few words to him," she answered.

People go to religious services only to fall asleep. Even those who suffer from insomnia sleep well in religious meetings. What happens? It's a trick of your mind. Sleep is like the soldier's armor; it protects you against all you

don't want to know. So you look as if you are listening, but
you are not awake; and without being awake how can you
hear?

While talking you are awake; while listening you are
not. And this doesn't happen only at a religious meeting.
As soon as another person talks to you, you are no longer
alert, but lost in an internal dialogue of your own. While
he talks to you, you pretend to be listening, but you are
really talking to yourself. Then to whom do you prefer to
listen? Definitely to your own self, because the voice of the
other person doesn't even reach you; your own voice is
enough to drown out all the other voices. And then you
fall asleep out of boredom with yourself, because what you
are saying inside you have said and heard so many times
before. Sleep is an escape from the repetitive talk that is
going on internally.

He alone is capable of listening who has broken this
conversation within. And that is the art of shravana. If
the internal dialogue stops even for a moment, you find
the whole expanse of space opening within you; all that
was as yet unknown begins to be known. You find the
boundary of that which was boundless; you become
familiar with the unfamiliar. He who was a total
stranger, with whom you were not acquainted at all,
becomes your very own! And it all happens so suddenly.
The universe is your home!

All gurus, all religions aim at one thing only: how to
break the constant dialogue within. Whether we call it
yoga or meditation or repetition of mantra, the aim is to
break the constant internal flow of words in order to
create an empty space within. If it happens even for a
little while you will understand what Nanak is talking
about.

Through listening occult powers and saintliness are gained.
Heaven and earth are made stable,
And the world and lower worlds revolve.
Through listening death does not touch.
Nanak says, Through listening devotees (attain) bliss,
And sin and sorrow are destroyed.

It is hard to believe what Nanak says—that by listening alone a person can attain *siddhis*, occult powers; or a person can become a *pir*, a saint; or a *devta*, a celestial being; or even Indra, the king of the devtas; that by listening, the sky and earth revolve and worlds and lower worlds exist, and death does not touch you.

It all seems a gross exaggeration, but it is not so in the least, because as soon as you learn the art of listening you learn the art of becoming acquainted with life itself. And as you begin to acquire the knowledge of existence, you find that the same silence you experience at the moment of shravana is the principle of all existence. It is the basis on which the sky and the earth are maintained; it is on the hub of this void that terrestrial bodies revolve; it is in silence that the seed breaks and becomes a tree, that the sun rises and sets, and moon and stars are formed and disintegrate. When words fall into silence within you, you reach the place where all creation is born and where it becomes extinct.

Once it happened: a Muslim fakir came to Nanak and said, "I have heard that you can turn me to ashes by your will, and that you can also create me by your will. I cannot believe this." He was an honest, genuine seeker who had not come out of idle curiosity.

Nanak said, "Close your eyes. Be relaxed and quiet and I will do for you what you wish." The fakir at once closed his eyes and became tranquil. Had he not been a serious seeker he would have been frightened, because what he had asked was very dangerous—to be turned into ashes and remade, because he had been told that creation and extinction lay in Nanak's hands.

It was morning, a day just like this. Nanak was sitting under a tree beside a well at the outskirts of the village. His disciples Bala and Mardana were also with him. They were very much perturbed, because never had Nanak said such a thing to anyone before. What would happen now? They too became alert and the very trees and stones also became alert because Nanak was about to perform a miracle!

The fakir sat, silent and tranquil. He must have been a man of great faith. He became absolutely empty within. Nanak put his hand on his head and pronounced the Omkar. As the story goes, the man turned to ashes. Then Nanak again sounded the Omkar and the man regained his body.

If you take the story at its face value, you will miss it, but this did happen within the seeker. When he became completely empty within, when the internal dialogue was broken and Nanak gave out the chant of Omkar, the sadhaka attained the state of shravana—there was nothing but the resonance of Om within him. And with this resonance the annihilation took place on its own. Everything within the man was lost—all the world and its boundaries—turned to naught, to ashes. There was nothing within, nobody. The house was empty. Then Nanak once again chanted the Omkar and the man came back to himself. He opened his eyes, fell at Nanak's feet and said, "I had thought this could never happen, but you have proved it possible!"

There are those who miss the point and believe that the man actually turned to ashes and Nanak brought him back to life, but this is a foolish interpretation. Internally, however, the annihilation and creation did take place. The fakir was capable of listening. When you develop the art of listening then it is not me you will hear. I am an excuse. The guru is just an excuse. Then you will be adept at hearing the breeze as it passes through the trees; in the silence of solitude you will hear the Omkar, the basis of all life. And in the resonance of Omkar you will find that everything depends on the void. The rivers flow in the void, the ocean becomes one with it. When you close your eyes you will hear your heartbeat and also the faint sound of the blood flowing, and you will know that you are not these; you are also the observer, the witness. Then death cannot touch you.

For those who have mastered the art of shravana there is nothing more to know. All existence comes into being through shravana. All existence happens through the void; and when you are listening, the stamp of the void falls on you. Then the void vibrates in you and that is the basic resonance of existence—it is the basic unit.

By shravana death cannot touch you. Once you know the art of listening, where is death?—because the listener attains the knowledge of the witness. Right now you think and think, and then listen. The thinker will die because he belongs to the flesh. The day you listen without thinking you will become the witness. Then I shall be speaking, your head will be hearing, and there will be a third within you who will simply watch that listening taking place. When this happens a new element begins to unfold within you, the beginning of crystallization of the witness; and there is no death for the witness.

Therefore Nanak says that through shravana death does not touch. It is through listening that the devotee achieves permanent happiness; it is through shravana that suffering and sin are destroyed.

How is this internal dialogue to be broken? How can you become silent? How can the clouds be made to disperse so that the clear skies can be seen? This is what the process is all about. When someone is speaking, there is no need for you to keep on talking. You can be silent, but this habit dies hard, so you go on and on, talking away.

I asked a little boy, "Has your little sister started talking?" He said, "Talking? And how! It's so long since she started to talk that now she won't stop. Now we are all busy trying to keep her quiet."

When you came into this world you were silent. Do you want to be talking away all the time till you leave it? Then you will miss life and even deny yourself the supreme touch, the supreme bliss of death. You entered this world in silence; prepare to leave it in silence, too. Talking is for in-between, and only in the mundane life is it useful, in relating to another person.

When sitting by yourself it is madness to talk since silence is the process by which we relate to our own self. If silent you will find it difficult to keep up outside relationships; it you talk, it will be difficult to relate to yourself. Talking is a bridge that is connecting us to others; silence is a bridge that connects us with our self. Somewhere, somehow, you err in your selection of the means.

If a person becomes quiet and talks to no one, he establishes no relationships and gradually people will begin to forget him. Dumb people are the most miserable, even more so than a blind man. Notice carefully that you feel more pity for the dumb than the blind. While it is true that the blind man cannot see, he does establish relationships; he can have a wife; he can talk to his children; he can be a part of society; he can have friends. But the mute is closed within himself with no way out, no way for him to establish contact with others. You can sense his difficulty in the agony of his gestures. When you cannot follow him, how helpless and miserable he feels. There is no one more pitiable than a dumb person: he cannot talk, he cannot open his heart to anyone, he cannot express his feelings of love or joy or sorrow and unburden his mind.

As the mute is incapable of establishing contact with others, so you have become incapable of establishing contact with yourself. Where you should be dumb—absolutely silent—you keep on talking. The other is not there at all, so to whom do you talk? You raise questions yourself and then answer them yourself. This is nothing but a sign of madness. The only difference between a mad person and you is that the mad person talks aloud to himself while you talk silently. Some day you too may join their ranks and begin to talk aloud. Right now you manage to repress the insanity within, but it can erupt any moment, because it is a cancerous ulcer.

Why does this internal dialogue go on? What is the reason? It is out of simple habit. All life long you are taught how to speak. A child is born and the first concern of all around him is that he should speak as early as possible since this is considered a sign of intelligence; the longer he takes, the duller he is considered to be.

Since talking is a social art and man is part of society, how happy the parents are when the child talks. Also many necessities of life are fulfilled by talking: when you are hungry, thirsty, you can express your need. It affords a protection in life.

What on earth is the use of silence? It seems to be useless. It holds no meaning in our day-to-day life. How can you go shopping if you are silent? How will you satisfy the various needs of the body without communication?

We are so habituated to talking that we talk even in sleep, all twenty-four hours of the day; talking is automatic.

We keep on talking and rehearsing. Before talking to someone we rehearse the dialogue internally; and then, after the conversation, we repeat over and over all that happened—what I said and what you said, and then what I said—and we gradually forget what we are losing by this useless talk. Externally you may be gaining something, but within you are certainly losing contact with yourself. You are getting closer to people while you are becoming further removed from yourself. And the more adept you become at this game, the harder it will be for you to go into silence. Habit! And habit cannot be broken just like that.

When a person walks he makes use of his legs; while sitting there is no need to move your legs. When you are hungry you eat; if a person keeps on eating when not hungry it is a sign of insanity. Similarly, if you try to sleep when you are not sleepy it is inviting unnecessary frustration. But we do not think the same way when it comes to talking. We never say that we shall stop all talk unless it is a necessity.

It seems as if we have completely forgotten that the process of talking can be begun or ended at will, which it certainly can, or else all religions become impossible. Religion is possible only through silence. This is why Nanak praises shravana so much, which is in praise of silence, to glory in silence so that you may begin to hear. But you go along merrily talking, carried along by your own momentum, and even if it comes to your understanding it is very difficult to stop, since habits take time to leave and often require the development of opposite habits in order to break them. So you will have to practice silence. To stay in the company of holy men means to practice silence. In the presence of the guru there is nothing to say and everything to hear. You listen and sit quietly. You don't go to the guru for a chat.

A few days ago a friend offered to come for a discussion. I said, "In that case, *you* talk. I shall listen but say nothing."

He said, "But I want to exchange views with you."

I answered, "I have nothing to do with your thoughts. If you are prepared to be without thoughts I can give you something. Or, if you have something to give, I'm prepared to take."

We have nothing whatsoever to give, but we are eager to carry out transactions in thoughts. We say exchange of thoughts and what we mean is you give me a bit of your insanity, and I give you a bit of mine. As both are mad enough, there is no need of any give-and-take.

We do not go to the guru to exchange views but to sit quietly next to him. Only when we are silent can we hear, and that requires a little practice. How can you begin? In the twenty-four hours of a day you need to be silent for an ✳ ✳ hour or so, whenever it is convenient. The internal dialogue will go on but don't be party to it. The key to it all is to hear the talk within just as you would hear two people talking, but remain apart. Don't get involved; just listen to what one part of the mind is telling another. Whatever comes, let it come; don't try to repress it. Only be a witness to it.

A lot of rubbish that you have gathered over the years will come out. The mind has never been given the freedom to throw away this rubbish. When given the chance, the mind will run like a horse that has broken his reins. Let it run! You sit and watch. To watch, just watch, is the art of patience. You will want to ride the horse, to direct it this way or that, because that is your old habit. You will have to exercise some patience in order to break this habit.

Wherever the mind goes, merely watch; don't try to enforce any order as one word gives rise to another and another, and a thousand others, because all things are connected. Perhaps Freud was unaware that, when he based his entire psychoanalytic method on this "free association of thoughts" as he called it, it derived from yoga. One thought comes, and then another, and each thought is linked to the other in a continuous chain.

Once I was traveling in a train that was very full. When the inspector came to check our tickets he looked underneath my seat, where there was an old man hiding. He said, "You, old man, come out! Where is your ticket?"

The poor man fell at his feet and said, "I don't have any ticket nor any money but I have to go to the village in connection with my daughter's wedding. I would be grateful if you let me go this time."

The inspector took pity on him and let him go; but when he turned to the next row he saw another man underneath the seat. This man was young. "Are you also going for your daughter's marriage?" the inspector joked with him.

"No, sir," said the young man, "but I'll soon be this old man's son-in-law, and I too am penniless."

This is how things are joined. Someone is the son-in-law; someone is the father-in-law. The connections are hidden and need to be brought out. There is a whole chain of them within you and you will often be shocked when you know how, and in what queer ways, your thoughts are interlinked. Sometimes you will also be frightened and think you are going mad.

This is, however, a very wonderful method. Whatever is happening, allow it to happen. If it is convenient and possible, speak your thoughts out loud so that you can also hear them, because within the mind the thoughts are subtle and there is the fear you may not be very conscious of them. Speak them aloud, listen to them, and be very aware and alert to remain well separated from them. Resolve to speak out whatever comes to mind, but be absolutely unbiased and neutral. If abuse comes—abuse! If Ram, Ram comes or Omkar, give voice to that.

It is absolutely necessary to empty the mind patiently for six months, because all your life long you have done nothing but load it with thoughts. If you persist patiently and diligently then only six months is enough; otherwise it might take you six years, or six lives! All depends on you, how wholeheartedly and sincerely you work at this method.

Many a time it will happen that you will forget to be a witness; you will ride the horse once again and set out on your journey of thoughts, involved once again. If you identify yourself with some thought, then you will have failed; as soon as you become aware of this, get off the horse and let the words, the thoughts, go where they will without riding them. Just keep watching.

Gradually, very faintly, you will begin to hear the footsteps of silence, and experience the art of listening. Then, when you are qualified to listen you no longer need look for a guru, because wherever you are, there the guru is. The breeze will stir in the trees, the flowers and the dry leaves will fall—you will hear all. Sitting on the seashore you will hear the waves. You will hear the river, the spate, the lightning in the sky, the thundering of clouds. You will hear the birds sing, a child cry, a dog bark—under all conditions you will *hear*.

When the art of listening is mastered, the guru is present everywhere. If shravana is not known, all the masters sitting before you cannot make you listen. The guru is—only when you can listen.

Nanak says, Through listening the devotee is full of bliss,
And sin and sorrow are destroyed.

If you have learned the art of listening you will be filled with joy, because then you have become the witness; and the witness is joy itself. Shravana occurs, the mind is no more, and its extinction is joy. Bliss is to go beyond the mind. At the moment when listening takes place, the chain of thoughts is broken and there is bliss, there is transcendence. You are no longer in the valley of thoughts but on the lofty peak where thoughts do not reach—beyond the dust and grime, where there is only unbroken silence. On this lofty, silent peak there is nothing but the resonance of bliss and you reach the supreme blessedness.

Through shravana alone suffering and sin are destroyed. Where is sin for him who has acquired the art of listening? For sin is connected with thoughts only. Understand this a little. A car passes you on the road and the thought occurs: I should have a car like that. Now you have become glued to the thought. There is only one refrain within you: how to get such a car. By fair means or foul the car must be had. You cannot sleep nights, your days are equally restless; your dreams are filled with the car, your thoughts are filled with the car; the car surrounds you on all sides.

What actually happened? The car passed and a thought arose within you, because everything that you see is reflected in the mind. But once you are identified with the thought, you cannot stand apart.

A beautiful woman passes and a thought arises in the mind. This is natural, because the mind is only a mirror; its function is to reflect whatever happens around it. When the woman passed, the mind registered the reflection. When the woman is no longer there, the reflection must also cease. Had you been just a witness there was no way to sin. But once you became identified with the thought you wanted this woman at any cost. By love or by force, by violence or by nonviolence, you must have her.

Thus a single thought catches hold of you, possesses you. Had you allowed the thoughts to rise and fade, and been only a witness, there would be no question of sin. All sins arise because of your identification with thoughts. Then the thoughts get hold of you so badly that you shake like a leaf in a storm. Thoughts have brought you nothing but unhappiness and suffering, but you are not even conscious enough to realize that all suffering coincides with thoughts, and bliss occurs only in the state of no-thoughts.

Nanak says: Through shravana suffering and sin are destroyed, because the fruit of sin is suffering. Sin is the seed and suffering is the fruit.

When sin is gone suffering is no more. What remains when sin and suffering are no more—that state is samadhi, which is bliss itself.

Nanak says, Through listening devotees attain bliss.
And sin and sorrow are destroyed.

He who becomes an adept at listening is absolved of all sin. Such a devotee, says Nanak, attains bliss and his bliss develops more and more each day. The word *vigasu* is used, which is very meaningful; it contains both bliss and the idea of its continuous flowering and development. So *ananda*, bliss, is a flower that keeps on blooming. The moment never comes when it is in complete bloom. It just blooms and blooms—from perfection to more perfection, as if the morning sun rises and keeps on rising, and never sets. Such is this ananda. It is like a flower that never withers, like a sun that never sets.

When the void begins to crystallize in the heart and silence is born, the ripples of ananda rise and, having arisen, keep spreading more and more. Remember, ananda is not an object that you are done with once attained. It keeps on increasing constantly, limitlessly, once it is attained.

Thus we say: God is infinite. Thus we say: God is bliss. Because bliss is infinite, you can never attain it completely; every moment you feel it increasing and increasing, and each time it satiates you completely. This is a riddle that cannot be solved by the intellect, which argues: If once attained, what is left to be attained? Satiation is also not a goal but a live happening.

Ananda is not something to measure in kilos; you can't buy a kilo or two and be done with it, because bliss is infinite. Once you step into it, you drown in it more and more, and the delight is that each time you feel you have got it in full measure, yet each time it feels so much more than before.

Purna, the whole, the perfect, is also progressive; it is not a dead thing. It stops nowhere but keeps spreading more and more. Furthermore, we have given existence the name of Brahma, that which is endlessly expanding. The word also means that there is no limit to its expansion, that it is not just as much today as yesterday, but it spreads and spreads endlessly.

Through listening Vishnu, Brahma and Indra came into being,
The most sinful will sing His praises,

And the secrets of yoga and mysteries of the body are revealed.
Through listening all the scriptures and teachings are known.
Nanak says, Through listening devotees attain bliss,
And sin and sorrow are destroyed.

He who has heard truth in the guru's words has known fragrance in sitting quietly next to him. He finds that the happening flows towards him through such a person, and begins to penetrate him. Knowledge is contagious; bliss is contagious. If your doors are open bliss enters into you like a breath of wind from a person who has attained it. While you stand to gain he loses nothing since it increases and expands to the extent that it is shared. If you are silent a space is created within you. Remember, existence prefers a vacuum. No sooner do you become empty than existence fills your vacuum. As the river water rushes in to fill your empty jug, create a vacuum and air will rush in to fill it. Prepare to be empty and you will be filled, but as long as you are filled with yourself you will remain empty. Empty yourself and you will be filled with supreme energy. As you depart from one corner, God will enter from the other.

Nanak says: Even those who lead sinful lives, whose lips have never spoken a good word, whose tongue has always uttered abuse, whose heads are filled with curses, if even these listen but once, they are filled with glory. An infinitesimal glimpse of shravana can make you fresh, can bathe your entire being.

Nanak does not tell evildoers to stop sinning. He just tells them to listen and the sins will fall away. He doesn't tell them to improve first and only then can they listen, because that would be impossible and then there would be no hope for people to listen.

Nanak says: Listen and forget about sin, forget about evil. And no sooner do you hear than a new sutra, a new path, begins to unfold in your life. A new spark will kindle a fire that will burn away your sins; your past turns into ashes as soon as you become silent.

What is sin? What have you been doing in the past? You have identified totally with your thoughts, constantly turning them into actions, and this is sin. Stand away from your thoughts; actions will crumble, the doer will be lost, and all connection with the past will snap. Then you realize that the past was no more than a dream. Through infinite lives everything you have done is because of the illusion of doing; the day that illusion is broken, all actions come to an end.

People will be unable to understand Nanak if they hold the common belief that each sin has to be wiped out by an equal virtue. For people of calculating minds this seems but fair—that for each sin you must atone with a corresponding virtue. But if this were so you would never be liberated; for infinite lives you have sinned, and where is the guarantee that in the course of your equalization you will not sin further? Then this chain is impossible to break and liberation is impossible.

Your sins spread over infinite lives. If God is a shop-keeper or a magistrate who insists on the cleansing of each sin, when will it ever end? And even assuming that all present deeds are virtuous, it will still take infinite time to make up for the past. And how can you be sure you will perform only good deeds? Wise men follow a different method of calculation altogether, because they say that the question is not of sin but of the basis of sin, its very roots.

Say you have watered a tree for fifty years. So you think you will have to starve its roots of water for another fifty years before it dies? The tree no longer depends on you for water; it draws its supplies directly from the soil.

Cut off its roots and the tree will die today, but you can tear off the leaves one by one and the tree will not die even in forty years; no sooner do you break one leaf than two new ones are born. No, by cutting leaves and branches you are merely pruning the tree. In the same way you cannot nullify sin by virtue. Eradicate one sin and four new others spring up.

Catch hold of the roots. Actions are the leaves, and the sense of doing is the root. Remove doing and the tree will dry up at once. All flow came from: I am doing. The art of eradicating the doing is witnessing, and to witness means shravana.

Nanak sings of such unique and wonderful glory! He says: Be silent and listen. In moments of such listening you are no longer the doer. Listening is a passive state since you have nothing to do in order to listen; it is not an action.

Now this is interesting. In order to see, one has to open one's eyes, whereas the ears are already open. You have nothing to do in order to hear. Therefore, there can be some sense of doing in seeing, but hearing does not involve doing at all. Someone speaks. You listen, sitting empty, motionless, passive; you are in non-action. Therefore that glory is not attained even by seeing which is attained by listening; hence the stress on shravana.

Mahavira speaks of *samyak shravana*, right listening, which Buddha also emphasizes. To Nanak it is a wonderful glory to hear. There is no doer there. No one is present at the moment of listening. If you are silent, who is there within? There is a solitude in moments of listening in which a voice resounds and passes away. There is no one within. If a thought comes, you come along with it; when thoughts are not, you are not. Since ego is the name given

to a collection of thoughts, shravana also means the ego-
less state.

Nanak says: Through shravana alone you know the
tactics of yoga and the secrets of the body. This is very
significant. The Western physicians have not been able
to understand where and how the East acquired its
knowledge of the human body and its secrets. Surgery
developed in the West mainly because the dead are not
burned by Christians and corpses were therefore available to be removed from their graves and taken for dissection.

Since Hindus burn their dead and no bodies were
available for dissection, then how did the East acquire its
knowledge of the human body? The East had no means:
no corpses, no scientific development, no technique, no
technology, and yet its knowledge of the human body is
perfect. There is much research and discussion on the
subject, but this sutra of Nanak provides an answer to the
mystery.

Through shravana alone you know the knack of yoga
and the secrets of the body. When you become empty and
are established within yourself, you begin to see your
body within. Right now all you have seen of your body is
the skin. Until now you have gone round and round your
house and know only the outside walls; you have no
knowledge of what is inside.

From within you begin to see the entire network of the
different systems. It is a unique experience to enter the
palace and see all the grandeur within. It happens when
you become silent and tranquil, when the mind poses no
problems. The mind is a door to the world outside, and the
moment you join it you move outward; whatever you
think will be outside of you—wealth, woman, house, car,
fame, status. All objects of thought are outside of you.

So as soon as you stop thinking, you withdraw from the outside and the energy is focused within. Now you sit on your own throne and see inside yourself for the first time. Then you know that this body is not as small as it looks; this small body holds a miniature universe within itself. It is a model of the vast universe, the vast existence. Therefore the Hindus say the whole of the universe is contained in an eggshell. Nanak says that he who becomes quiet, he who has become silent and learned the art of listening, and who has begun to hear his own body from within, comes to know the secrets of the body as well as the methods of yoga.

Whatever Patanjali has written in the Yoga Sutras derives from the experience of his own body and no one else's. His findings still stand totally correct even to this day. All the methods of yoga have been discovered with his own body.

I shall give you a few examples. If you become tranquil you will find that the rate of your breathing changes. As soon as thoughts stop, respiratory movements change; when thoughts start again the rate of breathing changes. If you begin to recognize the rate of breathing when you are tranquil, all you have to do is breathe in that rhythm and you will become tranquil. So you have learned one secret; you have the key to one mystery.

When you are absolutely peaceful, the spinal column becomes perpendicular to the ground you are sitting on. This happens on its own if the man is healthy and not ill or too old. Therefore, when you want to be peaceful, fix your spinal cord at a ninety-degree angle. Thus gradually a yogi comes to experience what is going on within him.

As you progress further you will feel energy rising upwards from your spine. You will feel it as a sharp warmth that flows through the spine. Ripples of electricity rise within, and as they climb higher and higher, you are filled with joy. Pain and despondency begin to vanish and a feeling of joy arises. As the electrical waves go even higher, all that is trivial and base in life falls away into the valley below and you are as if on a high mountain. The fog of the village, the talk of people and the mundane struggles of life are left far behind as you have risen.

This is why the spinal column is called the *Meru and*. Meru is a mountain in heaven; thus it is the Meru spine and it is said that he who climbs the heights of Meru and reaches the same height as Mt. Meru in heaven. The Hindu never shaves a tuft of hair at the top of the head; this is the last peak, the seventh door from which the energy then is absorbed into the infinite. When your energy begins to diffuse from this place you attain to *brahmacharya*, celibacy. You need do nothing to attain brahmacharya; whenever sexual desire arises you needn't actively suppress it. You have only to straighten your spine for all the energy to flow upward. The same energy that flowed into sexual desire becomes the energy of brahmacharya. It is the same whether it flows downward through the seventh door into nature, or upward through the seventh door to reach *paramatma*, the divine.

The person who develops the art of sitting quietly finds that his own body begins to provide a thousand experiences. You can know all of the Yoga Sutras through your own body. There is no need to read Patanjali. Actually, Patanjali should be read later on, only for corroboration, to show that you are on the right path. When you go within, many a time you will be frightened and not know whether the proper things are happening to you. By referring to scripture, it can be encouraging and reassuring to know that all who have attained have followed the same way. Such-and-such happened to them also and such-and-such will occur again in the future.

The scriptures are the evidence of the sages, but the authentic knowledge is attained only from within oneself and not through their words.

Nanak says:

Through listening, all the scriptures and teachings are known.
Through listening devotees attain bliss, and sin and sorrow are destroyed.
Through listening all truth and contentment are attained,
And the virtue of bathing at the sixty-eight holy places is gained,
And through listening again and again honor is earned.
Through listening spontaneous meditation happens.
Nanak says, Through listening devotees attain bliss,
And sin and sorrow are destroyed.

To arrive at the ultimate freedom, Hindus require that a person bathe at sixty-eight holy places. These holy places are marked on the map of India, but in reality they represent sixty-eight points within the body through which one must pass to attain virtue. The Hindus have performed a wonderful task that no other race has equaled in discovering these points. However, places on the map are merely symbols; unfortunately, wandering in these symbols as if real, the Hindus have lost their consciousness of life. It is said: "Get the water of the Ganges and offer it at Rameshwara." These really refer to points within the body; the energy is to be taken from one point and directed into another, which is the holy pilgrimage. But what do we do? We actually carry water from the Ganges up to Rameshwara!

The external map is a symbolic translation of man's internal world. Everything within man is very subtle. To exemplify it, these external symbols were created, but in mistaking the symbols for reality we went astray.

Symbols are never truths; they only hint towards truth. They are pointers when Nanak says: Through shravana truth is obtained, so also contentment and knowledge, and through it is attained bathing at the sixty-eight centers of pilgrimage. When you become silent you begin to find the holy places within the body. Then you do not have to ponder what truth is for you see truth directly. As long as you think, there is no truth—only opinions, concepts. Truth is an experience. And once you can see, why still think?

Contentment is attained. As long as you think, you are discontented, because thoughts lead to thousands of suggestions: do this, do that! Thoughts give rise to new desires and desires lead to discontent. It is very harmful to have thoughts as friends; they lead you astray. If there is any bad company worth giving up, it is that of thoughts. It is all right to use thoughts, but if you begin to obey them you are in for all kinds of trouble. They are like drugs; if you get addicted to them you go astray and will be so confused that you won't know what to do.

Mulla Nasruddin had so much to drink one day that he was afraid to go home. He knew he would have to furnish an explanation and he couldn't think of a plausible answer, so he wandered here and there aimlessly. A policeman came upon him in the middle of the night, demanding to know, "What are you doing here at this time of the night? Answer quickly or I'll have to take you to the police station." Mulla Nasruddin answered, "If I had an answer wouldn't I have gone home already?"

Thoughts are an addiction that has no answer. Had there been an answer you would have reached home long ago. Why are you roaming at such a late hour? You have no answer to explain your life. Thoughts have no answer. A real answer can only be found in the no-thought state.

Nanak says: Contentment and truth through shravana; the sixty-eight holy places through shravana; and through shravana alone you attain the natural samadhi.

If you were only to listen, it becomes meditation. Without meditation you cannot hear. What is the meaning of meditation? Meditation exists only where mind is not; where the internal dialogue is gone.

> Through listening the highest virtues are acquired,
> Sage, saint and king come into being,
> And the blind find the path,
> Through listening the fathomless is fathomed,
> Nanak says, Through listening devotees attain bliss,
> And sin and sorrow are destroyed.

Through listening alone the blind find their way, the beggar becomes a king, and you reach the depths of the boundless! Thoughts are like a teaspoon, and you try to measure the ocean with it! Listening is to enter into the ocean. You will reach the bottom only by drowning in it and not by measuring it with a teaspoon.

Aristotle, the Greek philosopher, was walking along the seashore lost in high thoughts. Suddenly he came upon a man who was trying to empty the ocean into a pit he had dug, with the help of a spoon. He became curious and asked, "Brother, what are you doing?"

The man replied, "If you have eyes you can see. It is as clear as day. I mean to empty this ocean into this pit."

Aristotle laughed and said, "Is it not madness? Are you in your right senses? Can oceans be measured by spoons? Can pits be filled by spoons? Why waste your life in senseless tasks?"

The man laughed and said, "I thought it was you who is mad, because aren't you engaged in filling the infinite with your spoonful of thoughts?" It is said that Aristotle tried to locate that man later but he never found him.

The man was correct: how small is a thought, how vast experience! How will you measure this vast existence with your measuring spoon? Where will you keep it? Your head is so small, the universe so vast. Look at your arms, how short they are—how far can they reach? You are engaged in a worthless task. Perhaps that man may have succeeded in emptying the ocean, because the ocean is finite. A spoonful of water does make the ocean less by a spoon, but the infinite you can never attain through thoughts.

Therefore, says Nanak, the beggar becomes a king as soon as he becomes silent. The depths of the depthless become known, the unknown becomes familiar, the stranger becomes the beloved, and the blind find their way—all through shravana.

Nanak says, Through listening devotees attain bliss,
And sin and sorrow are destroyed.

Chapter 6

Only Contemplating Can Know

The state of contemplation cannot be expressed;
Whoever attempts it will afterwards repent.
There is no paper, no pen, no writer,
That can penetrate such a state.
The name of the flawless one is such
That only contemplating can know it.

Through contemplation is remembrance born in mind and intellect,
And awareness of the universe acquired.
You cease to repent your words,
And gain freedom from the god of death.
The name of the flawless one is such
That only contemplating can know it.

Through contemplation the path is cleared of all obstacles,
And a man departs with dignity and honor;
One is saved from wandering astray,
And connection to religion is established.
The name of the flawless one is such
That only contemplating can know it.

Through contemplation alone the door to liberation is attained,
And the family can be saved;
Through it the guru is delivered and helps his disciples across;

They need no longer beg for alms.
The name of the flawless one is such
That only contemplating can know it.

L ET US FIRST understand what *manan*, contemplation, means. Thinking and contemplation are both processes of the mind, but they are very different, even opposite.

When a man swims from one bank to the other he remains on the surface of the river. His position changes but not the depth. Now imagine a diver; his position in the water needn't change at all, but his course is downward, further and further into the depths. Thinking is like swimming and contemplation is like diving. In thinking we go from one thought to another; in contemplation we go into the depths of the one word. The position does not change; the depth changes.

The process of thought is linear; whether you think of your business or your spiritual liberation, thinking of God or of your wife, you remain on the surface. But in contemplation the journey inward begins; you plunge into the very depths of the word. Its deepest recesses resonate.

Contemplation is the only true revelation of the mantra.

Understand well this one word, and the entire sutra opens for you. The quintessence of Nanak's teaching is contemplation—contemplation of the one name, Omkar. Ek Omkar Satnam. Omkar is the one true name, the only truth. He gave the mantra to his disciples not to be thought about, but to submerge themselves in. As the one word Om keeps resounding, the resonance itself increases the depth of the experience.

There are three levels: in the first you pronounce the word out loud—Om...Om...Om.... This is the level of speech. Making use of your lips, speech resounds outside. Then you shut your lips, not even allowing the tongue to move, and you pronounce the name in your mind— Om...Om...Om.... . The second level is deeper than the first. You do not make any use of lips or tongue; you do not use the body at all—you use only the mind. On the third level even the mind is not used. Om is not even pronounced. You become silent and listen to the resonance of Om that is already within. The mind is no more; and when it is gone contemplation begins. Contemplation means the absence of mind.

The resonance of Omkar is with you from your very birth. Have you noticed how happy infants are without any apparent reason? They lie in the cradle and throw their little arms and legs about and make cooing sounds. Mothers in India think they are remembering something from their past lives, for there is absolutely no reason for their happiness. Lying in their cribs they have yet to start their journey in life. Psychologists are confounded with the child's joy, but take it to be the expression of their good health.

Yogis have discovered a different reason altogether, for the wellbeing of the body is not enough. Within, the child hears the resonance of Omkar, a soft melodious strain. The child hears it and is captivated by it, enchanted by it. Hearing it, the child smiles and gurgles and feels happy. The child's health may remain good later on, but the melody within will be lost; this cheerfulness will be gone. Then it will become difficult for the child to hear the Omkar for the layers of words that surround it.

The resonance, Ek Omkar Satnam, is the first happening. In it lies the fountain of life. Then come the words brought about by our education, impressions, society, culture. Then the third level is actually pronouncing words

in speaking, conversation and dialogues. While speaking
you are actually farthest away from words. Therefore
Nanak stresses the necessity of learning how to listen.
For when you hear you are in between; you can go either
way, towards speech or towards silence.

So there are three states: the state of Omkar, the state
of speech, and the inbetween state of thoughts and feelings. When you are listening you are in the mid-state of
thoughts and feelings. If you begin to tell others what you
have heard, you have descended into speech. If you begin
to reflect, to contemplate on what you have heard, then
you are in contemplation, and you go into the void. The
distance is very subtle. Each person has to understand
well the distance between the two within himself and
provide for the equilibrium.

Contemplation begins as soon as you submerge yourself in any one word. Any word will do but no word is more
beautiful than Omkar, because it is pure resonance. The
words Allah, Ram, Krishna can also be used, but there is
no need to take big, big names. The English poet Ten-
nyson repeated his own name and lost himself in its
resonance.

As you enter into the depths of any word, the word
gradually gets lost; and as it begins to fade, contemplation
sets in. The word is always lost ultimately; all mantras
are lost for they are of the mind. The supreme mantra,
however, is forever resounding within. The first mantra
only helps to bring you into silence, but not into the
supreme mantra. Once you are silent you can hear the
resonance of Omkar within you.

All mantras teach you to swim and then from swimming they teach you to dive. But how long will you insist
on voyaging only on the surface? How long will you go on
from one life to the next? How long will you merely keep

changing your location, your situations? When will that
auspicious moment arrive when you will take the plunge,
from wherever you are? At that very moment contemplation will begin to happen. With this in view, now let us try
to understand Nanak's sutras.

The state of contemplation cannot be expressed;
Whoever attempts it will afterwards repent.

Why is this so? First of all, contemplation cannot be
talked about for there is no movement in contemplation—
it is non-movement. The journey does not start; in fact, it
ends. It appears like movement.

When you travel by train you see everything rushing
past you. In fact it is the train that is moving, and all else
is static. In a like manner, because of your habitual movement, when the mind begins to come to a halt, you feel it
is a movement. But when the mind stops ultimately, you
will suddenly find that everything has stopped, for nothing had moved.

He who is hidden within you has never walked—not
even a single step. He has undertaken no journey, not
even a pilgrimage. He has not stepped out of His house;
He has been there forever.

It is the mind that has always been on the run, and its
speed is so great that everything around that has never
moved appears to be running. When the mind begins to
halt they also begin to halt, and when the mind comes to
a stop, everything stops with it. While you can talk about
movement, how can you speak about non-movement? It is
possible to talk about a journey, for you can describe the
different places in your travel from one place to another,
but if you have gone nowhere what will you talk about? If
there has been no happening, no change of situations,
what is there to say?

You can write the life story of a restless man, but what can you write about a man of peace? It is the experience of novelists, writers and dramatists that things come alive only around the bad man. The life of a good man is very dull and uneventful.

Don't be under the illusion that the Ramayana is the story of Rama; it really revolves around Ravana, the villain. Ravana is the actual hero of the story and Rama is secondary. Remove Ravana and what remains of the story? Sita is not stolen, the battle is not fought—everything is quiet and uneventful. How much is there to say about Rama? Can you write an epic on God? He is where He ever was. There has never been any change in Him—the story just cannot take shape. Therefore there are no biographies or autobiography of God. To write about someone, a journey is necessary.

You can write a great deal on thoughts; what will you write in connection with no-thought? Whatever you say about it will be false and you will regret it later. Sages always repent after speaking, for they feel they could not say what they wanted to say, and they have said what should not have been said. What they tried to convey the listener could not follow, and what he understood had no meaning.

Lao Tzu has said, "Nothing can be spoken about truth, and whatever is spoken becomes an untruth." The more you know, the more difficult you will find it to express yourself. Each word becomes a challenge to utter for now you possess a touchstone within by which you test; as a result all words seem too shallow and petty to express. A big event has taken place inside which cannot be contained by words, a vast space discovered within that cannot be filled with the capsules of words.

And even if you speak, the regret becomes greater, for by the time your words reach the listener their meaning becomes quite different. Everything that you said gets completely changed—you gave a diamond; it became a stone. The genuine coin you gave, in changing hands became false. As you look into his eyes and see that the coin has become a fake, then you are filled with remorse for this man will now carry it along with him throughout his life.

This is exactly how all sects run, how the crowds of thousands move. They carry the burden of what was never given to them. If Mahavira were to return, he would beat his chest and weep at the state of Jainism; if Buddha returns he will weep for the Buddhists; if Jesus returns the fight will start again with the Israelites, for what each of them said never reached the people for whom it was intended. Something very different was received and digested.

If Nanak were to return he would not be as displeased with others as he would be with the Sikhs, for you can be angry only with those to whom you gave the word; it is they who have distorted it into something quite different.

We are very cunning. When a person like Nanak speaks, we add our meanings to his words, as it suits us. We do not shape ourselves in Nanak's words; we fashion his words according to ourselves. This is our trick to bring things back to where they were. There are only two ways.

There once was a very rich woman. She was very artistic but also fickle and obstinate. Being fond of an ashtray that was very expensive, she had decorated her room so that it became the focus of the room and every-thing was made to match: the curtains, the furniture, the walls. The ashtray was the center of everything. One day the ashtray broke. She called the best craftsmen to make an exact replica of the ashtray but try as they would, no one could recreate the original color which was also reproduced everywhere in the room.

One day a craftsman offered his services. He asked for a full month to produce an ashtray to match the original one, but he laid one condition—no one was to enter the room during this month, not even the lady. In a month's time he invited her to inspect the room. She was completely satisfied.

When the other craftsmen asked him what the secret was, he said, "It was simple. First I made an ashtray as close to the original one as possible, then I painted the walls accordingly." Impossible as it was to get the exact shade in the ashtray, this was the only way out.

When Nanak speaks there are only two ways open to you: either you merge into Nanak's color and attain to satisfaction, or else you are bound to become restless. To be near a person like Nanak is like standing next to fire. Either you burn yourself as Nanak burned, you turn into ashes as Nanak did, you lose yourself as Nanak did—like a drop falling into the ocean; or, the only other alternative is to color Nanak's words in your own shade. This is very easy, for we never actually hear what is told to us, but hear what we want to hear. We infer meanings that suit us. We don't stand on the side of truth, we make truth stand on our side; we make truth follow us.

The difference between a genuine seeker and a false seeker is that the legitimate seeker follows truth wherever it might take him—whatever be the outcome—even if everything is lost, even if life is lost. He is ready to lose his all. The inauthentic seeker bends truth to follow him; but then it is no longer truth, it is falsity. How can truth follow you? Only untruth can follow you, for you are false; your shadow is bound to be fake. You can follow truth if you desire, but truth can never follow you; it cannot be contained in your concepts, it is too big for your head. Therefore, Nanak says, whoever attempts it afterwards repents.

There is yet another reason which you should note, that I have mentioned before. When you almost reach contemplation you come to the midpoint from which there are two choices, one of which is to start talking of it to others. In that case you will regret it; therefore, whenever the urge comes to tell others, first consult the guru. Do not trust in your own judgment to talk about it till the guru tells you.

The ways of the ego are very subtle. No sooner do you make one small step than it proclaims great triumph. It gets a fistful and claims to have attained all space! A little glimpse of light and it says the sun has risen. A drop has hardly fallen and you begin talking of the ocean. Then the talk leads to more talk and the result is that even the one drop vanishes, the glimpse dissolves. The result is that the person remains a shallow pundit, full of nothing but knowledge; he seems to know too much. He talks a great deal without any experience. If you observe him carefully you will note that his actions are completely inconsistent with what he says.

Once Mulla Nasruddin was trying to catch a train that had already started moving. He caught hold of the handle and one foot was already in the door when the guard grabbed him saying, "Don't you know it's an offense to climb on a moving train?" The Mulla climbed down.

Then just as the train was leaving the platform the guard jumped into his compartment. The Mulla promptly pulled him down, saying, "Well, sir, doesn't the law also apply to you?"

This is exactly the state of the pundit. His statements apply to everyone else. He enjoys the taste of delivering discourses—bereft of the waters of life, unrelated to his own experience, and this danger is always there.

When you reach the midpoint you arrive at two paths: one is the path of the pundit, the master of words; and the other is the path of the wise. The path of the pundit leads you to the world outside via words and pronouncements. On the path of the wise you leave the word and immerse yourself completely in no-word. Therefore without the guru's permission do not go on telling others.

There was a disciple of Buddha by the name of Purna Kashyap who had attained knowing but still followed silently behind Buddha. After a full year Buddha called him and said, "Why do you still follow me like my shadow? Go out into the world and tell others what you have known." Purna Kashyap replied, "I was awaiting your orders. What about this mind? It might begin to take pleasure in preaching to others and then I might lose what I have attained only with so much difficulty! I know there is every possibility of the ego's returning."

It is very difficult to attain knowledge, very easy to lose it, for the path is very subtle and you can go astray any moment on the slightest excuse. So Purna Kashyap waited, knowing that Buddha would tell him when he was ready to preach to others. Do not set out to teach others before the guru tells you or else you will repent. And the repentance will be great for you were very close to the other shore when you went astray. The boat was just about to cast anchor when the shore receded. Wisdom and learning are the final temptations.

The state of contemplation cannot be expressed;
Whoever attempts it will afterwards repent.
There is no paper, no pen, no writer,
That can penetrate such a state.

Who is competent to express this state? For as contemplation goes deeper and deeper, the doer is lost, and the mind begins to end; contemplation is its death.

The mind can speak, the mind can tell. Its expertise lies in explaining what it knows, even telling of things you do not know; and frequent repetition leads you to the illusion that you know. If you keep explaining a thing again and again, you gradually forget whether you have known it or not and begin to feel and believe that you know. Just consider: do you say only things you know or do you also say things you do not know? Do you know whether God is? If not, do not tell anyone that God is. Have you known truth? If not, do not tell others about truth, for the danger is not that others will be deceived, but by constant repetition you yourself will be deluded into the certainty that you know.

This is a very subtle illusion. Once the thought takes hold of you that you know—when you have not known—your boat will never reach the other shore. A man who sleeps can be awakened, but he who pretends to be asleep is hard to awaken. The ignorant can be enlightened, but not a learned man who says he already knows all. Armed with this understanding, avoid the saints and scholars; only go to them when your knowledge gains sufficient strength to protect you. The pundit searches out the ignorant and avoids the sage. If Nanak comes to town the pundits will run away, for they are frightened that such a man may lay bare their actual state. He might lift the veil and uncover their ignorance; and this veil is so weak and thin that it tears at the slightest touch.

Where there is no paper nor pen nor even writer, then the state of mind does not exist, and who is to ponder over contemplation?

The name of the flawless one is such
That only contemplating can know it.

That is how it is, but only you will know. Just as a
mute cannot explain the taste of sugar, your lips will
remain sealed. Every time you think of it there will be a
lump in your throat, your heart will become full, so full;
tears will flow, or laughter, but you will not be able to say
a word. People will think your mind has lost its balance.
Your inside will be so overfull that it will pour out of every
pore in your body. You will dance, you will sing, but you
will not be able to speak. So it was that Nanak sang and
Mardana played. Whenever anyone asked Nanak about
his state he would look at Mardana and nod. Mardana
would pick up his instrument and begin to play, and
Nanak would begin to sing. Nanak said nothing, he only
sang.

When you hear a sage—if you hear him properly—you
will find he is singing, not talking. You will find poetry in
his words. Even as he sits he dances. You will find a kind
of intoxication in the atmosphere around him, an intoxication that does not lull you to sleep or into sense-
lessness, but rather awakens you. It takes you not into
forgetfulness but into wakefulness. And if you are ready
to flow along with it, it can carry you to unknown and
wonderful shores. If you are really ready to dive down
deep into the ocean it can take you on a long astonishing
journey—to the ultimate.

The sage's tune is more melody than words. He speaks
less, sings more, for what he has attained cannot be
expressed in words. It will perhaps be transmitted by a
tune, a low murmur; a slight glimpse and you may get
carried away by it.

Gurdjieff defined two kinds of art. In ordinary art the
artist, the singer, the sculptor expresses his feelings.

Even a great painter like Picasso does no more than capture his state of mind in his work. Gurdjieff calls this subjective art. Objective art includes the Taj Mahal or the Ajanta-Ellora caves. In this the artist does not portray his feelings but creates a condition that elicits certain feelings in the viewer.

There is the statue of Buddha. If it is truly a piece of objective art—which it can be only if the sculptor has known what buddhahood means—then you will find yourself getting connected with it in a mysterious way as you keep looking at it. You will find that you have descended deep within yourself and the idol will become contemplation.

The idols in the temples were not put there without a reason. They are all part of this objective art. Music also was not created accidentally; those who went into samadhi first gave voice to music. Having heard the melody of Om within, in various ways they tried to capture the melody of this resonance in the realm of sound, so that those who know not the music within may get some taste of it. Little children invariably come to the temple in order to partake of the offerings made to the deity. Whatever your reason, there is value in going to the temple. The external sounds of the bells and devotional songs can become a divine gift if they touch off remembrance of the music within.

The deep pleasure in music is a glimpse of samadhi. Dance also is an objective art, thus the tradition of dancing before the deity. Witnessing the dance, your boat may suddenly leave the shore and sail off to distant lands!

One thing you must keep in mind about Nanak is that whatever he has said, he has sung; whatever he wanted to convey, he has conveyed along with music. For the real thing is the music—the *nada*, the sound. What he says is

a mere excuse when his aim is to trigger the resonance
within you. If it begins to resound in the right way your
thought processes will break and you will find yourself on
a different plane of words altogether. If you have gathered
up enough courage to flow along, if you are not holding on
like mad to the shore, then the third happening—contemplation—will also occur.

> *There is no paper, no pen, no writer,*
> *That can penetrate such a state.*
> *The name of the flawless one is such*
> *That only contemplating can know it.*

It is like a dumb man tasting sugar; only he knows the
taste. And then this taste is never forgotten, not only
throughout this lifetime but for infinite lives.

Once you get the taste, you find the taste is much
more than you—you can never forget it. The taste is such
that rather than your containing it, you will be lost in it.
It is like the ocean; you will be lost in it like a drop.

In truth how can you taste God? It is rather God who
tastes you, provided you are ready. You get immersed in
that taste and a harmony, a unison, is formed with the
divine. Such is the name Niranjan, the faultless one.

> *Through contemplation is remembrance born.*

As you get more and more involved in conversation,
remembrance decreases. Perhaps you may have realized that. While you are observing yourself most of your
troubles drop off; it is only when you begin speaking again
that you land yourself in trouble. What happens? When
you are speaking remembrance is at its lowest and awareness is almost nil, because in speaking your attention is
on the other and not on yourself. Consciousness is like an
arrow. When you talk, the arrow is pointed towards the
other, so you are conscious of the one you are talking to,

and your attention is diverted away from yourself. In this state of your non-awareness of your own self you say things you may regret all your life.

In a moment of non-awareness you tell a woman you love her although you had never thought about it before. On the spur of the moment words fall out of your mouth and now you are caught in the situation; one careless event gives rise to a thousand more. If you try to pluck one leaf, four more appear in its place, and you are propelled on a journey you least wanted.

Though it may never have struck you before, you will find that all your troubles have their origin in words. When one word has been uttered, the ego in its pride makes you fulfill your words. You are in love and you tell your beloved, "I shall love you for ever and ever." You cannot know what the next moment is going to bring for you. How can you make a promise for the morrow, when you do not even know what is going to happen tomorrow morning, let alone speak of the distant future or of lives to come? If you have even the slightest awareness you would say, "This very moment I am in love with you. About tomorrow I can say nothing." But then the ego would get no pleasure in that.

Mulla Nasruddin's wife said to him, "You don't love me as you did before. Is it because I have become old, or because my body has become sick and clumsy? Have you forgotten your promise before the clergyman that we shall be together in sorrow and in joy?"

The Mulla replied, "Aren't we together in sorrow and joy? But I had made no promise about old age!"

When today you say "forever" do you realize the implications? If today you declare your love, the rest of your life you will spend fulfilling this promise—a hard task! If you cannot fulfill your word, you will be full of regrets; if you do, you will be thoroughly miserable. For when love has flown away what will you do? Can you bring it back by force? Instead you must invariably weave a web of deceit.

While speaking, it is difficult to be aware of yourself, for on the plane of speech your attention is on the other person. Speaking is all right only for a Buddha, a sage, who by his sadhana has developed the double-pointed arrow, the consciousness that is aware of the other as well as of its own self. This consciousness is called surati, remembrance or self-remembering. The mind is capable of looking in both directions simultaneously and it needn't be lost while talking. While speaking, the witness stands at attention all the time; then no word can possibly cause trouble for you.

There is a Sufi story: The guru sent for his four disciples to practice the sadhana of silence. The four sat in the mosque as evening fell and it began to get dark. No one had yet lit the lamp. As a servant passed by, one of the disciples called out and said, "Brother, light the lamp. Night is coming on."

The second disciple scolded, "The guru told us not to speak. You have spoken!"

The third could not contain himself, "What are you doing? You too have spoken!"

The fourth who had remained quiet now said, "I was the only one to obey the guru. I did not speak until now."

You may laugh at the story but it is really your own story. If you become silent for a while you will realize how much you long to talk, how you begin an internal dialogue. The slightest excuse and you lose your contemplation.

What is the meaning of the story? As long as no one was around they remembered to observe the silence. As soon as the servant came along, the other was present to attract their attention and all contemplation was lost.

Through contemplation is remembrance born.

Remembrance is a beautiful word. It corresponds with Buddha's right mindfulness. Whatever you do, do it mindfully. Be mindful when you talk, when you walk, even when the eyes blink. Do nothing senselessly, unconsciously; for whatever you do in such a fashion will invariably lead to sin. Whatever you do without awareness leads you away from your self. The only method of coming close to your self is to become more and more aware. Whatever the circumstances, whatever the situation, hold fast and never let go of your awareness—even should you stand to lose everything. Even if your house catches fire, move only with complete awareness.

Ishwar Chandra Vidyasagar, the philosopher and social reformer, has given the following account in his memoirs.

He was once invited by the viceroy who was about to confer an honor on him. He was a poor man, his clothes were old and threadbare, and he dressed in the Bengali style of kurta and dhoti. Friends advised him to get new clothes in keeping with the occasion. At first he refused but later thought better of it and let them order new clothes for him.

One day shortly before the event, as Vidyasagar was returning from his evening walk he saw walking in front of him a well-dressed Mohammedan in coat and pajamas, twirling a stick in his hand. He was walking at his own pace enjoying the evening. Soon a man—by all appearances his servant—came running and told him, "Hurry, sir, your house is on fire!" There was no change in the man's stride; he continued walking along as if nothing had happened. The servant, thinking maybe he hadn't heard, repeated loudly, "Sir, your house is on fire! Haven't you heard what I said?"

Even the poor servant, who stood to lose nothing, was trembling and perspiring with fear, but the master remained unaffected. "I have heard," he told the servant. "Should I change my habitual way of walking just because the house has caught fire?"

Ishwar Chandra was shocked. Here is a man whose house is actually on fire, and he is not prepared to change his lifelong walk; and there he was, ready to give up his lifelong attire just to see the viceroy! Ishwar Chandra was curious to know more about this unique man. As he followed, he saw him walking at the same pace twirling his stick; when he reached the house and saw the flames he calmly gave orders to put out the fire, directed it all, but himself stood on one side and watched without one iota of difference in his attitude.

Ishwar Chandra writes: "My head bowed in reverence to this man. Never had I come across the like of him."

What is it that this man was guarding so zealously? He was guarding his <u>surati</u>, his awareness, and he was not prepared to lose it at any cost. Whatever happens, happens. All that was required to be done was being attended to; that is enough. On no account can contemplation be bartered away. Nothing is so precious in life that you can afford to lose your remembrance for it.

But you abandon your awareness for the slightest thing. A one rupee note is lost and you go mad looking for it. You look for it even in places where it could not possibly be. A man has lost something and you find him looking in the tiniest box, much too small for such an object. You are always ready to lose your awareness, or it is better to say you have no awareness to lose—you are unconscious!

Nanak says: Through contemplation awareness is born within the mind and the intellect. As the Omkar settles more and more within, the external utterance stops first. The arrow now turns within, for now there is no one without to speak to; in other words, the external relations created by speech are no more. To speak is to build a bridge to reach others. It is the relationship between us and others. By not speaking, this relationship is broken; you have become silent.

To become silent means now the journey is reversed: the arrow has turned inwards, the journey within has begun. As soon as this happens, the first glimpse of awareness begins to appear, and for the first time in full awareness you know that you are! So far you could see everything except yourself. Only you were in shadow, as there is darkness directly under the flame. Now you will awaken. As the intensity of Omkar increases, contemplation settles on the word and awareness increases proportionately.

Take it this way: There are two sides to the scales; when one goes up the other comes down to the same extent. Proportional to your going inward, so awareness increases. On the third plane, when even the word is lost and only the resonance of Omkar remains—pure sound—suddenly the awareness becomes complete. You get up. You awaken, as if the sleep of a thousand years has been broken. Darkness flees and there is light, and light alone. It is as if you were in a deep slumber through innumerable lives and dreaming away. Suddenly the dream is broken, and lo, it is morning. You see the dawn as if for the first time in your life.

Through contemplation is remembrance born in mind and intellect,
And awareness of the universe acquired.

You cease to bear the brunt of life,
And gain freedom from the god of death.
The name of the flawless one is such
That only contemplating can know it.

The day you awaken you realize for the first time the
infinite space, the countless worlds, this existence, this
leela—play of the gods. As long as you are steeped in your
own desires, lost in the labyrinth of your own mind, you
are blind and see nothing. The mind is another name for
blindness; contemplation is the opening of the eyes, the
restoration of sight.

Nanak says: Through contemplation alone you become aware of all the worlds. All the heavenly bodies, the
whole universe becomes visible. Life manifests in its complete and perfect glory. Then you see His initials in all
things great and small. You will find His name on every
leaf, His resonance in every hair of your body; you will
hear His melody in the winds. Then the whole of existence
unfolds His glory to you.

Now you ask: What is the meaning of life? What is the
idea behind it? Why are we born? Why do we live? The
great French existential thinker, Gabriel Marcel, has
written that life has but one problem, and that is suicide.
Why do we live? Why should we not commit suicide? The
ultimate state of insensibility, of unconsciousness, is in
suicide, where the priceless gifts of life are thrown away
for you find nothing in them.

Just the opposite happens when you awaken into
awareness; then the glory is boundless. World upon world
opens before your eyes. Every stage abounds with mystery and wonder. Then you come to know the meaning of
life, the bliss which we call samadhi. Then you know why
life is.

In your present state you cannot know; however much
you may ask, however much you are told that to attain

God is the goal of your life, it does not solve your problem. No matter how much it is drummed into your ears that samadhi is the goal of your life, nothing strikes home as real until your remembrance awakens. You hear and you dismiss such talk as the words of those who are not very sound of mind. You trust your own understanding, but where has it taken you but to the brink of suicide? This valuable gift given to you is less than worthless, for you find no meaning in it. But no sooner do you become awakened than the mystery begins to unravel before you. A flower opens and each petal exudes nothing but joy— enchanting bliss!

Nanak is a simple rustic. He says: Through contemplation you cease to bear the burden of life. He speaks plain village language, but what he says is significant and to the point. Through contemplation you need not spit out your words only to take them back again, bearing the insults and abuse, or even a slap on the face for whatever you said in your dullness. You speak through your ego-sleep, unaware of what you say, what you do, where you are going. Then it is only natural that you get slapped in the face.

Today you say you are in love; before morning dawns your love has flown away! One minute you feel like murdering someone and in a short while you rack your brain how best to please him. One instant you say one thing, the next minute you say the opposite. You cannot be trusted. You are as changeable as the seasons. There is nothing stable within you, nothing crystallized, so you have to bear a slap in the face every moment.

Nanak says: Through contemplation alone you need not bear that slap on the face, and you no longer have to go along with the god of death. Everyone dies but all don't have to follow Yama, the god of death. Understand the symbol. Everyone dies, but once in a while a man dies consciously and then he need not follow Yama. As long as you live in non-remembrance you are a prisoner of Yama. The meaning of Yama is fear. One who lives in non-awareness, dies in non-awareness. He trembles and wails for someone to save him from death. He holds onto the very last breath of life, wanting to be saved from the jaws of death by any means. This state of fear, this dark face of fear, is symbolized by the god Yama astride a black buffalo.

But a person who dies in full remembrance and awareness is not obsessed by fear. Without fear he comes to realize that death is the culmination of life and not its end. Far from being fearsome, death is the gateway to His abode, an invitation to His dwelling, a process of merging into Him. There is no need to weep and lament; rather, he enters into the faultless beauty of death, filled with joy and celebration—as if going to meet his beloved.

Nanak's last words are priceless. As he was about to leave the body he said, "The flowers are blooming, spring has come. The trees are vibrant with the songs of the birds!"

Which realm is he talking about? Some people thought it a nostalgic remembrance of his childhood, his village, where—that very season being spring—he imagined the trees in full bloom and the birds singing in them. It is a matter of coincidence that it was springtime, that the flowers were in bloom, and the birds were singing, and the air was filled with gladness. But this was not what Nanak had in mind. Nanak was seeing something else, but had to use familiar metaphors in talking to mortals. In the last moments he was entering into the supreme beauty, the incomparable loveliness where flowers bloom perpetually and never wither, where the birds sing eternally, where there is everlasting loveliness.

No sooner does a person become enlightened than he discovers death to be no annihilation but the ultimate flowering, the highest state of existence. He realizes that in death we lose nothing. One door closes, another opens. The sage enters dancing, singing; the ignorant man weeps and wails. If any man follows the emissaries of death, he himself is responsible, for there is no Yama, much less his emissaries. It is your fear that is your Yama; once you become fearless, God spreads out His arms for you.

Your actual experience of death depends on what you are. Death is the statement, the test, of how you have lived. If at that moment a man is cheerful, serene and filled with bliss and thanksgiving, know that his life was incomparable, for death is the ultimate offering to God. If he weeps and wails it is a sure sign that his life was a tale of anguish, a veritable hell.

> Nanak says, Through contemplation you
> ...gain freedom from the god of death.
> The name of the flawless one is such
> That only contemplating can know it.

> Through contemplation the path is cleared of all obstacles,
> And a man departs with dignity and honor;
> One is saved from wandering astray,
> And connection to religion is established.
> The name of the flawless one is such
> That only contemplating can know it.

All obstructions are within you and not outside of you. Obstacles are there because of your insensibility and they cannot simply be removed. The only way is to awaken within; then all obstacles vanish.

Now suppose your house is in darkness. As you enter, every corner of the house seems filled with danger; maybe there are ghosts or goblins or burglars, or even a murderer.

Everything seems so ominous; the house holds a thousand perils; there might even be snakes and scorpions around. How will you possibly overcome all these hazards if you set out to deal with them one by one? Who knows how many thieves, how many criminals, lurk within this darkness? You cannot deal with them individually. The only way is to light a lamp. One single lamp illuminates the whole interior and all fears flee. Once the house is lighted and you can see whatever danger there is, you can always find ways to deal with it.

The fact is, as Buddha has said, "The dark house attracts the burglar." A thief avoids the house that is well lit. If the lamp is burning within and if the awareness stands guard, no obstacle or hindrance dare enter within you.

One day, early in the morning, Mulla Nasruddin came running to me. He held a paper in his hand and seemed terribly disturbed. He handed me the paper and flopped into a chair. The anonymous writer was warning Mulla that if he did not refrain from following his wife within the next three days, he would shoot him.

"What should I do?" asked Mulla.

"Why, that's simple," I said. "Just leave his wife alone!"

"But which wife shall I stop following?" he asked. "If it were only one woman I'd been following I'd know which one to stop!"

If there were only one hindrance you could get rid of it, but they are infinite. You are stalking an infinite number of women; your desires are inexhaustible. Destroy one, ten more take its place. If you keep grappling with each, hoping to eradicate them one by one, you never will succeed. A method is needed to finish it once and for all. And he who shows you this method, the *gur*, is the guru.

So Nanak says: Through contemplation all hindrances on the path are eradicated. Continue the repetition of Omkar and let it reach the non-repeating state, then you find your eyes have opened. Then there are no obstructions, for these are but your creations. There is no outside enemy to be vanquished. You are your own enemy. Your insensitivity is your enemy, and because of it you are enmeshed in endless entanglements. No matter how cautious you are, you keep adding fresh hindrances at every step.

There are people in this world who regulate their lives with control and restraint. They must take each step carefully so as not to go astray. But restraint is not the end; awareness is the ultimate goal. The invitation to wander is always beckoning inside. However much you impose restraints, the raging passions will bring you down at the slightest opportunity. A person who practices self-denial and controls his every action must always be afraid, for within him the imprisoned passions continue boiling.

Through contemplation the path is cleared of all obstacles,
And a man departs with dignity and honor.

There is a different kind of honor that does not depend on others; it is the respect that arises out of internal dignity. He dies with majesty who feels death to be the union with God. He departs with joy and celebration in his heart, being grateful to existence for the life granted him. His air of thanksgiving for everything around is stamped on his face and in his every hair. Then it is not significant how many followed his coffin or where he died. None of this matters to his real dignity, his glory, his nobility, which are intrinsic qualities.

When death is no longer fearsome to you, you die with dignity; otherwise you cannot. For how can you be dignified when you weep and wail, entreat and beg? Then what does it matter how many people follow your funeral? All the pomp and ceremony cannot erase your anguish. All the flowers showered on you cannot smother the stink within you; the booming salute cannot overcome the uproar of sorrow and woe within you. Your death will be empty of honor all the same.

When Nanak says that through contemplation a person departs with honor, he talks of that internal honor, an internal reverence, a feeling of thanksgiving.

One is saved from wandering astray,
And connection to religion is established.

No matter how many scriptures you read, you cannot establish contact thereby with religion. No temple or mosque or church can connect you with religion. Slumbering, insensitive you go to worship; the same you who runs the shop, also goes to the house of worship. Your attitude should change, and once it is altered, everything else is transformed accordingly; otherwise you will keep on trying everything and yet remain your same old self.

Nanak went to Hardwar during the month of offerings to the dead. People were filling vessels with water, and then, facing East, were throwing them into the sky in order to reach their forefathers in heaven. Nanak picked up a bucket also, but he turned towards the West, and each bucket of water he poured, he cried out, "Reach my fields!"

After emptying a number of buckets, the people round him remonstrated with him. "What are you doing? You are turned in the wrong direction. You should face towards the rising sun! And why do you say, 'Reach my fields'? Where are your fields?"

Nanak replied, "About two hundred miles from here." The people began to laugh. "And you expect the water you throw here to reach your fields two hundred miles away? You are really out of your mind."

"How far away are your forefathers?" Nanak asked.

"They are infinitely far away," they replied.

"If your water can reach your ancestors an infinite distance away, why can't my water cover a mere two hundred miles?" asked Nanak.

What is Nanak trying to say? He is asking them to think a little, ponder: "What is this foolishness you indulge in? Become a little aware; what do you gain by such actions?"

Unfortunately all religion is filled with such stupidities. Some send water to ancestors, some bathe in the Ganges to wash away sins, yet others sit before idols without any feeling of worship or adoration, merely to ask for worldly things. A thousand foolishnesses prevail in the name of religion.

Therefore Nanak insists that religion is not attained through scriptures, nor through tradition and customs, nor through blind following. Contact with religion is established only when a person attains contemplation.

When a person awakens, awareness appears within him. When the resonance of Omkar first sounds, our relationship with religion begins. The day you are capable of hearing the resonance of Om within yourself, without any longer saying it, you are filled with joy, you are the witness, the observer. That very day you establish your connection with religion, not with some creed or sect. It is religion that Buddha calls dharma. It is religion that Mahavir and Nanak talk about.

Religion—dharma—means nature, the natural order of things. What Lao Tzu means by Tao, so Nanak means by religion. To be removed from one's nature is to be lost. To return to one's own nature is to return homewards. To be established in one's own nature is to be established in God.

The name Niranjan—God, the spotless, the flawless one—is such that only he who contemplates his heart knows.

> *Through contemplation alone the door to liberation is attained;*
> *And the family can be saved;*
> *Through it the guru is delivered and helps his disciples across;*
> *They need no longer beg for alms.*
> *The name of the flawless one is such*
> *That only contemplating can know it.*

The gateway is within you, the wandering is within you, the obstructions are within you, the paths are within you. When once the lamp is lit you can see in both directions: what is truth and what is untruth. Under the light of the lamp all desire is seen as untruth, and to follow desire is the mundane world. As the light burns within, you will see that desirelessness is truth and also the gateway to liberation.

You are tied because of your desires. Desires are the chains that hold you. Each desire forms a fresh link in the chain, and God knows how long and intricate is your chain of desires. You desire and you enter the prison; you desire and you are tied down. And the more you desire, as you invariably do, the stronger become the shackles that bind you and the thicker become your prison walls.

Nanak says: Through contemplation alone the door to salvation is attained. As soon as you awaken, your eyes are open completely and you see clearly. Cease desiring and the bonds are severed; there will be neither expectations nor attachments. When desire is missing there are no fetters; only then are the portals of liberation open. Desirelessness is the door to salvation.

And through contemplation alone the family can be saved. Which family is Nanak talking about? Certainly not of wife, children, brothers and sisters, for Nanak could not save them; nobody can. There is another kind of a family, that of guru and disciples, that is actually the family, for it is here that love occurs in its pristine purity. This love is born out of desirelessness; it happens without any reason.

You love your father because you are born through him. You love your wife because of your bodily desire. You love your son for you see in him a part of yourself or support in your old age. But what of the relationship with the guru? It is so difficult to find a guru, for you seek love without cause, without reason. With the guru there is love and love alone—no desire, no expectation. If you desire or expect something from him, you cannot be a part of his family. You will have to appear before him in all the simplicity and artlessness of a child.

Faith is called blind, and so it seems to those who are given to thinking. People come and say: "Our parents ask, 'Why are you mad about Osho? Are you out of your mind?' "

As a matter of fact they *are* mad and their families are right, for the head that had managed the worldly affairs has really gone out of order. A new love is born within them that cannot be argued about. They cannot even plead a reason for this love. Even if they try, they find it impossible!

Nanak says: Through contemplation alone can the family be saved. A family grows up around a guru; but when this family becomes a sect, deterioration begins. As long as it remains a family, it is different altogether. When a Buddha is born, thousands of people unite to form his family. Admission to the family of the guru is a very big event, for it signifies entry into a causeless world, a causeless love.

Nanak's followers are colored by him and drowned in his essence; his rhythm has caught their hearts and they are mad with ecstasy. But then Nanak will pass away and so also will those who joined his family of their own free will. When their children become Sikhs in turn, it has no genuine meaning, for the love that you have not chosen yourself cannot transform you. To choose Nanak is a great revolutionary act, but to be born into a Sikh household and call yourself a Sikh is no revolution.

A Mohammedan is born in a Mohammedan house-hold; a Christian is born in a Christian household; so also with a Hindu or a Jain or a Sikh. Your sect or faith is acquired through your birth, while family in this sense denotes what you have chosen yourself. A religious man always makes his own choice. An irreligious man is a sect-arian; he identifies with the religion he was born into.

You are a Jain by birth or a Christian or a Hindu, but how can you be a Jain or Christian or a Hindu by birth? Birth gives you blood and bones and muscles; it does not give you your soul. An insoluble riddle follows.

When a guru is alive there is a light around him in which he floats and allows others to float also. When the guru is alive there is a live phenomenon, a happening taking place around him. When the guru departs, and also those who had offered their lives unto him, the children born into their families identify themselves with the sect of their parents and call themselves Sikhs or

Christians or Buddhists; but they have no personal connection with the religion they profess.

One thing you must understand well: Religion is a ✓ personal decision. No one can be religious from birth.

> *Through contemplation alone the door to liberation is attained,*
> *And the family can be saved;*
> *Through it the guru is delivered and helps his disciples across;*
> *They need no longer beg for alms.*

As contemplation crystallizes, desires fall. What is the mundane world but an eternal round of begging for alms? Just observe yourself. What are you doing in your neediness? All twenty-four hours of the day you are wanting, your arms stretched out in desire. You are a veritable beggar. Nanak says through contemplation, your begging ceases. Remembrance makes a king of you, an emperor; it releases you from begging. Contemplation gives all and moves you beyond all desires.

Through contemplation God is attained. What else do you seek? Having reached the ultimate, there is nothing more ahead. Having attained all, what is still left to desire? You have reached samadhi. Having attained all, the need to beg disappears.

> *The name of the flawless one is such*
> *That only contemplating can know it.*

Chapter 7

The Journey Ends

Five are the tests and the ministers;
They gain shelter and respect at His door;
They decorate the king's court.
Attention is the guru of the five.
Whatever you will say, consider well first,
For the doings of the doer are impossible to assess.
Religion upholds the earth and is born of compassion.
Establish contentment and create the balance.
Whoever understands becomes the truth
And knows the burden religion bears.
There are many worlds and many more beyond them;
What power assumes their weight?
Creatures of all forms and colors are created by his writ,
But only few know the rule to tell it.
Can anyone write the account of this mystery?
If it were written how great it would be,
What strength and power! How beautiful His appearance!
How great His charity; who can conceive it?
His single word creates this vast expanse—
Infinite mountains and rivers, the animate and inanimate.
How shall I think about it?
However much I offer myself could never be enough!
Whatever pleases You, O Lord, is best for me.
You are the formless, the almighty—You who abide forever!

T HE WORLD BEGINS when the one is lost, and it is natural that the journey ends when the one is found again. And this one can be found in many ways because it had been broken in many ways. When they pass through a prism, the sun's rays break into seven parts, the seven colors that form the spectrum; so also existence becomes fragmented.

The world is full of colors; color belongs to multiplicity. The color of God is white, the one being colorless. All sadhanas are only devices and techniques that seek out the one in the many—that reunite the fractions into the undivided, the integral. The Hindus contend that the one has broken into two: matter and spirit. If you get even a slight glimpse of the one within these two, your journey is complete.

There is another theory that the one has divided into three: truth, goodness, beauty. If you can see truth in beauty or vice-versa; if you see goodness in truth or in beauty; if you get a glimpse of the one within these three, so that all the three are lost and only the one underlying them all, Ek Omkar Satnam, remains, then your journey is over.

Nanak says the one is divided into five because of the five senses. If you seek the one within these five you shall attain, you become the *siddha*, the emancipated one. It is of no consequence in how many parts you divide the one, because it is already divided into infinite parts. The important thing is to discover the undivided, perfect whole within the fragments.

The senses are five, but within these five, meditation is one: to understand this is to grasp the sutra. Telling the beads in a rosary has no meaning, but if you can get at the thread that holds the beads together, then you will have taken refuge in God. Holding on to the beads is to remain in the mundane world; but <u>to grasp the thread of the beads is to attain God</u>.

There are five senses, but who is within these senses? When you look, who is it that sees through your eyes? When you hear, when you touch, when you smell, when you eat, who is it that experiences the perception, the experience? <u>Nanak answers that attention lies at the center and unites it all</u>.

There is an ancient anecdote: A sannyasin was sent by his guru to the palace of a king with the instructions, "The king may perhaps be able to make you understand what I could not." The disciple doubted this, but he had to obey the guru's order. When he reached the palace he found it flooded with light, wine was flowing and dancing-girls moved to sensuous music. He was terribly pained, thinking surely he had been sent to the wrong place; so he asked the king to allow him to go back, explaining that his search was something different. How could the king who was himself lost be of any help to him?

The king said, "I am not lost but you will understand that only after you remain here awhile. Just to see from the outside is fruitless. If you take the trouble to look deep inside perhaps you may grasp the key. Your guru sent you here only after great deliberation." The key is already hidden within, and not in the sense organs themselves.

The king persuaded him to stay overnight. He was put in a wonderful room that was the last word in comfort, but there was only one snag: from the ceiling just over the bed hung a naked sword on a slender cotton thread. The sannyasin could not sleep a wink because the thread was weak and the sword could drop any moment. He was dismayed by this cruel joke.

In the morning the king inquired whether he slept well. "Everything was fine," said the sannyasin with some sarcasm. "It couldn't have been better, but what was the big joke of dangling that sword over my head? I couldn't sleep a wink with my attention glued to the sword all the time."

The king said, "In exactly the same manner the sword of death hangs over my head constantly calling my attention. The girls dance but my mind is not on them; the wine flows but it gives me little pleasure; the tables overflow with all kinds of delicacies, but I can't enjoy the food with the sword of death always hanging over me."

The five senses are the five openings through which you contact the outside world. Without them you cannot relate to life, but the more you enter into them, the farther away from yourself you go. *Dhyana*, attention, is hidden within each of the senses. When a particular sense points outward your attention moves outward through it. Therefore, when your attention goes out through one sense organ you become oblivious of the other senses. This happens because you know only through your attention, and not through your senses. Knowledge itself is attention. For example, you are sitting at a feast but a thorn has got into your foot and the pain is unbearable. You can never enjoy the taste of the food for the terrible pain engages your full attention, which flows only in that direction.

Another example: You have just been told that your house is on fire and your whole mind is on how to get home as fast as you can. Though you are walking on a road with many people you are aware of nothing around you. You don't notice the people rushing by, pushing one another, pushing you, or even that you are pushing others. You have no interest in what is being sold in the shops or what people are talking about. While your ears hear all, you hear nothing; while your arms touch the others you feel nothing. Your mind is entirely on the fire at your house.

The senses do not experience anything without your mind; their experiences rely entirely on your attention. When you pour your attention into a sense organ, then only is it motivated and gains strength. But if you withdraw your attention from all five senses, what remains is the one, because all the five will be lost instantly. And the real search is for this one alone. In these sutras Nanak has shown the method of removing the attention from the five senses.

Now let us try to understand the sutras:

Five are the tests and the ministers;
They gain shelter and respect at His door;
They decorate the king's court.
Attention is the guru of the five.

Dhyana, attention, is the one guru of the five senses. If you remain scattered among the five you are misled, but if you catch hold of the one you will arrive.

Looking at a woman grinding wheat, Kabir said, "No one can remain whole between the two slabs of the millstone." Kabir was telling his disciples that he who is caught in the millstone of duality is similarly ground to bits and cannot be saved.

Kabir's son said of this, "But there is something else in the millstone—the middle shaft. What if someone were to hold on to that?"

In his next couplet Kabir refers to this shaft, saying that he who takes refuge in it, he who seeks protection by holding on to the one amidst the two grinders, cannot be ground by them.

Whether you say two, like Kabir, or five like Nanak, or nine, or infinite, the meandering routes are many but the destination is one. On whatever path you choose to wander, the method of passing through will be specific for this path. Nanak's method means that when you eat you must be aware of your attention: the food is going in, various tastes are forming in the mouth, so experience it all with careful attention. If you taste your food attentively you will find that eventually the taste fades away and only attention remains. Attention and observation form a blazing fire which turns taste to ashes.

While seeing a beautiful flower, observe very attentively and you will find that the flower is gone and only observation remains. The flower is like a dream, attention is eternal.

When you see a beautiful woman and observe her without getting lost in a maze of thoughts, you will soon find that she is no more—like a line drawn on water—and only attention remains. If you thus remain alert and attentive with each of your senses, the forms of the senses fade away and the formless alone emerges. Once a person arrives at this dhyana, nothing can destroy it.

Nanak says there is only one master of the five senses, and that is attention. All the five senses, like five rivers, pour their waters into this very dhyana.

Psychologists also study this phenomenon: eyes see, ears listen, hands touch, the nose smells; but neither eyes nor ears nor hands nor nose can perform these tasks on their own. Then who is it that joins them all?

Someone is speaking; you are listening as well as looking. But how can you be sure that the person you are seeing is the same one you are hearing? Eyes and ears are different from each other. One indicates that it can see someone; the other indicates that it can hear someone. But how do you connect both of these? Who is it who combines the two experiences and conveys to us that they refer to the same person?

There must be a common ground where all the senses combine their experience: the visions sent by the eyes, the sounds sent by the ears, the smells gathered by the nose, the touch felt by the hand. It is the focusing of attention that provides the common point determining the experience. Were it not so, life would be very jumbled and confused. You could never be sure whether you are seeing the same person who is talking, and whether the odors you smell also come from him. You would be broken into bits if there were not one to unite the five. All five paths must meet somewhere where their experiences are collected. This place is dhyana, attention.

Nanak says that attention is the guru of these five, who are disciples; but you have made gurus out of the disciples and forgotten the guru. You have turned the servants into masters and have no knowledge of the master at all. You heed your senses and don't give any thought to attention. You have completely forgotten that the senses are only superficial extensions of attention and you do not know what lies deep within.

If you want to lead a truly beautiful life, do not listen to the senses, because they are incomplete and only land you in trouble. In most cases people are slaves to one sense or the other. Some are mad after the sense of taste—food, food and food—they can think of nothing else. It is said about emperor Nero that he was a fiend for food. It was not just that he ate many times a day, but he kept on eating all day. Doctors were attending him permanently to make him vomit after each meal so that he could eat again.

You might say that he was mad, but this kind of madness exists more or less in all people. Some are addicted to sight—looking out for beautiful faces, beautiful bodies, even if they suffer in the process. They are slaves to their eyes.

You are blind if you are a slave to your eyes, because the authentic seeing organ is not the eye, which is merely a window. The one who looks out from this window is someone else. Do not ask questions of the window, but ask the one who peeps through it. People who are addicted to sounds and smells or to adorning the body, who are lost in music, or have the addiction of touching are all mad after their senses, and have accepted their slaves to be their masters. Listen rather to the owner who is the master within, because once he departs, the senses lie useless.

In 1910 the King of Kashi had to be operated on for appendicitis. Since the king had taken a vow not to partake of anything that induced unconsciousness, he refused any anesthesia. The doctors were in a dilemma, since the operation was absolutely imperative and so also the anesthesia. They tried to explain to him that it was a matter of opening his abdomen, but he persisted and asked only to be allowed to read the Gita while they operated, and that was enough. The doctors had to give in because delay in operating could be fatal. The king read the Gita throughout the operation, and when it was all over the incredulous doctors asked didn't he feel any pain. He said, "I was so engrossed in my Gita, I was not aware of what was happening."

You only know a thing when you apply your mind to it; you see only what you want to see. When your attention is diverted, everything changes. You are unaware of things that you really want to avoid. If you wander through the market, you will see only those things that interest you: a cobbler will concentrate on leather goods, a jeweler will have eyes only for diamonds. You only see those things that are illumined by your attention. All else remains in darkness.

The most profound art of living is to attain mastery over attention. If you are flowing towards God the world will be lost to you, and it is for this reason that sages call the world maya, an illusion. Maya does not mean that the world does not exist. It exists very much, but sages discovered that as their awareness flows Godward, the world fades from perception. And where awareness is not, the existence or nonexistence of that place becomes irrelevant. Existence is born in the act of perception. It fades when the attention is withdrawn.

The sages say: God is truth, the world is non-truth. Does this mean that the world we see around us is not there in actuality? It is very much there, but the sage no longer perceives it. If you are greedy, wealth is real to you; when greed is gone, riches become like clay. Wealth is not wealth because of itself, but because of your perceptions. Or, with sensuousness the body becomes very significant; without sensuousness it becomes secondary.

Existence shifts with attention; it manifests only in the path of attention. Once you understand this you become your own master. Having discovered the master within, you no longer obey your servants, the disciples, because what is the sense in asking those who do not know themselves? Now you follow and do the bidding of the master within.

Nanak says one alone, dhyana, is the guru of the five. On the superficial level dhyana means attention; on the deeper level dhyana refers to meditation. It is meditation that leads to discovery of the master within. There is nothing more profound, nothing deeper than meditation, so ponder over it and make no casual passing remarks about something so significant. But people are such that they talk about attention and meditation without any direct knowledge. People who do not know in themselves enjoy talking just for the sake of talking and they cause a great deal of confusion in the world.

We are experimenting with hundreds of different methods of meditation. Someone came to me saying so-and-so asked, "What is this thing that you are doing? Do you call that meditation?" I told him to ask his friend whether he knows what meditation is, and if he does, to learn from him. For the question is not whether you learn from me or from someone else; the aim is to learn meditation. He went back and asked his friend, who replied that he had no experience with meditation and didn't know what it is. Now this same gentleman is very eager to advise his friend on what meditation is not. Not knowing himself what it is, he is ready to give his opinions. So irresponsible we are!

Nanak says ponder well before you speak. Be fully aware and say only if you know yourself. The world has gone astray not because of ignorant people, but because of those all wise and all knowing people who really know nothing, yet love to talk and advise others. Not being conscious of what they are doing, or why, they are just a plague with their opinions and views.

It is not difficult to gather fools around you; you have only to start speaking and continue speaking, no matter what. In a few days you will have gathered a whole band of followers, because there are always people more stupid than you in this world. To find disciples all you need is a little madness in you, some arrogance, and the strength to speak your loudest, and people will flock around you. As people begin to hang around you, many happenings will be attributed to you. The very people who are in total darkness, never having known the light, get caught in your trap when you begin to speak on light, because they feel there is certainly something in you.

Also, people are very imaginative: whatever they wish to happen, they begin to imagine. When the process of imagination begins, dreams are born. If someone imagines his kundalini rising, he may begin to see light or see colors, and when this happens, faith increases in the man who proclaims himself the guru. That is why we find so many gurus.

I know many such gurus who have no knowledge of meditation. When they meet me in private their question is the same: How does one meditate? What is meditation? And these persons have followings of thousands!

Nanak says that whatever you say with regard to meditation, you must ponder well before you utter, because it is like playing with fire. Nothing could be more subtle, nor more valuable. The path that leads from the mundane world to God, the supreme spirit, is very thin and fine. You have to contemplate a great deal before you venture to express your thoughts.

Whatever you will say, consider well first: "Do I know myself? Have I the experience?" If each person in this world were to take a vow to speak only of that which he has knowledge, all deceptions and misconceptions would end. When man is ready to acknowledge his ignorance of things he does not know and realize that he has no right to talk on such matters, then life will become simple and it will not be so difficult to realize truth.

But there is so much untruth all around, such a network of deception and false gurudom that you will not be able to find a true satguru, a perfect master. You will not come across a true Nanak because there are so many impostors vying to be gurus. How can you discern among them? There are no criteria to go by.

Therefore, Nanak says, speak only after great deliberation, and only after you have known and experienced directly. Don't play with the life of others. This is exactly what you are doing when you advise others on things you are ignorant of yourself. There is no sin greater than misleading a person from the path of knowledge. Theft, murder, deception are nothing compared to it. When you steal you only deprive someone of some earthly possessions, which is hardly of any consequence. When you kill a person you deprive him of his body, but there is no shortage, since new bodies are obtained; you merely snatch the covering, not the *atman*. When you deceive someone what do you gain by it? Something very paltry, nothing of value.

But if you pose as a guru and lead your disciples along paths you have no idea of yourself, you can cause them to wander for endless lives. There can be no deception greater than this, no sin more heinous. There is no greater sinner than an ignorant guru.

Remember, a person can wander from guru to guru and, finding them worthless, his faith is shaken and his hope is lost. He begins to feel that there is nothing but hoax and hypocrisy in the name of religion. When ninety-nine out of one hundred are hypocrites how can one trust the one who is genuine? Such a person, even if he meets a satguru, a Nanak, will invariably be very wary of him, naturally suspecting him to be like the others.

A major reason behind much of the rank atheism in the world is the prevalence of false gurus. Atheism is not an outcome of science as is generally believed, nor does it get its impetus from the atheist philosophers. People have lost faith because of the impostors who masquerade as gurus. It is no longer possible to convince them that there is someone like a genuine master. They also refuse to believe that there is a power that is God.

When the gurus are fakes, how can God be true? This God, and these methods and practices, are merely devices to exploit gullible people—such is the experience of seekers, good people who have been so badly misled.

Thus Nanak exhorts us to speak only after due contemplation because it is like playing with fire, like laying a wager on other people's lives. Think well before you speak or else hold your peace.

Whatever you will say, consider well first,
For the doings of the doer are impossible to assess.

How can we say anything about God? For He has no beginning, no end, nor any limit. The only thing we can possibly do is to be silent about Him. What will you say? What can you say about Him? What can you say in connection with meditation? Then give it great deliberation and thought.

Understand that meditation is the method; and God, paramatma, is at the completion of the experience, the knowledge. You may be able to say something about the path if you have traversed it, but nothing about the destination, which is boundless; it has no limits, no direction. I cannot tell you what God is but I can certainly tell you how I have reached Him; the path can be spoken about.

Buddha has said that a buddha can only give a hint and show the path, nothing more. Nanak has said again and again: I am only a physician who can prescribe the medicine. I know nothing about health. The doctor's knowledge is confined only to the treatment of a certain ailment; his medicine cures the disease but he has no knowledge of health, the wellbeing which fills a person with joy and gratefulness when the illness is gone—he knows nothing about that!

Whatever is spoken about God can only be negative. At most we can say, "He is not this...He is not that...." As soon as you say, "He is this," you confine Him within a boundary, because only that which bears an outline, a boundary, can be pointed out. The limitless cannot be pointed out. Therefore, Nanak says, you can say nothing about God, so it is best to keep silent about Him.

But nowhere in the world do we find people silent on the subject of God. In fact it is a constant topic of heated discussion. There are seminars and meetings where pundits debate on the existence or nonexistence of God. Busily proving their points, no one worries about the fact that God cannot be proved, much less disproved. God can be known, He can be lived. We can become God, but He cannot be proved nor disproved.

How will you prove that God is? Whatever you say of Him will be wrong—absurd and wide of the mark. Or how will you prove that God is not? That will also have to be absurd and irrelevant. Whatever you say about Him can only be absurdly incomplete, because God is the totality, the whole. The vast space that spreads all around you and far out into infinity is referred to in that simple word God. God is not a person sitting somewhere on high—God is an experience of being drowned, of being bathed in divinity, of being lost in it. God is a state in which you no longer are, and yet you are very much there.

It is a strange and wonderful contradiction: on the one hand you are absolutely annihilated, and on the other hand you are a perfect whole, the ultimate perfection! So God is neither an individual nor a conception nor a hypothesis. God is an experience, the ultimate experience!

It is such an experience that you are absorbed in it completely, so lost that there is no one to return and speak
about it.

So, says Nanak, nothing can be said about him. Only
something can be said about meditation—but that too
only if you have experienced it, and after due contemplation. Make it a rule for yourself to speak only of that
which you know, and this small rule can transform your
life. Forget about the rest of the world; worry only about
yourself and don't budge from this rule.

We love to exaggerate. Say we know an inch of something, we want to give a mile's worth of information about
it. We know only a grain and we set out to discuss a
mountainful. The state of mind is a state of exaggeration,
because the ego revels in overstatements.

Mulla Nasruddin fell down on the road. He became
unconscious and was taken to a hospital. When he was
placed on the operating table, they found a piece of paper
in his pocket on which was written in large letters: "I
suffer from epileptic fits. Please do not operate on me for
appendicitis. My appendix has already been removed
many times."

The mind elaborates with great zest and alacrity. It
gets a great kick out of it. A slight knowledge of something and you begin to elaborate, adding spice and color;
and the more you color the falser your knowledge becomes
till ultimately the essence is lost and only the color
remains.

Always say proportionately less of what you know and
that will harm no one. Beware of the urge to exaggerate.
And this holds good not only in talking about God, but
also about meditation, about life and existence. For existence is vast; whatever you have known of it is but an

infinitesimal part, not enough to give you the authority to pontificate.

For instance, you are a shopkeeper. You have known only your shop, whereas existence is a vast thing in which there are infinite ways of living. You have not known life in its entirety. While there are thousands of shops dealing in thousands of things, you have only dealt in one particular kind of goods. Even as a shopkeeper you can at most claim to know only one kind of shop, and of the thousands of customers, you can claim to have known but a few; that is the sum total of your experience—a mere grain.

Newton has said: People think I know a great deal. My own feeling is that the knowledge I have attained is like one grain of sand on the seashore. This one grain is my knowledge, whereas my ignorance is as much as the remaining grains on the shore!

Direct your attention to what you do not know, what is as yet left to be known. This will make you humble; whereas if you concentrate only on what you know, your back will become stiff with arrogance, as your ego is strengthened. Always concentrate on what is yet to be known, what is yet to be experienced. There you will find endless vistas of knowledge yet to be explored and you will feel the futility of keeping count of the knowledge of things you know, because it will look ludicrous, almost nothing!

Therefore Socrates says: When the sage attains the supreme knowledge he finds there is only one thing that remains to be known—that I know nothing! This is the characteristic of a sage: he knows he knows nothing.

Therefore Nanak says to keep within limits, be simple, be humble. Say only what you know and, on the subject of God, hold your peace! For what can you say about him? Whatever you say can be no more than gossip. Can an ant speak of the ocean? Who are you to prove His existence or nonexistence? Who has appointed you the judge? Does God depend on your arguments to make Him or break Him?

Keshav Chandra came to visit Ramakrishna to debate on the existence or nonexistence of God. He elaborated many points to prove that God does not exist. As Ramakrishna listened his heart thrilled with joy. He embraced him lovingly and said, "You have been very kind to come to me, a simple villager. I have never witnessed such magnificent intelligence, and looking at you now I am thoroughly convinced that there can be no greater proof that God is. How can a flower like you ever bloom if it were not for Him?"

Keshav Chandra had come expressly to prove that God is not. His arguments were very lucid and clear, his reasoning so subtle. Such a great logician and genius is born only once in a thousand years. It was very difficult to answer him, and Ramakrishna did not put forth even a single counter-argument. Ramakrishna was so filled with love and delight at the sight of Keshav Chandra, and was so genuinely convinced thereby of the fact of God's existence that Keshav Chandra was struck dumb by his pure ecstasy. Ramakrishna told him, "That you exist is proof that the world is not just material. If such a process of intelligence can be, if reasoning can be so subtle, then this world is not of matter alone; it is not as gross as the stone; there surely is a consciousness hidden within it. For me, your very being has proved that God is."

Keshav Chandra returned home and wrote in his diary that this man had won him over. It is difficult to defeat a religious man who offers no arguments. You can only defeat a person who reasons and argues, where all that is required is to be a better debater, a cleverer speaker.

A religious man gives you no ground for a debate when he refuses to compete with you. He says: I believe in God. I have faith in God. I have no opinion or decisions to make about Him. God is my feeling, not my thought. God is in my heart and not in my head. And the heart keeps silent. A religious man is always silent when questioned about God. Ask him about meditation and he will speak, but only as much as he knows directly.

People in ancient times were honest. There is a beautiful story in connection with Buddha's search for truth. For six years Buddha had gone from guru to guru. After each guru taught him all that he knew, he would move on to another. Then the moment came when Buddha knew all that the gurus knew. Buddha asked the last guru, "What shall I do now?"

"I have taught you all that I know," said the guru. "You will have to look for someone else."

This last guru of Buddha was Alar-Kalam. As Buddha took leave of him Alar-Kalam said, "I have revealed all knowledge that I have attained and have no more to give. Go forth and seek another who can direct you further, but do not forget to impart that knowledge also to me!"

This is the reason that many people of the past attained wisdom, for honesty was a part of their nature. In today's world who worries about honesty? If you can put forth your arguments impressively, it doesn't matter whether you really know what you are talking about, because people are bound to flock around you. It is a matter of how you advertise yourself, like any marketable commodity. If you advertise well, if you succeed in awakening the passion and the greed of the people, you are bound to attract a formidable clientele. It is so easy to become such a guru!

Therefore Nanak says to be very careful what you say about meditation, because it is religion that supports the earth. By even a few right or wrong statements you can upset the lives of thousands of people; one wrong statement can sow confusion for endless births. Religion is not a small matter; it is the basis of your life, the support of all existence. Only speak what you truly know about religion. To develop a false conception of religion is to lose all that supports and maintains your being. Religion upholds and maintains the earth. It arises out of compassion and pity, and the establishment of contentment forms its equilibrium.

Let the following lines go deep within you:

Religion upholds the earth and is born of compassion.
Establish contentment and create the balance.

Religion is the basis of all life, of all existence. Without it existence cannot hold together; the world would fall apart. It is the foundation on which stands the mansion of existence. All else is like the other building materials, like bricks, mortar, cement. Religion is the foundation, the innate quality of our nature. It is in the very nature of fire to give heat; without heat there cannot be a fire. It is the nature of the sun to give light; if it does not it will no longer be the sun, it will have lost its quality, its innate character, its dharma.

Jesus often said: If salt loses its quality of saltiness, how can you make it salty again? There is no way. Anything that loses its intrinsic quality is no longer that thing; it was what it was because of its very nature, its quality.

The sun is the sun because it gives light; fire is fire because it gives heat. And man is man because of meditation—that is his nature! The person who loses the quality to meditate is a person in name only. Though he still looks like a human being he is actually an animal, because he lives like an animal. We never criticize an animal who lives according to its nature. We never tell the dog he is behaving like a dog; that has no meaning to him. But we sometimes tell a person he is behaving like a dog or, "Don't be an ass!"

We can say this to a human being because he is not an actual human being unless he becomes properly established in meditation; that is his natural self. A Buddha, a Kabir, a Nanak are proper human beings. But the bulk of humanity has fallen so low that we call such special people *avatara*, incarnations. Naturally we do not look upon them as human beings, for then what are we? We would have to rate ourselves lower. But to maintain that we are human beings, we have to create a special place for them just a little above us, that of the incarnation. It solves our problem to call them godlike—no, gods—and remain human beings ourselves. But we are not human beings.

Manushya means man. It contains the root *mana*, which means mind. The words must be understood. When a person is deeply established in meditation, he becomes manushya, because consciousness and awareness as a higher state of mind is the nature of man. When you attain your own consciousness, you find that it is the portal to the consciousness of all of existence. So the only way for man to reach God is to discover the innermost basis of his own nature.

Religion upholds the earth and is born of compassion.
Establish contentment and create the balance.

Religion is the support, the nature, the basis of all life. It is the son of compassion. Establish contentment and the equilibrium is established.

Compassion, contentment are two very valuable words, because the whole life of the seeker can be contained within them. Contentment within and compassion without must be balanced on the scales. Be always satisfied within your own self and ever-compassionate towards others, never contentment based on others nor compassion for one's own self.

Understand that we do just the opposite. We see a man dying of hunger, or lying on the streets writhing with pain, and we say: Life is as it should be—you have to take it as it comes. Though we may have been taught that contentment is the satisfaction that things are as they should be, we misuse it. It should be contentment in what one has, but compassion for others. On the other hand, if I know that I am where I should be, and there is no need whatever to change, that whatever fate has given me is enough, then I am satisfied and fulfilled as I am.

Unrest and turbulence follows in the wake of dissatisfaction: when I feel things are not happening as I would wish them to happen, that I am not as I should be; that I have not been given what I am worthy of receiving; that God does not seem to be pleased with me; that there is some injustice; that I am not appreciated as I should be; that I definitely deserve more fame, more wealth...as soon as these thoughts of dissatisfaction begin to gather in your mind, you will feel the lack of things and your restlessness begins. Your mind will concentrate on all that you do not have and see only insufficiency and misery.

When there is satisfaction towards one's self, then you begin to feel and notice all that you have. And when you begin to realize all that you have, you are filled with thanks and gratefulness towards Him who has given you so much, thinking "Surely I don't deserve all of this!"

Contentment towards oneself, and compassion towards others. You must do whatever is possible for you to do for others—and more; give happiness and peace, whether they receive it from you or not, and don't worry or be discontented on that account—it is your own affair. So keep it to yourself if you tried your best and could not relieve a person of his pain or suffering. Let it not dishearten you; don't reproach yourself, but maintain your contentment.

But we tend to become contented about the lot of others and sympathize with ourselves. This is what has happened in India and caused its downfall; this is why India is poor, sick and miserable. Where others are concerned we say, "It is God's will." But where we ourselves are concerned, we are not prepared to take what comes to us and fight to the bitter end. There we do not say: God's will.

Self-centeredness and selfishness lead us to proclaim: "Thy will be done!—as long as He has made me wealthy and the other poor. Whatever is written in our destiny we get—as long as I am the master and others are slaves." We are without pity for the lot of the destitute, having wasted all our feelings of compassion on ourselves.

The words compassion and contentment are priceless; only change their direction and they become dangerous. If we are satisfied with our own lot we enjoy infinite peace and tranquility in life; we become wholly fulfilled. If we can be compassionate and sympathetic towards others, we shall wipe out poverty and misery. Kindness and compassion develop into a sense of service to others that fills you with prayer and worship, because it then becomes the path that leads to God.

If you are kind to others. but dissatisfied with your own self, you will end up a social worker; you will never become religious. If you are satisfied with yourself but have no compassion for others, you become a lifeless holy man. Having lost all that is precious and meaningful in life, such people run away to the jungles. They are satisfied with their own selves but without an iota of compassion. They succeed in finding their own happiness but they are the ultra-selfish people. If you look into their eyes there is no sign of pity, only a ruthless stare.

Ask the Jain muni, who is busy accomplishing his own self-contentment, "What of kindness and sympathy for others?" "We all have to reap the fruits of our actions. What can I do about it?" he will reply. While he is cultivating his own satisfaction, his sadhana is incomplete; there is no balance.

Look at a Christian missionary. He cultivates compassion and kindness: he does not mind the jungles, or the Adivasis, the poor primitive tribal man whom he serves with such fanatical zeal; no work is too mean for him. But he is dissatisfied within himself.

All these people are incomplete: the Christian missionary has compassion, the Jain muni is self-contented, but there is no balance. If one side of the scales is heavier than the other, because of this lack of equilibrium the instrument of existence cannot be tuned to resonate with the divine melody.

> So Nanak says:
> Religion...is born of compassion.
> Establish contentment and create the balance.
> Whoever understands becomes the truth.

He who embodies both compassion and contentment—in their right proportion and the right direction—attains the supreme comprehension of life. He will then

know what religion is; he becomes truth incarnate. The
ideal is: satisfaction within and compassion without; meditation within, love and kindness without.

Buddha describes a similar ideal utilizing the words
compassion and wisdom: wisdom within, compassion
without. Until such time that both of these are present,
whatever the knowledge, it can only be false. The lack of
either leaves knowledge incomplete.

By merely being compassionate to others you do not
reach anywhere; you have to do something within yourself also. No matter how many difficulties you endure to
serve the downtrodden and the sick, if you do not cul-
tivate contemplation within, awaken your remembrance
and meditate, you can reach nowhere. If you have not
found the One within the five senses, you yourself are still
an ill person.

Just as you walk on two feet and birds need two wings
to fly, just as you need two eyes to get a proper view of the
world that surrounds you, so in exactly the same manner
you need two wings for the ultimate journey. Nanak calls
them compassion and contentment.

Whoever understands becomes the truth
And knows the burden religion bears.
There are many worlds and many more beyond them.

Scientists acknowledge that there are at least fifty
thousand worlds within the limits of their discoveries,
and how many more beyond these? Life does not exist on
this planet alone but probably on tens of thousands of
other planets. How can you perceive an expanse so enormous with your limited mind? You will have to put it
aside.

As soon as the mind becomes silent the window falls
away and you find yourself under the open skies. Then
you begin to see how vast the expanse of existence is, how

infinite! And when you realize the exquisite glory of existence, you wonder why you were lost in feeble nothings all
this while: someone abused you, someone insulted you, a
thorn pricked your foot or you had a headache—such is
the story of your life! While the magnificent phenomenon
of existence is taking place every moment around you, you
are involved in futile matters. Your calculations were all
of the wrong kind; while infinite wealth was raining
around, you were counting shells.

> There are many worlds and many more beyond them;
> What power assumes their weight?
> Creatures of all forms and colors are created by his writ,
> But only few know the rule to tell it.
> Can anyone write the account of this mystery?
> If it were written how great it would be.
> What strength and power! How beautiful His appearance!
> How great His charity; who can conceive it?
> His single word creates this vast expanse—
> Infinite mountains and rivers, the animate and inanimate.
> How shall I think about it?
> However much I offer myself could never be enough!
> Whatever pleases You, O Lord, is best for me.
> You are the formless, the almighty—You who abide forever!

As soon as you step aside from your silly involvements
you will see your present state. It is as if it were raining
rubies and diamonds outside while you have shut yourself
inside your house, holding your rubble and stones tight
against your chest for fear you might lose them.

Where in your thoughts do you abide? What engages
your attention? What discussions and arguments are
going on within you? If you examine these you will find
them very petty and insignificant, so trivial as to be
unworthy of any consideration, but you have wasted all
your life in them.

And Nanak says: When the mind is set aside, when you are in the no-mind state and the sound of Omkar begins to vibrate within you, you begin to witness the glory of existence, its vastness; you see the infinite life, the overflowing boundless nectar, the limitless beauty and the unaccountable power that has no beginning, no end. All this you see when you enter His court. And then you realize you can never even imagine such vast existence or guess at its wonderful taste. But alas, how foolishly we are frittering away all chance of this wonderful experience.

Nanak asks: How shall I think about it? It is to stand dumbfounded, the eyes filled with surprise and wonder. The trouble is we never lift our eyes upwards, having kept them firmly focused on the pebbles and stones.

How is one to think of nature? Even if I offer myself in sacrifice a thousand times it is but a paltry gesture. And how shall I repay the limitless phenomena that happen every moment, the infinite nectar that showers incessantly? I cannot, I cannot, even if I offer myself on the sacrificial fire a thousand times. Such a feeling of gratefulness is born, and such thanksgiving is the real prayer.

The words Nanak uses in prayer are priceless: "What pleases You, O Lord, is best for me." Thy will be done! In such moments your desires and wishes will drop off and there will be only one prayer on your lips: O Lord, do not fulfill my wishes; let only Your will be done! For whatever you ask is bound to be mean and insignificant. Children always ask for toys and foolish people ask for foolish things.

Then you will say to Him: Let not my desires be gratified, O Lord, because what you have ordained is best for me. Who am I to decide what should be and what should not? Whatever You will is always the best. What does not come to pass is surely not for my good. There is only one criterion, one proof—whatever You will is forever the best. You are the formless, the almighty, the birthless one!

The Lord is forever. It is I who exist at specific times and become nonexistent at others. My being is like a bubble of water. He is the ocean, I am a wave. And what can a wave ask? It lives but for a moment, then how can its desires be real? The last words of Jesus are truly priceless—Thy will be done, O Lord!

> *Whatever pleases You, O Lord, is best for me.*
> *You are the formless, the almighty—You who abide forever!*

Doubt raised its ugly head even within the mind of Jesus when he was being hung on the cross. At the very moment that the nails were being hammered into his limbs and the blood began to flow there was a moment— just a single moment that is so very valuable because it demonstrates how weak man is. All of humanity mani- fested its complete helplessness through Jesus. And Jesus said in that moment, "What are You showing me? What is this You are doing unto me, O Lord?"

The question arose, and though Jesus did not really doubt his Lord, even so there is a slight suggestion of doubt. It is a very personal question which Jesus asks, "What is this You wish to show me?" And doubt lurks behind the question. One thing is certain, that Jesus was not happy about what was taking place. He did not ap- prove of the cross, the hammering of nails. Something was happening which should not be happening.

So it is a complaint, all right; and the complaints of all humanity manifested in the words of Jesus. You will also experience these moments in your own life when all your faith will be shaken and your mind will cry out, "What is happening?" You will doubt the bona-fides of God; you placed so much faith in Him and is this the result? But this in itself proves that you have not trusted Him wholly, or else you would accept whatever happened. If your acceptance bears even a little hesitation within, it is not perfect acceptance. If you accept complainingly, your acceptance is incomplete; your faith must be whole-hearted—whatever He wishes.

But Jesus pulled himself together. For just one single moment the entire race of mankind trembled through Jesus, for only one moment; then Jesus raised his head and said, "Thy will be done, O Lord! Thy will, not mine." At that moment the man faded and Christ was born. Jesus disappeared and Christ manifested in his place. So small is the distance between Jesus and Christ, the distance of a single moment. How great a difference lies between ignorance and knowledge, between Buddha and you, between Nanak and you! No matter how high you ascend, one fear always nags at your heart: Is my wish being gratified? The devotee also always keeps an eye on God: is He doing his bidding? If not, he complains. No matter how tender the words he uses, a complaint is a complaint, and the thorn keeps pricking within.

The perfect devotee has no complaints; his confidence in Him is complete: Whatever You will is best for me. You are my protection. You are the eternal, the formless, the almighty. I am but a wave; where is there any question of my will? Thy will be done. Thy will is my will. The wave's desire cannot be different from the ocean; the leaf's desire cannot be different from the tree; the limb's desire cannot be different from the body's. In this manner one should let go of one's self like a drop in the ocean.

However, this is possible only when you discover the One behind the five. As you are now, you do not exist; then who will you seek? Right now you are so divided

within yourself that there is a crowd within, not one
whole integrated individual. Then how will you take the
jump when some parts are going right and some left, and
others in other directions? You do not exist as one individual. Scattered in many fragments, your being has no
meaning.

So the first thing Nanak says is: Seek the One behind
the five—seek attention, awareness, meditation! And the
second thing is: As meditation grows stronger, let there
be contentment within, compassion without. As compassion firmly takes root, contentment will become more
profound, and you will experience the dawning of the
feeling of gratitude and thanksgiving, and you will say,
"Thy way, not mine, O Lord!" This is the ultimate, the
culmination of perfection.

Chapter 8

Countless Ways

There are countless ways to repeat His name and express devotion,
Countless ways of worship and purification.
There are countless scriptures and countless mouths to recite them,
Countless ways of yoga to make the mind dispassionate.
There are countless devotees who contemplate His virtues and
knowledge,
Countless who are virtuous and generous.
There are countless brave men who risk their lives for Him,
Countless who vow to silence and meditate on Him.
Nanak says, How shall I praise Him?
However much I offer myself could never be enough!
Whatever pleases You, O Lord, is best for me.
You are the formless, the almighty—You who abide forever!

There are countless ignorant fools and countless who are blind,
Countless thieves and shirkers.
There are countless numbers who ruled by force before they departed,
Countless murderers who earn only by murder.
There are countless sinners who commit nothing but sin,
Countless liars who live by their lies.
There are countless barbarians eating only filth for food,
Countless fault-finders who fill their heads with scandal.
Thus Nanak ponders on the wicked and the low.
However much I offer myself could never be enough!

Whatever pleases You, O Lord, is best for me.
You are the formless, the almighty—You who abide forever!

Countless are the names and the places where You dwell,
Countless worlds that have never been reached.
To say countless is to burden the mind.
Through the letter comes the name, and all the prayers.
Through the letter is all knowledge and songs in His praise.
Through the letter is all writing and speaking,
Through the letter are all events destined.
All destiny has already been written,
But He who writes is beyond destiny.
All creation is His name;
There is no place that is not His name.
Nanak says, How shall I praise Him?
However much I offer myself could never be enough!
Whatever pleases You, O Lord, is best for me.
You are the formless, the almighty—You who abide forever!

T HERE ARE INFINITE paths open to the seeker. Which
one should he choose? And on what basis? Is there
some criterion for choice? Not only are there infinite paths
to truth, but there are equally infinite paths to non-truth.
What protection is there from taking wrong paths, to
escape futile wanderings? The greatest problem for a
seeker is how to choose the right path and distinguish the
wrong ones. Once we recognize that a path is wrong, we
begin to steer away from it, for how can one continue
along a road which is known to go in the wrong direction?
You are bound to shun it. The knowledge of non-truth is
in itself freedom from it. But how is one to decide among
such infinite choices?

The moment of recognition of truth is also the first
leap into experiencing it. No sooner is it recognized than
it imparts its color to you and you develop wings and the
flight begins. But again—there are innumerable truths.

Infinite paths have been discovered in the course of centuries—so numerous, so very complex and involved as to defy any solution. So Nanak asks what is the seeker to do? These verses deal with this problem.

There are countless ways to repeat His name and express devotion,
Countless ways of worship and purification.
There are countless scriptures and countless mouths to recite them,
Countless ways of yoga to make the mind dispassionate.
There are countless devotees who sing His praises and contemplate the knowledge,
Countless who are virtuous and generous.
There are countless brave men who risk their lives for Him,
Countless who vow to silence and meditate on Him.

What is the seeker to do? How is he to choose his path? "Which path is right for me? Since I am truly ignorant, therefore I seek; and in my ignorance I have no way to test what is gold, what is dust. What can my best be worth when I am so ignorant and uninformed?" A person who has never seen gold, though he possess a touchstone will never know the value of gold. He who has known only mind all his life, will also take gold to be an aspect of mind. We can only recognize what is within our field of experience. We have not known God; we have not reached that far. Which way will lead up to Him?

There seems to be only one way, what scientists call trial and error. Seek, experience, wander again and again, and with constant trial and error you will find the right path.

But if we follow this trial and error method we may never arrive, because life is so short and the paths so numerous; we can barely complete a simple path in the course of one lifetime. How is one to gather experience? Who is the guru? How is one to know and recognize him so that we may follow him?

The problem gets more and more intricate. Were it only a question of choosing one among many right paths, it would not be so hazardous, because whichever one we chose would ultimately lead to reality. But there are so many false paths for every right path, that only one in a million attains truth. The rest wander about blindly creating their own paths, writing their own scriptures.

Things were easier in ancient times when the Vedas were the only texts on spiritual science; then there were no Mohammedans or Christians or Buddhists. Whenever there was a question the Vedas provided the answer. It was so convenient to have only one single book of scripture offering the gospel truth. Now there are infinite Vedas, infinite scriptures. It is impossible to thread your way through them. Which scripture will you consult? The Jains have their own scripture, so also the Mohammedans and the Hindus, the Catholics, the Jews. And they do not have one but many. The Gurugranth Sahib is a scripture that has been added to many times. As the number increased, so also our problem of deciding on a path.

Perhaps this is why mankind has turned atheist. It is well nigh impossible to choose a path, or even to believe in God, under the influence of so many philosophies running at cross purposes, each trying to disprove the others.

Ask the Jains; they say Vedas have nothing in them. Ask a Buddhist, he will say Vedas are meaningless. Ask the Vedantist and he proclaims that everything besides the Vedas is useless and trivial and leads a person astray. Ask the Hindu and he says Buddhists and Jains are atheists. If a single word from them enters your ears, you are lost. The Hindu says the Vedas are the oldest scriptures and hence worthy of our trust. Ask a Mohammedan and he says: the Koran is the latest scripture and therefore the most authentic, because when a new order comes from above, all old orders are automatically superseded.

The Hindu says that once only did God send down the Vedas. There is no need for any new scripture since God is not a human being who errs or needs to improve upon His work. He is the ultimate knowledge, the Vedas are His only true words, and therefore all else is false. God, having once made His order known, all else that follows is merely a device of man. The Christians and the Mohammedans however say that the universe undergoes perpetual change; since man changes, God must change too. Orders change because situations change. Therefore believe in what is new, not in what is old and outdated.

Whom will you heed? Whom will you believe? You are ultimately left with your own understanding. You stand with legs trembling in the midst of this vast entanglement.

Man has turned to atheism because it is becoming infinitely harder to have faith in something. Some way has to be found by which a simple, innocent human being can believe, can again become a theist. While the greatest of philosophers have failed to decide on the choices, what is a simple human being to do? He has neither the means nor the time nor the armor of reasoning and logic. Which path is he to choose and how?

Nanak's suggestion is priceless: It is futile to wander in these infinite paths. I know of only one solution and that is:

Whatever pleases You, O Lord, is best for me.

Therefore I leave myself entirely to Your pleasure. I cannot choose for myself, for I am ignorant and stand in darkness; I am blind. I have nothing on the strength of which I can set out to seek. I have no means to test the authenticity of my path. What shall I do? I surrender myself at Thy feet—Thy will be done.

Thy will be done: I sit at Your command, I stand at Your command; whatever I do is Your command. I do not bring myself into it at all. If You make me wander I shall wander; if You make me reach the destination, it is Your will. I shall not complain if I wander, nor shall I pride myself if I arrive, because all is Your will. I shall not be the decider. This is exactly what Krishna means when he says to Arjuna in the Gita: "Leave all religious duties aside and surrender unto me." These are words spoken on behalf of God.

What Nanak says are the words of the devotee: What pleases You is best for me. The path You choose is the path for me. In Your will lies my salvation. I shall not care to choose, lead me where You please. If it is Your will that I should wander, then that is the path for me. If it is Your will to leave me in darkness then I shall take it to be the light for me. If You make the day into night, I shall accept it as night. Thy way, not mine, O Lord!

This is very very difficult, because your ego will keep interfering time and time again. Your mind will keep asking what is all this? Could it be that God has made a mistake? Am I wrong in placing my faith completely in Him? When things are going well, you will put your trust in Him, but when things do not go as you wish, trouble starts; and that is the true time of test, that is the time for your practice.

For instance when there are flowers spread everywhere before you, you will say with Nanak: Your will is my will. But when you are caught in the midst of suffering, when there is nothing but insult and failure all around, then is the real time to test your faith, your practice. In sorrow and pain also, you should be able to say with Nanak: Thy way, not mine, O Lord! I am happy in whatever you choose for me! In sorrow and suffering you must also accept what He gives.

But this acceptance must not be a pretended show of contentment. Keep in mind that sometimes we assume a false sense of contentment when we find ourselves helpless. When there is suffering and unhappiness with no way out, then the easiest thing is to say, "Thy will be done." But our dissatisfaction lies hidden behind our words. Outwardly we accept but inwardly we feel that it should not have been! What we wished for did not come to pass, we could not do anything about it either. We are helpless, powerless, impotent—so the best thing is to accept His will.

Had you uttered these words of Nanak in a state of helplessness and resignation you would not have understood the real meaning of these words. Contentment is not a pitiful state; it is the state of the highest blessedness. These are not words spoken for consolation when nothing else can be done, but as the manifestation of truth. Understand well that it should not be an act of deceiving and consoling one's own self.

Generally this feeling comes about after a person has tried his very best to get out of some trying circumstances. Having made full use of his sense of doing, he finds himself defeated on all sides, and then he turns to Him in desperation, leaving everything to Him; but this is no real surrendering. From the very beginning you should not make any effort to change your circumstances, but leave everything in His hands.

Nanak's concept of supreme surrender is the ultimate spiritual path, the highest practice of a devotee. Then you needn't worry about choosing a path or method or scripture. You needn't worry about logic or proof of any philosophy; you have no use for any of these. The devotee rids himself of all these in the one stroke of surrender. He leaves everything at one time and cries out: "Thy way, not mine, O Lord! Thy will be done!"

Experiment a little and you will understand. Nanak is no philosopher. He has not written a scripture, his words are the expression of his inner feelings. He is giving voice to his own experience. You will have difficulty at every step because of the ego, whose very cry is: I know what is right and what should be.

There is a short story by Tolstoy. The god of death sent his angel to earth as an emissary to bring back the soul of a woman who had just died. The angel found himself in a dilemma because the woman had given birth to triplets. All three were girls: one was still sucking milk from the dead mother, another was crying and the third was so exhausted that it had fallen asleep. Such was the state— three little babies, the mother lying dead and no one to look after them, since the father was already dead and there was no one else in the family.

The angel returned without the woman's soul and told the god of death: "Forgive me, I did not bring back the woman's soul. You can't be aware of what I have just witnessed: there are three little babies that this woman has given birth to, one still suckling at her breast. There is no one to care for them. Can't you allow a little time to the mother so that the girls are big enough to look after themselves?"

"So you have become very clever and wise, it seems," said the god of death, "perhaps wiser than he who wills both death and life to all mortal beings. You have committed the first sin for which you shall be punished. You will have to return to earth and, until such time as you laugh three times at your own foolishness, you shall not return."

Understand this: laugh three times at your foolishness. The ego always laughs at the nonsense of others. When you can laugh at your own absurdity, the ego breaks. The angel readily agreed to undergo the punishment. He was quite certain he was right under the circumstances, and wondered how he would find an opportunity to laugh at himself. He was ejected from heaven.

It was almost winter. A cobbler, who was on his way to buy warm clothes for his children, came upon a poor man, bare to the bones and trembling in the cold. It was none other than our friend the angel. The cobbler felt sorry for him. Instead of buying the children's clothes with his hard-earned money, he went and bought clothes and a blanket for the naked man. When he also came to know that he had nothing to eat and nowhere to go, he offered him the shelter of his own house. However, he warned him that his wife was bound to get angry but he should not be upset, everything would be all right later on.

The cobbler arrived home with the angel. Neither the cobbler nor the wife had any idea who he really was. As soon as they entered the door the wife fired off a volley of abuse at her husband for what he had done.

The angel laughed for the first time.

The cobbler asked him why he laughed. "When I have laughed again I shall tell you," he answered, knowing that the cobbler's wife was unaware that the very presence of an angel who was her unwanted guest would confer a thousand benefits.

But how far can the human mind see? For the wife it was a loss of warm clothing for the kids. She can only see the loss, but not what had been found—and free of cost, at that. So he laughed, because she didn't know what was happening around her.

Within seven days he learned the shoemaker's trade, and within a few months the cobbler's fame had spread far and wide. Even kings and noblemen ordered their shoes here, and money began to flow in an endless stream.

One day the king's servant came to the shop, bringing special leather in order to have a pair of shoes made for the king. "Take care you make no mistakes, for this is the only piece of leather of its kind," said the servant. "Also, remember, the king wants shoes and not slippers." In Russia, slippers are worn by a dead person on his last journey. The cobbler gave special instructions to the angel to be extra careful with the king's orders, or else they would be in trouble.

In spite of this the angel made slippers for the king. The cobbler was beside himself with rage. He was certain now he would be hanged. He ran to beat the angel with his stick. The angel laughed out loud at the very moment that a man came running from the king's court, saying, "The king is dead. Please change the shoes into slippers."

The future is unknown; only He knows what is to be. Man's decisions are all based on the past. When the king was alive he needed shoes, when he died he required slippers. The cobbler fell at the angel's feet and begged forgiveness. The angel replied, "Don't worry. I am undergoing my own punishment." And he laughed again.

The cobbler said, "What makes you laugh?"

The angel said, "I laughed for the second time because we do not know the future and we still persist in desires which are never fulfilled, because fate has different plans. The cosmic law works, destiny is set out, and we have no say in the matter. Yet we raise a hue and cry about things as if we are the makers of our destiny. The king is about to die, but he orders shoes for himself! Life is drawing to a close and we keep planning for the future."

Suddenly the angel thought of the triplets: I did not know what their future was going to be. Then why did I intervene unnecessarily in their affairs?

Soon the third event took place. Three young girls, accompanied by an old rich woman, came into the shop to order shoes. The angel recognized the girls as the daughters of the dead woman who had been the cause of his punishment. All three girls were happy and beautiful. The angel asked the old woman about the girls, and she said, "These are the three daughters of my neighbor. The mother was very poor, and died while nursing her new-born babies. I felt pity for such helpless babies and, since I had no children of my own, I adopted them."

Had the mother been alive, the girls would have grown up in poverty and suffering. Because the mother died the girls grew up in riches and comfort, and now they were heirs to the old woman's fortune. They were also to be married into the royal family.

The angel laughed for the third time.

He told the cobbler, "My third laugh is because of these girls. I was wrong. Destiny is great, while our vision is limited to what we can see. What we cannot see is so vast. We cannot imagine the enormity of that which we cannot see and of that which is to be. Having laughed at my foolishness three times, my penalty is completed and now I must leave."

What Nanak says is that if you stop putting yourself in the middle, and stop getting in your own way, you will find the Path of Paths. Then you needn't worry about other paths. Leave all to Him and be thankful for whatever He has caused to happen for you, for whatever He is making you do this moment, for whatever He will cause you to perform. All praise unto Him! Give Him a blank check of gratitude. Whatever He has chosen for you and through you, whether you liked it or not, whether you were praised or blamed, whether people called it your good fortune or misfortune, let there not be even a trace of difference in your thankfulness.

Nanak sees only one path and that is: You are the formless, the almighty, You who abide forever. I am too small, like a wave in the ocean. I leave everything to You. You have given me so much. Your bounteous grace pours all the time everywhere; so much so that if I were to give myself as an offering a thousand times, it would be too insignificant. He knows only one path: Whatever pleases You is best for me.

There are countless ways to repeat His name and express devotion,
Countless ways of worship and purification.
There are countless scriptures and countless mouths to recite them,
Countless ways of yoga to make the mind dispassionate.
There are countless devotees who contemplate His virtues
and knowledge,
Countless who are virtuous and generous.
There are countless brave men who risk their lives for Him,
Countless who vow to silence and meditate on Him.
Nanak says, How shall I praise Him?
However much I offer myself could never be enough!
Whatever pleases You, O Lord, is best for me.
You are the formless, the almighty—You who abide forever!

On the one hand is the congregation of saints and philosophers who have with great deliberation devised untold methods for finding truth; but unfortunately, just because of the countless methods, truth was lost.

There are countless ignorant fools and countless who are blind,
Countless thieves and shirkers.
There are countless numbers who ruled by force before they departed,
Countless murderers who earn only by murder.
There are countless sinners who commit nothing but sin,
Countless liars who live by their lies.
There are countless barbarians eating only filth for food,
Countless fault-finders who fill their heads with scandal.
Thus Nanak ponders on the wicked and the low.
However much I offer myself could never be enough!
Whatever pleases You, O Lord, is best for me.
You are the formless, the almighty—You who abide forever!

On the other hand, there is the crowd of the wicked, the sinners, the murderers and the lustful. They too, with all the skill of their egos, have found countless paths to circumvent truth. They are creative innovators of lies. They are great discoverers who have uncovered delightful untruths, created beautiful tantalizing dreams. Anybody can be caught by their hypnosis and led astray.

One can go astray either by choosing a wrong path or by remaining undecided about which right path to follow; in both cases you will fall into error. Says Nanak: I care for neither. Whatever You choose is best for me. I care not what the virtuous say, I care not what the sinners say. I choose neither sin nor virtue, neither the right path nor the wrong. I choose nothing; I leave all to You. Whatever You make me do is auspicious. Wherever You take me is favorable for me. Whichever path You indicate is the path for me. It matters not whether the goal is reached or not reached.

Understand this: if the desire for attainment lurks within, you will not be able to leave everything to Him. Then all your attention will remain on the goal and you will always be anxious about your progress. Your surrender will be incomplete and half-hearted, which is worse than no surrender at all.

No! There is no question of either reaching or not reaching the destination, because there is no longer any destination. To abandon all thought of destination is the destination itself. Surrender is the ultimate quality for the devotee. Nothing remains after this. Then if He makes the devotee sink to the lowest depths, the seeker feels himself raised higher and higher. If He throws him in the darkest pit, the devotee feels the sun rising from a thousand directions. The question is not where you are going, nor what you are attaining, but what is your innermost feeling?

Nanak's method is totally a method of surrender.

Countless are the names and the places where You dwell,
Countless worlds that have never been reached.
To say countless is to burden the mind.
Through the letter comes the name, and all the prayers.
Through the letter is all knowledge and songs in His praise.
Through the letter is all writing and speaking,
Through the letter are all events destined.
All destiny has already been written,
But He who writes is beyond destiny.
All creation is His name;
There is no place that is not His name.
Nanak says, How shall I praise Him?
However much I offer myself could never be enough!
Whatever pleases You, O Lord, is best for me.
You are the formless, the almighty—You who abide forever!

His name! There have been almost as many discovered as there are people in the world. Each makes his choice. There is a Hindu scripture, Vishnu Sahastranam, which is nothing but the names of God. Mohammedans have their own names. It is both a Hindu and Moham-medan tradition to name their children after some name of God: we find Rehman, Rahim, Abdullah, which are all Islamic names of God; and Ram, Krishna, Hari, which are Hindu names of God.

If we were to consider all the various names, we would find them to be as varied as there are people in the world. And yet there is a way out: no matter how many names we coin, they are all the product of the human mind. He is without name. Therefore, whatever name we give Him, that will do.

So Nanak says: Which name of Yours shall I repeat? Which name shall I call You by? Which name should I take that will reach You? The seeker is always worried about which name would be best. It is common knowledge that when we write a letter we have to write the address and so we pay the utmost attention to the name and address.

It happened once that Mulla Nasruddin was working for a man who had a weakness for writing anonymous letters. He sent them to ministers, newspaper editors, and also to the intellectuals of the town. One day he wrote a letter and gave it to Nasruddin, who promptly went and posted it.

"Where is the letter? Have you posted it?" he asked Nasruddin.

"Yes," said Nasruddin.

"But I hadn't yet addressed the envelope. Couldn't you see that?"

"I did notice it," said the Mulla, "but I thought this time you wanted to keep the address anonymous as well."

If you keep the address secret how can the letter be delivered? How will you address a letter so that it reaches Him? Thus His name is essential. There is a constant search for a name befitting Him, which would evoke a response from Him. Says Nanak: Either all names are His or no name is His. The *akshara*, the letter, is His name. Akshara means the letter and also that which cannot be erased. A, B, C, D can be rubbed out after they are written. And the reason for calling the letters akshara is very meaningful. It implies that which is meaningful, that which is authentic and inexpressible; what is written is only the reflection thereof.

It is like this: there is the moon in the sky, and there is a lake below in which the moon is reflected. Disturb the water and the reflected moon breaks in a thousand pieces, because it is perishable. But no matter how much you try to stir things up, it has no effect on the moon, which is indestructible. Our language is only an echo of the language of God. Whatever we write in books and on boards is mere reflection which can be erased at any moment. But the source from which the words come is beyond extinction. You who are speaking are destructible, but that which speaks through you is beyond extinction.

So Nanak says akshara is His name, and the letter can be neither written nor erased. Other than akshara, all is man's creation. What is this akshara, this letter, the word?

We do have a very close echo of akshara in Omkar. The whole philosophical system of Nanak is based on this one focal point, Ek Omkar Satnam—that is all. Know these three words and you will know the whole Japuji; you will then understand Nanak in his fullness, because that is the essence of his verse. Akshara, according to Nanak, is Omkar—there is one resonance that vibrates

even without being expressed or written. And this
resonance is beyond annihilation, it is the very music of
existence; therefore there is no way of destroying it. When
everything else is destroyed, it will still go on.

It is said in the Bible, what is invariably repeated in
all scriptures: In the beginning was the word. What is
referred to as the word, the *logos* in the West, is Omkar.
In the beginning was the word; all the rest followed later,
and when all else is no more the word will still resonate;
everything will be absorbed in it.

India has developed various methods of *shabd* yoga,
the yoga of the word. The practice consists only of the
word. Its significance is to make oneself wordless so that
the speaker is silenced, and then what is heard is the
voice of God. This is what the yoga claims.

Nanak says: Countless are Your names and the places
where You dwell, and countless the realms where no one
has yet been. What is the sense in saying countless when
it only increases the burden on your mind? In truth, to
speak about God is only to increase the load of words;
because whatever you say only magnifies the burden on
your mind, because whatever you say will be basically
wrong.

Suppose a man stands at the shore of an ocean and
pronounces: "This ocean is boundless." If he has not tried
to measure the ocean and is only making a statement,
what is the use of it? The Pacific Ocean is said to be five
miles deep, yet you cannot say it is boundless, because
that means that which is truly without a boundary.

If we ask him what he means, he may say, "I was just
standing at the shore and made the statement." Then he
has used the wrong words. If he says, "I dived down but
could not find the bottom," then too it would have been

incorrect, because only as far below as he dived was there
no ground. Perhaps if he had gone a little deeper he might
have reached the ocean bed. In that case what he should
have said is, "I went five miles below the surface but did
not find the bottom of the ocean." If he had said he went
all the way down and still there was no ground, it is a lie.
When you go the whole distance you are bound to hit the
sea bed because then nothing is left of the sea.

What can you say with regard to God? For you to say
He is boundless you must know Him in his entirety. But
at that point all words become meaningless, for the depth
has been reached, the ultimate attained. Or you might
say you went very far but you did not reach the depth.
There, too, you should not use the word boundless. For
who knows, had you traveled a little more you might have
reached the destination.

How can you say innumerable? Is your counting over?
If so, no matter how imposing the figure, it is still not
beyond counting. If you say that you are still counting,
then wait; don't be in a hurry to make statements because, who knows, your calculations still may be completed.

So to call God innumerable is to call the innumerable
by its own name; you merely add to the weight of your
thoughts. Whatever you call Him—fathomless, infinite,
boundless—makes no difference. It is useless and meaningless to say anything about God. Whatever you say is
only a statement about yourself. The man who says God
is fathomless is only admitting that God is beyond his
capacity for measuring.

Different people have different measures of determining the innumerable. There is an African tribe whose
counting does not go beyond three. When there is no
numeral beyond three, all things after three become

countless. In fact this tribe only counts up to two. Three became too many, too much. Beyond three—which is already too much—comes infinity.

Is God really countless or does our counting come to a stop? Is He immeasurable or do our measuring devices run out? Is He boundless or do our legs give way so we can go no further? Whatever we say, we are saying about ourselves; we cannot say a single thing about Him. It would be better to limit our talk to speaking about ourselves, because that can be the truth.

We become absolutely incapable and incompetent before Him; none of our methods or approaches work. We fail, having been vanquished completely; in our complete defeat we call out: "Thou art boundless, infinite, fathomless!" Then we are speaking of our inability to fathom Him; if we feel we have said something about Him, we only increase the load of our thoughts.

You cannot—just cannot—say anything about God. You can only remain silent with regard to Him. Complete silence alone gives an inkling of God. Therefore, says Nanak, even calling Him countless, unfathomable is only increasing your load of words. Say nothing—absolutely nothing! *Become* something. Do not say a word. When your personality undergoes a transformation, you come nearer to God. A labyrinth of words merely adds to your confusion and you are nowhere near God.

When Nanak was admitted into the school the first question he asked of his teacher was, "Will your teaching help me to know God?" The teacher was taken aback because he never expected such questions from children. He replied, "By learning you shall come to know a great deal, but this learning will not enable you to know God."

"Then show me the method through which I can know God. What shall I do with knowing so many things? If I know the One I shall know all. Have you known this One, teacher?"

The tutor must have been an honest person. He took Nanak back to his house and told his father, "Forgive me, but there is nothing I can teach this child. He already knows so much that he asks questions to which I have no answer. This boy is superhuman and is destined to be great. We cannot teach him anything. It would be better for us to learn something from him."

How do we explain this? In India we have a specific philosophical explanation for just such occurrences: Nanak's body is that of a child, but the consciousness within the body is ancient. Through innumerable births his consciousness searched and struggled until he came to understand that He cannot be known by knowing. You cannot establish contact with Him through words. Only through silence can you hope to communicate with Him. What the child Nanak says is the outcome of knowledge attained by his consciousness over infinite births.

No child is completely a child, for no child is born with a blank slate. He brings along with him the impressions of all he has gathered through infinite births. So give the child his due respect; who knows, he may know more than you! Your body may be older than his, but the age of his experiences can be greater than yours. Many times we find children asking questions that baffle us, and we have no answer; but because we are older and stronger, we think we should know, and therefore we smother their curiosity with a heavy hand.

Nanak was fortunate that his tutor was an honest person, so they went back to Nanak's house, because it became absolutely clear to him that what the child said was true. He realized that if all the scriptures had not made him wise, what was the sense in teaching the same useless things to this child? It would only increase his burden.

In knowing the One all burdens drop. To know everything is only to overload the mind; to say countless is only to load the mind. The word, the letter, is the name.

The word is His name. Omkar is His name, and that alone is His praise and the prayer. Say nothing—just nothing. Just fill yourself with the resonance of Omkar and the prayer has begun! Do not say anything. Do not say: I am a sinner, I am lowly; You are the redeemer! There is also no sense in kneeling, falling to the ground, crying and wailing—that is no sign of prayer.

Man has devised such prayers for God as he would use to praise and flatter an egoistic person. Go to a king, fall at his feet, join your hands and call him your redeemer, call him your savior and he is very pleased with you. So you have made up prayers for God accordingly.

Nanak says: This is not prayer. God is no egoist. Then whom are you trying to flatter? Whom are you trying to deceive? You must be trying to get something out of Him by singing his praises, or else what reason lies behind all this praise? No, prayer does not mean praise. What value has praise? Therefore Nanak says again and again: What is one to say of creation or nature? How is one to express the wonder that is? There are no words to describe it.

What else can be meant by prayer? The only meaning is to be filled with Omkar. There is no prayer, no worship besides the resonance of Omkar. Temples have been so designed that the cupola reechoes with the resonance of Om and throws the vibrations back to you. Special attention was given whenever a temple was built so that if you pronounce Om in the correct manner a single resonance bounds back to you a thousandfold.

The West has recently introduced a new scientific technique, biofeedback, which may prove very useful in the future. It is a training method that can help calm the mind by showing it what is happening inside. When the mind is very very busy and excited, electrical currents are produced that reflect the level of activity. By means of small wires this current can be transmitted to a biofeedback machine, whose job is to show you how busy the mind is by measuring the current and turning it into a sound that you can hear. When the mind is filled with thoughts and the body is tense, a high pitched tone is repeated very rapidly. When the mind becomes more quiet, the sound slows down and drops in pitch. Slowly, slowly, it helps you to become more and more aware of the changes that are happening within, until eventually you are able to control the sounds, and thereby you produce a state of total relaxation and quietness within. Finally, when the body is trained to hear itself, you don't need the machine any more. This biofeedback technique can also be used for training in meditation.

The East was well versed in biofeedback techniques for ages. The vault of the temple is one proof of it. It collects the resonance of Om and sends it back to the center of its origin. The sound is created by you and it showers on you. Then, as the resonance of Omkar begins to approach nearer and nearer to the actual Omkar, the speed of the feedback will increase as well as its intensity. As you become more advanced, you will feel the resonance forming within you; then your Omkar will be more from the heart than the throat. Simultaneously there will be a change of tone of the echo resounding in the temple. You will find its quality to be more tranquil.

As the resonance of Omkar sinks deeper into your heart you will feel more pleasure in the echo of the temple. When the sound comes only from the mouth it will seem like so much noise at first. When the utterance begins to come from the heart you will begin to sense the music in the resonance. When it becomes absolutely perfect you will find the resonance taking place by itself; you are no longer producing it. Then will every atom of the temple shower its bliss on you.

The temple is like a small pool for you to practice. It is just like learning to swim in shallow waters. When you have completely mastered the art of uttering Omkar, step out into the vast ocean of space. The whole world becomes one big temple for you, with the cupola of the blue skies above. Wherever you stand and pronounce the Omkar, the vast vault of the skies will respond to your utterance and bliss will shower from all sides.

Says Nanak: From the letter, from the word alone can He be praised. From akshara alone all knowledge is attained. From akshara is all writing and speaking. From akshara all destiny takes place.

This is a very subtle point to understand. Nanak says through the letter alone are all events destined. As the word opens within you, your destiny changes. The key to changing your life lies within in the form of Omkar. The further away from Omkar you go, the deeper you plunge your life into misery. As your coalition with the sound, the word, the name develops, good fortune comes your way accordingly.

To be removed from Omkar is to be in the seventh hell; to come nearer to Omkar is to approach closer to heaven, and to be one with Omkar is to realize salvation. These are the three directions your destiny can take, and there is no other way to change your fortune. No matter how much wealth you attain, if you are in hell you remain in hell—only your hell will be the hell of the wealthy. If sorrow is your lot it will remain so even if you build a palace for yourself; you succeeded in changing the hut into a palace, but not your misery into happiness. Your suffering remains the same. Your destiny does not change because the wavelength of the vibrations that determine your destiny have not changed.

There are two types of people in this world. There are some who constantly strive to change the conditions of their lives: a poor man strives to get rich, a small-time clerk struggles to become the head of his firm, a man living in a tenement wants his own house, another wishes for a more beautiful wife—and so on. They try to change the situation, but the wavelength of their life currents remains the same; there is no change in them whatsoever.

The other class of people are the seekers. They do not care to change the conditions around them, but get down to changing the wavelength of their life vibration. No sooner does the wavelength change, whether in a shack or a palace, the person finds himself in the highest kingdom. Throw him into hell, he experiences only heaven. The resonance of Omkar fills him with bliss and celebration. You could not take his happiness from him even if you throw him into the fire!

There was a woman who was a Zen monk. Before she died she told her disciples: "I want to sit on my pyre while I am still alive. What way is it to go on other people's shoulders? I don't want it said of me that I had to be carried by others. All my life I have never taken anybody's help. The One alone is my only help. To whom else should I now turn, and why?" She would not listen to reason. Her disciples had to construct the pyre. She sat on it and ordered that it be lighted. People ran away, the heat was so unbearable, but she sat unperturbed.

"How do you feel?" someone called out from the crowd. She opened her eyes and said, "Only such as you can ask such a foolish question."

The expression on her face never changed. Whether a bed of flowers or a bed of flames, it was all the same to her.

Once the inner wavelength is adjusted, no fire can burn it, no flowers can increase it. It is this inner current that Nanak calls destiny. Your fate is not written on your forehead; rather it is written in the wavelength of your life current, your vibration. And the pursuit of this life current is possible through Omkar alone.

Through the letter is all writing and speaking,
Through the letter are all events destined.
All destiny has already been written,
But He who writes is beyond destiny.

There is no destiny, no fate for God. God has no des-ires, no motives. He is beyond destiny. He has nowhere to go. He is in no search of a destination. Therefore the Hindus speak of God's leela, which means God's play. God plays with His creation as a child plays with his toys; a child has no other motive than to play for the sake of play. He is happy and cheerful always.

Flowers bloom—what for? The moon shines and the stars twinkle—what for? What reason is there to love? Why do rivers and streams flow?

God is. He goes nowhere. The day your life current gets adjusted to the right wavelength, you will find all purpose disappearing from your life. This is why we refer to the lives of Rama and Krishna as leela and not as biography. Their lives are a play, a sport, a frolic, a festival!

He who writes is beyond destiny. We receive only what He orders. All creations are His name. Therefore why search for His name? In the trees, in the plants, in stones and pebbles, is His signature. Jesus used to say: Pick up a stone and you will find me pressed under it.

Break the branch and you will find me hidden within it.
Everywhere is His name; He vibrates in every sound, and
all vibrations are forms of the One—Omkar. Its intensity
and subtlety give birth to all sounds.

The One is hidden in the many. All creation is His
name. There is no place where His name is not...in what
way shall I praise Him, the creator of creation? Nanak is
overflowing with wonder. Again and again he is filled
with gratitude and awe—how should he express nature?

> *Nanak says, How shall I praise Him?*
> *However much I offer myself could never be enough!*
> *Whatever pleases You, O Lord, is best for me.*
> *You are the formless, the almighty—You who abide forever!*

Leave all to Him. The only grip you have to loosen is
the grip on yourself, and everything is solved. Your only
trouble is that you listen to your own advice. You have
accepted yourself as your guru. The solution is also only
one: make Him your guru and stop meddling in your own
affairs; step aside, let Him take over the reins of your
destiny. Then whatever happens, do not judge or draw
conclusions, because nothing happens against His will.
Whatever happens, happens for the best. What pleases
Him is the most auspicious. Thy will be done!

Chapter 9

Dyed in His Hue

If the body is covered with dirt,
Water can wash it away.
If the clothes are soiled and polluted,
Soap and water can wash them clean.
Even if mind is filled with evil,
Love for His name can dye you in His hue.
Saint or sinner are no empty words;
All our actions have been recorded.
Man sows and he himself reaps the harvest.
Nanak says, By divine order are some saved and others reborn.

By visiting holy places, austerities, compassion, and good deeds,
You may gain respect from others;
But he who listens to God and meditates on His name,
His heart is filled with love and he is deeply cleansed.
All virtues are Yours, O Lord. Nothing is in me.
Without virtuous actions, no true devotion exists.
Yours is the only true word. You are the sound.
You are Brahma. Your power is magnificent and self-directing.
What was that time, what date, what season,
What month when You assumed form and creation began?
The pundits knew it not,
Or they would have written it in the holy books;
Neither did the kazis know,

Or they would have put it in the Koran;
Nor did the yogis know the day, the time,
The season and month when it happened.
The creator who creates all creation,
He alone knows.
How should one praise Him and express His greatness?
How can one know Him?
He is supreme. His name is great.
Everything happens as He ordains.
Whoever credits himself as worthy,
Gains no honor before Him.

R ELIGION IS AN internal bath. When we travel from place to place our clothes become dirty and collect dust. This is easily removed by washing. But as we travel through time, dust gathers on the mind, which is not as easy to remove as the dust in the clothes. Because the body is external the water required to cleanse it is available outside; since the mind and its dust are within we have to acquire some cleaner within.

Every moment the dust keeps gathering within, even if you do nothing but sit. A man may indulge in no activity, yet his body requires a bath each day. The mind is never inactive, but always doing something or other; a tranquil mind is rare. So dust is gathering on your mind every moment, which, no matter how many times you bathe during the day, cannot be cleansed by the outside water.

This sutra relates to water within. It is priceless. If you understand it well enough to recognize the lake within, you will have acquired a key to transform your life. Whatever keys you hold now, none is effective. Had even one worked, there would be no further need to understand Nanak. Though you have many keys, your ego will not allow you to admit that they are useless.

Mulla Nasruddin was a servant in a rich man's house. One day he told his master, "I wish to retire. I can serve you no longer. After all there's a limit to one's endurance. You have no faith in me, and I cannot bear it any longer."

"How can you say, Nasruddin," the master asked, "that I do not trust you? Aren't the keys of my safe always lying on the table?"

"Yes," said the Mulla, "but none of the keys fits the safe."

You also have many keys; so much information have you gathered. When your information works, then knowledge is attained; otherwise you are merely burdened with it.

Carrying the burden of so many keys, it is necessary to ask yourself whether any of them works. Does the gate of life open with it? Does light come in? Do I experience bliss? Have I heard the enchanting notes of divine music? Or, for that matter, do I express joy and gratitude to the Lord who has given birth to me? Do I cry out: "Your compassion is great. You have given me life!"

Our complaints are many, our thankfulness nil. And how can you be thankful when no key fits? Throw away these keys and listen to Nanak who speaks of the key that works, and it is not Nanak alone who has spoken of this key but also Mahavir, Buddha and Jesus. Isn't it strange that you carry a load of useless keys and leave out the one key that works? It is also not correct to say "the key that works" because it is a master key that can open all the doors of life. Since time immemorial man talks about useless keys and never bothers about the one that really matters.

The reason behind this is very clear: the keys that you are willing to use do not require you to undergo any transformation. You remain as you are. There is no danger of your changing or losing yourself. Besides, the pleasure of jingling keys and making loud noises is very enjoyable, so you are satisfied to have the keys and yet save yourself from the difficult process of transformation.

You do not listen to Nanak or Buddha or Mahavir, because the key they offer is dangerous—it works! And once it is set in place the lock will open and you will no longer be the same. You have invested heavily in yourself as you are, so a lot is at stake; if you change, all your work till now will have been in vain. The mansions you raised will fall like a house of cards; all the boats you set sailing will capsize. Whatever you have treasured within your mind, the dreams you dreamed, will all prove false.

Your ego refuses to accept this. Your ego says it may be that I am not a super-wise man, but I am wise. Maybe I have committed some errors, but it can't be that everything I have done is wrong! And it is but human to err sometimes—who doesn't? You put forth all these old sayings and console yourself. To err is human, you say.

The one thing, however, that you are not prepared to admit under any circumstances is that you are ignorant. If you erred—it just happened. Don't the wise sometimes make mistakes? A well-informed person can also go astray, or fall into a pit, or knock his head against the wall. You are not prepared to own to being blind.

Try and understand this: whenever you make a mistake you say something bad has happened. You protect the doer and blame the action. You get angry and say what a terrible thing to happen that I got angry, as if the anger happened to you—that the conditions were such that it was necessary—you don't acknowledge that you are an angry person. If you hadn't been angry someone would have suffered, or you were angry for someone else's sake, never admitting the violence in your temperament. Or, you admit that sometimes you tend to get angry though you are aware that it is a mistake. You somehow manage to save the doer and blame the action. You admit the wrongness of the act, but never the person behind it.

Exactly that is your ego. Because of that ego you guard yourself against the genuine key, because as soon as the master key turns and the lock opens, the first thing to fall away is your ego. You become an insignificant nobody. Whatever you had earned and amassed suddenly proves to be meaningless rubbish. All this falls and the you with it. When the ego is annihilated, then you know that the key has worked; therefore, keep miles away from the key.

Rabindranath Tagore has written a beautiful poem. He says: "Since infinite births I have been seeking God. I do not know how many paths I have trodden, how many religious orders. God only knows how many doors I knocked on, how many gurus I served or how many yogas and penances I performed. One day, however, I ultimately succeeded in reaching His door. I used to get glimpses of Him, though; but that would be as near as some distant star. By the time I reached there, the star had long gone.

"But today? Today I stand before his gate. I read the name outside—it is His. I climb the steps so overjoyed that the destination is reached. I hold the knocker, I am about to knock, then....

"Then a fear catches hold of me! What if the door opens? What will I do then? And if I do meet God—what then? What will I do next? Till now there was only one aim in life—to attain God. Then there will be no more goal to work for. Till now there was only one obsession, one occupation—it will all be destroyed! And what when I have met Him? Then there will be nothing left to do, no future to look forward to, no journey to undertake—nothing for the ego to work on.

"Fear made me tremble. I quietly put the knocker down. So gently did I let it go for fear lest a slight jerk may cause a sound and the door might open! Then I removed my shoes so that I could go down the steps noiselessly. Then I ran! I ran for my very life, so to say, and never even looked back once!"

In the last verse the poet says: "I am still searching for Him. You will find me searching for Him on different paths though I know full well where He abides. And yet I ask others, Where can I find Him?" And I know where he stays. I seek Him even now. Far away near the moon and the stars I catch a glimpse of Him. But now I am confident because I know He will have gone far, far away by the time I arrive. Now I seek Him in all places save one— where He abides; and I never go anywhere near it. I guard myself...only from Him!"

This poem is a very significant statement, and it describes exactly your condition. Do not ever say you don't know where God is. He is everywhere; then how can you not know where He is? Do not ever say the lock is closed and you don't know about the key, because the key has been given to you a thousand times, but you always forget where you kept it. You leave it somewhere; your unconscious self tries to run away from it. Until your doubts are cleared away you will be seeking Him on one hand and losing Him on the other. You will be raising one foot to step in His direction and the other in the opposite direction.

You keep alive the myth that you are a seeker, because it satisfies you and appeases your conscience. It gives you a sense of importance to feel that you are not an ordinary base person who seeks wealth or position. You feel yourself above them because you seek God, truth, religion. While others are involved in lesser things, you have opted for the vast universal existence.

So you keep claiming that you are seeking Him, while secretly from within you are trying to escape Him. Unless you understand and confront this duality within you, you will never be able to seek Him.

Your state at present is like that of the man who builds a house during the day and destroys it at night. He repeats the same process day after day. Or, you might say, he lays a brick with one hand and removes it with the other; or he may employ two workers, one to lay the bricks and the other to remove them. When will his house ever be completed? For infinite lives you have been trying to build your home and yet it is not yet built. Surely something is basically wrong that makes you do two opposing things at the same time!

You carry your false keys that do not work. You bathe in the sacred rivers but your mind remains unwashed. You offer rituals in temples, but that is no worship. You offer flowers; you do not offer yourself. You give in charity, you feed the poor, you do these little religious deeds and take cover behind them.

Remember, you will be purified only if you are prepared to be annihilated; therefore you need waters that will make you extinct, that destroy every bit of you. Here we are discussing these waters. Try to understand:

If the body is covered with dirt,
Water can wash it away.
If the clothes are soiled and polluted,
Soap and water can wash them clean.
Even if mind is filled with evil,
Love for His name can dye you in His hue.

The hue of love. No word is more significant, more meaningful than the word love. After the names of God, love is the next most significant word, so try to understand.

We all know the word. You might say we all know love. What is so special to make it the key? Though we already know the word, mere acquaintance with words will not do. You have learned your words from the dictionaries of language but not from the dictionary of existence. The dictionary gives various meanings, but love has nothing to do with any of them. When love arises in your book of existence, the experience suffuses the word with life—so different from the lifeless words in the book. Now for instance, the dictionary describes fire as a thing that burns, but this fire does not burn you any more than, similarly, the water in the dictionary can quench your thirst. If you try to understand love in a like manner, your sins will never be washed away.

Love is a fire. Gold is purified by passing it through a fire in which all but the gold is burnt away—only that remains which is worth preserving. So also, when you pass through the fire of love, all that is worthless and useless in you goes up in flames. All sins are burned away and only the purposeful you, the meaningful you, remains. You become purified, perfect virtue.

So understand love well. First and foremost you must clearly distinguish love from sin, then only can you eradicate sin. Perhaps you have not recognized the relationship between these two very deep-seated conditions within you. You can sin only when love is absent. Sins are born in the absence of love. Where love is, sin is impossible.

So it is that Mahavir says nonviolence. Nonviolence means love. Buddha says compassion. Compassion means love. And Jesus' words are direct and clear. He says, Love is God!

Someone asked Saint Augustine, "What is the essence of religion? Please tell me as briefly as you can. How shall I save myself from sin? Sins are so many and life is so short."

The significance is that since life is short and sins are many, could he rid himself of them one by one in the short span of a lifetime? So he pleaded for a master key that opens all locks.

You can steal only if you have no feeling of love towards the person whose possessions you are coveting. You can kill only if you have no feeling of love towards the person you kill. You can cheat, you can deceive, you can commit all other sins—only when love is absent within you. Sins are born only in the non-presence of love. Just as an unlighted house attracts thieves, robbers, snakes and scorpions—and spiders weave webs within it and bats make it their home—but when light is brought in they all make a hasty retreat.

Love is light. No lamp of love has been lit in your life—therefore the sins. Sin has no positive energy of its own. It is a negative, a non-presence. You can sin only when that which should be within you is absent.

Understand a little: you get angry though all religious books exhort you not to. But if your life energy does not flow towards love, what else can you do but be angry? You will have to be angry, for anger—if you understand it well—is that very love that has lost its direction. It is the same energy that could not become a flower but instead became a thorn. Love is creation. If there is no creativity in your life, your life energy turns destructive.

The difference between a saint and a sinner is only that the life energy of one is creative and the life energy of the other is destructive. Thus, whoever creates can never act satanic. And one who creates nothing can never be a saint, no matter how much he deludes himself. The energy within has to be utilized one way or the other, for energy cannot remain stagnant; it has to flow. If you can love you dig new channels for your energy to flow towards love. If there is no love within you, what will your life energy do? It can only disrupt and destroy. If you cannot create you will destroy. Virtue is the positive state of the life energy; sin is the negative state of the same energy.

People come to me and say there is so much anger within them, what should they do? I tell them to stop thinking about anger. The more you think of anger the more energy you supply to your anger. Energy begins to flow in the direction of our thoughts. Energy flows and thoughts are its channels. Just as canals direct water from reservoirs to the fields, the canal for life energy is attention. Wherever your attention is, there your life flows. If your attention points in a wrong direction your energy flows in the wrong direction. If it is directed towards the right direction, your life flows in the right direction, and the right attention is love.

Nanak says the day your love is directed towards His name you shall be dyed in His hue; you shall be cleansed. Not only will your past sins be washed away but also future possibility of sin; you will be washed and cleansed before you can even get dirty. You are bathed and cleansed every moment.

You must have had this feeling when in the presence of a saint—a sense of freshness of the morning dew, as if he has just come out of his bath. The reason is simply that the presence of love does not allow dust to gather on him.

Love incessantly washes away all dirt—even before it can touch him.

So the first thing regarding love is for your life energy not to become destructive. Destruction is sin when it occurs for its own sake. There is another kind of destruction: a man tears down a house in order to build a new one. This is not destroying but a part of constructing. When you break for the sake of breaking, it becomes a sin.

If you have a small child whom you love very much, you sometimes give him a whack or two—because of your love you have beaten him for his good, to improve him. You hit him because you care. If you did not care for him you would not have bothered what he did and what he didn't do; you would have been indifferent. But you love him enough not to allow him to go on doing what he pleases. You will stop him from going near fire; you will even hit him if he does not listen. This hitting is not sinful but creative. You want to make something of him.

When you hit an opponent, it is the same hand; the slap is the same, the energy is the same. When the feeling within you is that of enmity, when you are hitting to destroy and not to create, it becomes a sin. An act in itself is not a sin. If the feeling within you is positive and creative, no act is a sin; if the feeling within is destructive, the same act becomes a sin.

There is a Sufi story: A Sufi came to a village on his way to a temple hidden somewhere in the nearby mountains. He went to a tea stall on the roadside and asked, "Can you tell me who is the most truthful man and the most untruthful man in this village?" The stall-keeper gave him the two names. In a small village everybody knows everything about everybody else, so it was not difficult to guide him.

The Sufi went to the most truthful man and asked him for directions. The man looked at him and said, "The easiest way is through the mountains." Then he gave him detailed directions in order to reach the temple.

Then the Sufi went to the untruthful man and asked him to show him the easiest way to the temple. The Sufi was shocked when this man showed him the same route as the truthful man. He did not know what to believe! He went back to the village square and asked if there was a Sufi in their settlement.

The traveler was directed to a Sufi saint. A truthful person and an untruthful person are two extremes; when a person reaches sainthood he goes beyond both. The fakir heard the problem and responded: "The answer is the same but the angle of vision is different. The truthful and righteous man directed you across the mountains, although it is easier to cross the river to reach the other side. He took into consideration the fact that you have no boat, nor any means of going through the river. Since you have a donkey on which you ride, how would you carry him across? In the mountains the donkey would be useful to you, in the boat he would cause you problems. Seeing all this, he suggested what was best for you under the circumstances.

"The unrighteous man pointed out the same path, but his intentions were dishonorable. He wanted to cause you trouble. He took delight in the fact that you would be harassed." The answers are the same, the intentions are different. Actions can be similar, therefore they tell you nothing; it is the feeling behind them that is the deciding factor.

Therefore we never keep count of the number of times a child gets punished by his father or mother. The truth is, say the psychiatrists, if a mother has never beaten her child, there cannot be any deep connection between the mother and child; it shows she does not truly recognize him as her own; there is a distance, a gap, between them.

A son never forgives the father who complies with all his demands. Later on in life, he realizes that his father has injured him. The child is not experienced, so his demands have less value. The father has to think and decide what would be good for him because he is more experienced in life. If he really loves his child he will decide on the basis of his own experiences rather than the child's demands. If a man gives his child full freedom, the child will never be able to forgive him.

Nowhere in the world has a child been given so much freedom as recently in the West. During this century Western psychologists have been teaching people to give total freedom to their children. The result has been an unbridgeable gap between the parents and the child. In former days sons feared their fathers; in the West today, the father is afraid of the son. In the past parents were revered and respected. In the West today, the child knows no respect for the elders, not an iota of love or caring. What is the reason? It is only this: as the child grows up he begins to realize the harm his parents have done to him by letting him loose to do as he pleased. He should have been stopped when he did anything wrong. It was their duty to prevent him from going astray, since they were experienced and he was not. They should not have listened to him; they should not have given in to his wishes. This revelation comes but, alas, then it is too late.

Remember this: love cares. Love cares that your life should be good, beautiful, truthful, and attain the highest glory. Indifference is a sign that there is no relationship, that your being born to your particular parents is a mere coincidence for all of you. There is no give and take. There is no feeling of oneness or belonging, with the result that in the West all intrinsic relationships are breaking down.

Love can also punish, because love is so strong and so self-confident that it can bring about creation through destruction. The important thing is that the aim is always creation. If destruction is necessary, there is bound to be a creating aim behind it.

The guru kills the disciple—completely! He kills him outright—no father's blows that fall only on the body. Just as water cleanses the body from outside, the father superficially cleanses the life of his son, but the guru hits hard and deep within. He bores inside you to your utmost depth, and will not rest until your ego is completely melted. Until you find such a guru, know that whatever master you follow you will never be able to forgive. Sooner or later it will dawn on you that this man has been wasting your time.

The mark of love is creativity. As long as you are creative in your relationships, you cannot commit sin. How can I sin when I am filled with love? The love gradually spreads and you find yourself hidden in each living being. Then whom will you rob, whom will you cheat? Whom will you deceive, whose pocket will you pick? As love increases you discover that all pockets are yours, and when you harm someone you find you have harmed yourself.

Life is an echo: whatever you do comes back to you. He whose love increases becomes aware that there are no strangers in this world. It is common knowledge that when you love someone you feel one with him.

You will not want to harm your wife when you realize that by harming her you ultimately harm yourself, because when she is unhappy you also become unhappy.

You would wish her to be happy when her happiness increases your potential happiness. One day you comprehend that the sorrow we give others makes us equally sad; the joy we give others makes us equally happy.

But we think in opposite terms—saving joy for ourselves and wishing sorrow on others. And we feel, perhaps, that in that way our own quota of happiness will be greater. The end result is that you find your own life filled with sorrow because whatever you give returns to you. If you have sown thorns for others, your own life gets surrounded by thorns. And if you go about sowing flowers unconcerned with what others are doing, your life becomes filled with flowers. You reap what you sow. But we do not seem to understand this formula of life.

A woman came to me wanting to divorce her husband. I will never forget what she asked of me. She said, "Show me a way of getting a divorce so that my husband remains miserable for all time to come." She knows very well that her husband will be the happiest person in the world the day she divorces him; she has pestered him endlessly. Now she wants that he be made miserable even after she leaves.

When we are together we wish to give sorrow; when we are apart we wish to give sorrow. Together or apart, if our aim in life is to create sorrow and pain for others, then it can only gradually create a painful wound within ourselves. The wound is of our own making. It comes out of constant attention to provoking pain.

This is what we call karma, the process of actions. Fate, destiny, only mean that whatever you do comes back to you. Though there may be a certain lapse of time, eventually it is bound to bounce back to affect you. Therefore do only what you want to obtain for yourself. If you

find yourself in a veritable hell, it is of your own making—
the fruit of what you have been doing for countless births.

People come to me and say, "Bless us so that we may
attain happiness." There would be no problem if it were so
easy, if one man could just bless everyone and they would
find happiness. How could my blessings wash away your
misery? Try to understand me and not ask for blessings;
that would be mere deception. You have given pain and
suffering to others, now you must reap the fruits of your
actions; and you come to ask for blessings? And your
attitude is that you suffer because I do not give you my
blessings. No blessings can remove your suffering. If
somebody's blessings help to improve your understanding
and sow seeds of love within you, that is more than
enough. Sins can be washed away only with love, and
suffering can end only when you give happiness to others.

Nanak says: If the mind is filled with sin, only the love
for His name can purify it. When you begin to love a
person, you find it impossible to harm that person, because then the other's happiness becomes your happiness;
the other's sorrow becomes yours. The barrier between
your life and your beloved's exists no more; you flow into
each other.

When that phenomenon takes place between a person
and God, it is called prayer, worship, devotion; it is the
ultimate form of love. When it gives so much joy to make
someone happy and so much pain to make someone unhappy, the same holds true in the case of you and God. If
the relationship is one of love you are in heaven; in the
absence of love you find yourself in the depths of hell.

God means totality. You have to love this vast expanse, the whole universe, all that is, as if it were a
person. All your sins will be washed away when you fall
hopelessly in love with all that is. Then whom will you

deceive? Wherever you look He is there; in whatever eye you look you will find Him seated.

Devotion is a revolutionary process. It means now there is none but He. Your life has suddenly become simple, uncomplicated. Now there is no more need to sin, no more need to deceive. Do not think that devotion implies going to the temple to offer worship. Reciting the Japuji early in the morning is not devotion; nor is going to the mosque or church. This will not lead you anywhere.

These are the false keys. The genuine key is to fall in love with the infinite. Now every particle of dust on this earth is entitled to your love. Every inch of this earth is my beloved; every leaf bears the name of my beloved; through every eye He looks at me. Everything is His, everywhere.

When you reach this recognition, however you live your life will be through devotion; it will transform your very way of life. You will sit differently, walk in a different manner, because everywhere you see Him present. You will speak differently if whomever you speak to is He. Now how can you annoy or tell lies about someone, how can you insult someone? How will you escape serving others, because in the feet of others you find Him hidden!

When this knowledge dawns on you, you will be in a perpetual ecstasy—what Nanak refers to as being dyed in His hue. You will possess nothing yet have everything. You will find yourself absolutely alone and yet all the world is with you. There will be a rhythm, a harmony between you and existence; you will have established an intimate contact with existence.

Nanak says only such a love can cleanse you of sin. All worship and recitations, all sacrifices and incantations are of no avail for the basic factor is missing.

I was once traveling on a train. A woman got on at a station with about ten children, who immediately ran from one end of the compartment to the other, upsetting everyone's luggage, getting into everybody's way; there was complete chaos. At last one passenger could bear it no longer when the kids had overturned his bag and torn his newspaper. He turned to the woman and said, "Sister, it would be much better if you didn't travel with so many children. If you have to travel it would be more comfortable for all of us if you left half of them at home." The woman flared up, "Do you take me for a fool? I *have* left half of them at home!"

When basic understanding is missing, it doesn't matter how many children you leave behind. If the woman did not use her discrimination while producing twenty children, how can you expect her to use her understanding when traveling?

Sins there are thousands, virtue is only one; illnesses are thousands, health is only one. It is not that you have your kind of health and I have mine. You can be ill with tuberculosis, cancer or some other complaint; there can be differences in illnesses. There can be originality. An illness can carry your individual stamp because illness is part of your ego. For different egos there are different illnesses, but health is one. Virtue is one, because God is one. You cannot be different in this context.

What is this health, this wellbeing, that is one? It is the feeling of love. Try to drown yourself in life, immerse in it little by little. When you get up from your chair, do so as if the beloved is present. Even when you enter a vacant room, do it as if God is present all around.

There was a Sufi fakir by the name of Junnaid. He would tell his disciples, "When in a crowd remember your aloneness, then the remembrance of God will be with you.

When you go into solitude, go as if God is present all around."

He is right. If you can remember your aloneness in a crowd you can maintain the remembrance of God; otherwise the crowd will seize hold of your attention and you will be led astray. And if you do not maintain the remembrance of God when you are alone, you will lead yourself astray.

There are two hazards: you can either lose yourself in others or get lost in your own self. God is beyond both. If you remember your aloneness in a crowd and are aware of His presence in your solitude, you will never go astray.

Nanak says: He who is dyed in the hue of love becomes pure within. He has undergone an internal bath.

To be saint or sinner are no empty words;
All our actions have been recorded.
Man sows and he himself reaps the harvest.

To claim you are trying hard to be virtuous brings about no change within you. By thinking or by speaking about it nothing ever happens. It is not strange that we talk a great deal about virtue and good deeds, whereas we never think or speak about sins, we only do them. If you are told to hold yourself back for a minute when anger comes, you will say it is impossible, anger cannot be postponed. How can you withhold anger when the withholder is not present when anger comes? Where are we when anger comes?

If you are told to meditate you say: Not today, I have no time. Besides, you feel, what's the hurry? We still have such a long way to go in life and these things are intended for the end of life when death is about to come. Remember you can never feel death coming; not even the dying man feels death.

A politician died and Mulla Nasruddin was called upon to make a condolence speech. The Mulla said something noteworthy: "God's kindness is so great. Whenever we die, we die at the end of life. Imagine what a disaster it would be if death came at the beginning or in the middle of life!"

And we keep putting off the end. It never seems to come until it actually arrives. Others come to know when one's end has come; the one who dies has gone before he knows it!

So, if you understand correctly, you never die. You remain always alive in your thoughts. The occurrence of death you do not know—others know it. You are weaving fresh plans for life even in the moment of death. You put off death for the morrow. All that is auspicious we keep putting off; all that is not we do immediately.

The day you do the opposite, you will be dyed in the color of His name. Then you will put off the inauspicious and carry out the auspicious immediately. When the feeling to give arises, give immediately. Don't trust yourself too much; your mind will devise a thousand tricks in a second to make you forget.

Mark Twain wrote that once he went to a convention to hear a minister speak. After five minutes, being very impressed and moved, he decided to donate the hundred dollars he had with him to the minister's cause. After ten minutes, he wrote, the thought arose in him that a hundred dollars was too much; fifty would do equally well. As soon as the thought of the hundred dollars appeared he lost all connection with the clergyman, because the internal dialogue had taken over. Before half an hour had elapsed he was down to five dollars. When the lecture was over he thought: "No one knows I intended to give one hundred dollars. And who gives so much? People don't even give one. I think one dollar is more than enough." By the time the collection plate came to him, he writes, "The dollar didn't come out of my pocket. Instead I picked up a dollar from the plate...who was watching? No one. No one would ever know."

Don't trust yourself too much about doing the right thing; it is often rather difficult. At certain moments, when you are on the peaks, the impulse to do good arises within you. If you lose that opportunity it may never come your way again. Never indulge in righteous thought, because the auspicious is the very thing which is not to be thought about but acted on. When you feel like giving, give! When you feel like sharing, share! When you feel like renouncing, renounce! When you feel like taking sannyas, take it! Do not lose a moment, because nobody knows when that moment will come into your life again, or whether it will come at all.

And when the inauspicious, the evil, arises within you—stop! Defer it for twenty-four hours. Make it a rule: if you want to harm someone, do it a day later. What's the hurry? Death is not standing at your door; and even if it is, what is the harm? At the most, the enemy will not have been damaged, that's all!

If you can put off a negative act for one day you will be incapable of doing it, because the frenzy to do harm is momentary. Just as the impulse to do good comes in a moment, so also the frenzy for evil is momentary. If you can bring yourself to desist at that moment, you will realize how futile your action would have been. Restrain a murderer for a moment, and he cannot kill. If a man is about to jump into a river to drown himself, interrupt him for a short while and he will no longer try to kill himself. Certain acts are possible only in certain moments. Within you are moments of both dense insensibility and intense awareness.

At times of heightened awareness you are filled with love and creativity. In moments of intense insensibility you are overwhelmed with senseless destruction. In your frenzy you wish to destroy; then later you repent, but this is empty and worthless. If you must repent, repent after doing some good. What is the sense of repenting after sin? But that is what you always do—first sin, then repent. And good deeds? Since you never do them, the question of repentance doesn't arise.

Nanak says nothing happens by thinking, nor by saying. Sin and virtue have nothing to do with words, but with acts. Your account before God is not in words but in deeds. He judges you by your actions, by what you are. What you have said, what you have learned, what you have thought, has no relevance here. The final outcome rests on your actions. Nanak says man sows and reaps the harvest himself.

Generally we say others cause our trouble, but success we achieve for ourselves. Failures are due to obstruction by others; all that is good is my own attainment. This way of thinking is absolutely wrong. Whatever happens in your life is part of the chain of your actions, part of your karma; you are responsible for all that is good or bad, auspicious or inauspicious, flowers or thorns. The day a person accepts and experiences total responsibility for himself a transformation begins to take place within.

As long as you blame others, there can be no transformation. If others are the cause of your misery, what can you do? Until such time as they all change, your misery must continue unabated. And how can you change others? There is no other way but to bear your sorrow. There is no other alchemy than religion to transform misery.

It takes time for seeds to bear fruit; and because of this, you completely forget that you had sown the seed

when the fruits begin to appear. Because of this forgetfulness, you attribute your woes to others. Remember,
nobody is worried about you. Each is worried about himself: others are plagued by their own ills and you are
plagued by your own. Each person must seek out the
thread of his own actions. Recognize well this fact and
only then is a profound transformation possible. As soon
as you understand that you are responsible, something
can be done. The first thing you must do is recognize and
accept quietly the reactions and results of your past actions. It makes no sense to produce fresh turmoil while
reaping the fruit of your past actions. Only this way can
your past actions be neutralized.

A man spat on Buddha. Buddha quietly wiped his face
with his cloak. The man was very angry, and so were
Buddha's disciples when it happened. After he left Ananda could not contain himself. "This is sacrilege!" he exclaimed. "Moderation doesn't mean that anyone can get
away with doing whatever he wants to you. That way
would inspire others to do likewise. Our hearts are burning! We cannot bear the insult."

Buddha answered, "Don't be unnecessarily excited,
lest that become a link in your chain of karmas. I must
have hurt him sometime and now he has cleared the debt.
I may have insulted him somehow and now we are quits.
I came to this village expressly for him. Had he not spat
on me I would have been in a quandary. He has solved my
dilemma. Now my account is closed. This man has freed
me from some past action of mine. I am grateful to him.

"And why are you all so excited? It had nothing to do
with you. If your wrath is stirred up and you do something
to this man in your excitement, you will have created a
new link in your chain of karmas. My chain is broken,
yours will be made anew—and for no reason. Why are you

intervening? I have to reap the result from the one I have troubled. Before my total, highest annihilation, before I merge completely with the infinite, I must settle my account with all people, all things, all relationships formed in anger, insolence, hatred, attachment, greed, etcetera. For only he whose actions have been equalized is a completely liberated being."

So remember, let your past actions be discharged peacefully. Accept them cheerfully and be contented. Remember you are settling your accounts and do not create fresh links; then gradually your connection with the past is loosened and disintegrates.

Now the second thing to remember is: do not do any fresh harm to others or else you will simply be binding yourself to your actions. We create the fetters within ourselves. So remember that you have to break the old links and not create new links.

For this Mahavir used two very beautiful words: *asrava* means do not allow the new to come in, and *jirjara* means allow the old to fall off. By and by a moment comes when nothing of the old remains and nothing new is being formed; you are free. Ultimate bliss occurs only in this state.

> Man sows and he himself reaps the harvest.
> Nanak says, By divine order are some saved and others reborn.
>
> By visiting holy places, austerities, compassion, and good deeds,
> You may gain respect from others;
> But he who listens to God and meditates on His name,
> His heart is filled with love and he is deeply cleansed.

All outward ablutions bring no transformation. At most you may gain a little respect in the eyes of others. But this reverence can be dangerous because your ego will try to make a mountain out of it; it won't stop recounting how many pilgrimages you undertook, how many fasts you have observed.

Bodhidharma went to China from India. The Emperor of China came to him. This king had become a Buddhist and then had constructed thousands of monasteries, ashrams and temples. He had printed and distributed thousands of treatises on Buddhism. He fed millions of beggars every day. All this he recounted to Bodhidharma. He also told him how many images of Buddha he had had made. In fact there still remains a temple constructed by him which bears ten thousand statues of Buddha. He had whole mountains dug up for this purpose. His charity was immense, and all this he made a point of telling Bodhidharma.

Bodhidharma listened completely unmoved. The king could wait no longer. "What will be the fruit of all these good deeds?" he asked.

Bodhidharma replied, "Nothing. You will rot in hell."

The king was dumbfounded. "What is this you say? I in hell?"

"The deeds in themselves are not the problem. They are indeed good deeds, but your feeling of having done them is the difficulty. The good deeds have happened; leave them at that. Don't take upon yourself the doership of them. If you presume that you have done them, all virtue in your actions turns to dust; the medicine will turn to poison. As it is, medicines are made from poisons."

In the days when rupees, annas and pies were still in use, Mulla Nasruddin went to the doctor because his wife suffered from insomnia.

"Help me please, doctor," said the Mulla. "She keeps bickering all night long, as if it wasn't enough all day."

"Take this powder," said the doctor, "and each evening give her as much as would cover a four-anna bit."

After about a week the doctor came upon Nasruddin on the road. "Tell me, how's the wife?" he inquired.

"Your medicine worked wonders, doctor. She is still fast asleep!"

The doctor was worried. "How much of the powder did you give her?" he asked.

"Well," said the Mulla, "I did not have a four-anna bit so I took four one-anna coins, covered them with the powder and gave it to her—so much peace in the house! What wonderful medicine."

Medicine can become poison if you aren't careful about the quantity. Virtue can also become poison beyond a certain proportion. Remember, as long as virtue remains simply an action it is all right. When the doer is involved the proportion can become dangerous. If good deeds are performed to counteract one's evil deeds it is all right. But if good deeds are performed with the idea of earning or accumulating virtue, it is dangerous. You may gain some respect, but that is all. Don't take this to be religion.

I was once traveling with Nasruddin on a bus. Suddenly Mulla got up in the moving bus and cried out, "Brothers, has anyone lost a bundle of notes tied in a string?" Many people claimed the bundle was theirs; they vied with each other to reach Mulla. "Peace, Peace!" exclaimed Mulla, "So far, I have only found the string."

Religion is like the bundle of notes; good deeds are like the string. Don't pride yourself on them. The string in itself has no value, only when tied around the rupee notes does it assume value. What worth has a string that is tied around a stone? When good deeds unite with a selfless attitude they become the boat that takes you to the other shore. When good deeds are tied to the ego, they become like a rock on your chest that invariably drowns you. So there are people who are drowned in their evil deeds, and people who drown in their good deeds.

This is why it often happened that a sinner arrives while the virtuous man lags behind. An evildoer more easily becomes egoless because he knows he is a sinner; he knows it is well nigh impossible for him to reach God. He is convinced he has no good qualities and is only a storehouse of evil. He doesn't even dare to think that his voice could ever reach Him. In the absence of ego, even the sinner can reach; but when ego is present even the virtuous person drowns.

> By visiting holy places, austerities, compassion, and good deeds,
> You may gain respect from others;
> But he who listens to God and meditates on His name,
> His heart is filled with love and he is deeply cleansed.

Such should be your attitude. Don't allow pride to creep in over being a renunciate, or giving charity, or doing this or that. Don't let the pride of the emperor find a foothold in you, or, as Bodhidharma says, "You will rot in hell."

> All virtues are Yours, O Lord. Nothing is in me.
> Without virtuous actions, no true devotion exists.

I am not even worthy of worshipping You. I have no eligibility, no capacity. Therefore, Nanak says, all things are obtained through His grace. What is our capability? All devotees have said the same. It is always through His grace whatever you attain, since you are not capable of attaining by yourself.

To feel yourself capable implies that He has to give. If He does not give in spite of your capability, then we have reason to complain; and if He gives, what reason to be thankful? You have attained by your own merit. Within you a complaint arises out of considering yourself capable yet not having achieved.

On the other hand the devotee's mind is always filled with gratitude, because he always feels unworthy of all he has attained. His whole way of thinking is different. By singing and chanting one doesn't become a devotee; rather your attitude toward life should be: Unworthy I am, He has given me so much! The devotee's prayer is always filled with thanksgiving and gratitude—never with complaint.

Nanak says: I have no talents and without talent I cannot perform worthy actions, so how can I worship You? All I can do is sing Your praises, O Lord. All glory be! That is all I can say. I can only sing your praises O Lord. I am unworthy, I deserve to get nothing. I am so worthless that all I can do is sing Your glory—that is all.

> Yours is the only true word. You are the sound.
> You are Brahma. Your power is magnificent and self-directing.
> What was that time, what date, what season,
> What month when You assumed form and creation began?
> The pundits knew it not,
> Or they would have written it in the holy books;
> Neither did the kazis know,
> Or they would have put it in the Koran;
> Nor did the yogis know the day, the time,
> The season, and month when it happened.
> The creator who creates all creation,
> He alone knows.

And I? I am devoid of all talent. The pundits don't know, nor the *kazis*, the Mohammedan priests. The scriptures give no information; if all the wise men don't know who You are, where You are, how You assumed form, how

You fashioned creation, then how can I, a poor ignorant fool, know what to do?

The devotee never bothers about what He is; the pundit, the learned man does. The knowledgeable man tries to seek Him by analysis; he tries to lay everything bare in order to get at Him. The devotee remains blissful in His grace, because his contention is: How can anyone besides You know how all this came about? You alone can know, all else are foolish surmises. So the devotee never claims that he knows. His only claim is love. Remember, to claim knowledge is the claim of the ego; the claim of love is ego-less.

How should one praise Him and express His greatness?
How can one know Him?

Nanak says: You alone know; how shall I call out to You? I know no form of greeting! What words shall I use? I am afraid of using wrong words. Which aspect of Yours shall I glorify? What praise will be fitting? What words would be worthy for You? I know not. Clever people have expressed praises in Your honor, and each has striven to outdo the others.

But all expressions are incomplete. The really intelligent person has realized that He cannot be expressed because any name will fall short of Him and seem hollow and insignificant when compared to His glory.

He is supreme. His name is great.
Everything happens as He ordains.
Whoever credits himself as worthy,
Gains no honor before Him.

Whoever considers himself to be something invariably misses Him, because there can be only one: either you or He. In one scabbard there is room for only one sword, not two.

There is a very well-known poem by the Sufi poet Rumi: The lover went and knocked at the door of the beloved. A voice asked "Who is it?" He said, "Open the door. It is I." There was no answer, all was silent within.

The lover knocked again. He called out again and again, "Open the door. It is I, your lover," but there was no response.

Finally a voice came from within, "Two cannot be contained in this house. This is the house of love, it cannot accommodate two." Then again there was silence.

The lover turned back. He wandered for years in the jungles. He undertook many fasts and practices; he performed many rites and holy works. He purified himself and thus cleansed his mind. He became more aware; he began to understand the conditions. After many, many years he returned once again and knocked at the door. The same question came from within, "Who is it?" But this time the answer that came from outside was, "You alone are."

And, Rumi says, the door was opened.

If you go to the gates of God as somebody, then even if you appear as a sannyasin, a renunciate, a wise man, whatever, you will fail. The gate opens only for those who are nothing, nobody, who have annihilated their selves totally.

In ordinary life also, love opens its doors only when you are not, when you are completely merged in the other and the voice of I has stopped. Then when this I becomes less important than You, and when You becomes your whole life, then you are capable of destroying yourself for the beloved; you willingly and happily enter into death. Then only does love blossom. In everyday life we thus get a glimpse of the one when two are no more.

When the ultimate love arises, there should remain no sign of you; your name, your designation, your very self should turn to dust. Only when you annihilate yourself completely can this happen. Remember the words of Jesus: He who saves himself will be lost; he who loses himself will be saved. In His kingdom, he who destroys himself attains everything and he who saves himself loses everything.

Nanak says he who considers himself to be something is unworthy before Him. The truth is, he never even reaches Him.

Proud eyes are blind eyes. He who has even a single thought of being someone, his personality is deaf, inert; he is already dead. He cannot appear before God. God stands ever before you but as long as you are, you cannot see Him. You are the obstruction, the obstacle. When this hindrance drops, your eyes become pure and open, devoid of I-ness. You are as if you are nothing, a mere emptiness. And in such emptiness He enters at once.

Kabir has said the guest arrives in the house of one who is empty. No sooner do you become empty than the guest arrives. You miss Him as long as you are filled with your own self. The day you empty yourself He fills you.

Chapter 10

The Lure of the Infinite

There are millions of underworlds
And infinite skies above.
The Vedas say millions have searched and searched,
Only to end in exhaustion.
The holy books claim eighteen thousand worlds
But only one power behind all creation.
If anything could be written we would keep the account,
But all estimates are destructible.
Nanak says, He is the greatest of the great.
He alone can know Himself.

Those who worship praise Him,
But have no remembrance of Him,
As rivers and streams know not the ocean
Into whose vastness they fall.
Even kings and emperors of great domains,
Who possess enormous treasures,
Cannot compare with the lowly ant
With remembrance of God in his heart.

A N INCIDENT OCCURRED at a research institute where they were investigating various types of poison. The institute became infested with rats, their number increasing every day. Every possible method was used to kill them, but to no avail. Whatever poison they set out the rats ate merrily. The rats had learned to feed and thrive on poisons, because that was all that was readily available to them there, and they had become immune.

Then someone suggested the age-old method of setting traps, as for mice. So traps were brought and fitted with pieces of bread and cheese, but the rats ignored them completely! So accustomed to poison were they that they did not like anything else. Not a single rat was caught.

Finally someone came up with the obvious solution and covered the bread and cheese bait with poison. The rats immediately were caught in the traps.

This strange sounding story is nevertheless true. It actually happened at a research institute. Man's state is almost the same. He has become so habituated to words that even if silence is offered to him, he has to seek respite in words—just as the rats went only for the food covered by poison.

When the infinite is to be explained we need the help of pitiful words. Even when man is to be led into the void, the base language of words must be used. When explaining the ocean, one can speak only of the drop, and discussion of a drop cannot even hint at the ocean. It is not possible. Look at the mighty ocean, and look at the insignificant, tiny drop. Similarly, where are words compared to the void, where the intelligence of a lowly human being and where the immeasurable expanse? There is space and space, there are worlds and underworlds, all without end.

But these have to be measured in terms of man's feeble understanding, because man has become so

કે ના કરું ફપુ ફપુ એાપાં છે આંત.

addicted to the mind, and it is very difficult to break out of any addiction. Truth is not so far away; only our habits are the hindrance. Truth is very near, even closer than one's own heartbeat, closer than one's very breath. God is closer to you than your own self. But we have woven an intricate web of habits, and because of them it is difficult for us to see. The mind is nothing but a collection of habits. Therefore all saints have striven to eradicate the mind, to bring about the state of no-mind.

As soon as you let go of the mind, let go of the shore, you enter the ocean. There is no other way of knowing the ocean than to become the ocean—nothing less will do. While standing on the shore, no matter how much you speculate or expound on the ocean, it is all useless babble. The very fact of your standing on the shore shows that you are not directly acquainted with it. Once you are really acquainted, why remain on the shore? Once a person becomes familiar with the infinite, no power on earth is strong enough to chain him to the shore. The attraction of the infinite will pull him away. There is no power more magnetic than the lure of the infinite; all other attractions fade away when it pulls.

But we sit and just talk. We remain closeted in the room and talk of the open skies...outside! We lock ourselves within our own cages and talk of freedom. We are imprisoned by the web of our own words and we talk of the formless.

These verses of Nanak are very valuable:

There are millions of underworlds
And infinite skies above.

There is space...and space...and nothing but space. It is one sky that becomes infinite, because there is no boundary to space. It is one boundless space. Says Nanak:

There is the sky, and the sky, and only the sky...infinite times infinite.

There is not just one single infinity; there are infinite infinities. Wherever you go you will find space. Whichever direction you may take, you will find boundless space; whatever you touch you will find it is space. The boundless abounds everywhere.

In the midst of this boundless you are trying to trap God in your tiny cage of words? You try to imprison Him in books like the Vedas and the Koran. It is just like trying to imprison the vast skies within your palm. The wonderful thing about this is, when your palm is open there is space in it, but the moment you close your fist, whatever space was in it evaporates. The tighter you make the fist, the emptier it is.

Use words like an open fist, not like a closed fist; but words that are like an open palm no longer remain logical. The more logical you want to make an expression, the more you have to enclose it. The greater the definition, the more constricted the expression. Whenever a thing is well defined, it becomes limited; you create a wall around it.

The more rational the words, the less are they indicative of God. It seems as if they tell you a great deal but they really tell you nothing; the palm is closed. When words are free of reason they seem to tell little but they tell all. Keep in mind this difference.

The words of Nanak are not the words of a logician; they are the words of a poet, a bard. They are the words of a lover of beauty. Nanak is not giving any definition of God through his words. They are like the open palm— hinting at something, not telling anything. They point towards something that cannot be said. Don't hold on to

the words or else you will miss Nanak's message altogether.

If I point to the moon with my finger and you catch
hold of my finger and refuse to look beyond it, how will
you see the moon? The finger means nothing in itself; it is
only a means to point at the moon. You have to let go of
the finger to look at the moon, but people are such that
they cling to the finger.

This is why books are worshipped. Some worship the
Vedas, others the Koran and yet others the Guru Granth.
They direct their attention towards the book, and miss
what the book points to. The harder you hold on to the
book, the further away from the truth you go—the fist
gets tighter. Then words become more important;
whereas the greatness lies not in the words but in the
silence, for through silence alone you can know.

The Vedas say millions have searched and searched,
Only to end in exhaustion.

Man is incompetent when he seeks through his intelligence. All who set out to seek His depths were themselves dissolved, while He whom they sought remained
undiscovered. The Vedas are one long story of man's
incapacity. All scriptures agree that whatever man does,
his field of action is so small that God cannot be ensnared
in the web of his maneuvers. The harder you try to catch
Him, the emptier you find your hands.

The way of attaining God is different. Your method of
grasping will not work; rather, you have to let go of your
hold completely. Nor will your thinking and pondering
help; you must discard these too. Your reasoning and logic
will be a hindrance rather than a help, and your intelligence will act more like a wall than a stepping stone. On
this path the more you rely on your understanding, the
further astray you go. You have to leave it all to Him.

To trust one's intelligence is the way of the ego. It means that you have taken upon yourself the task of finding Him. Have you ever realized that whatever we set out in search of must be less, smaller than ourselves? Whatever you attain or acquire must be small enough for your fist to hold. And if God comes within your grasp, He can no longer be God.

Then how is one to attain God? It is quite the opposite way: he who is ready to lose himself attains Him. The only way is to put yourself in the palm of His hand. Our usual attempt is to tie Him in a bundle and bring Him home to show off to others: See, we have attained Him! The attempt must fail. Such a vast expanse can't be tied into a bundle. Space cannot be wrapped up in a packet. The packets and the bundles will reach home, but the space will not. Leave yourself in His hands if you wish to attain Him.

Nanak never tires of saying: "Endless sacrifices of myself are too little" ... "Whatever pleases You is best for me" ... "Whatever You make me do, that is the path" ... "Whatever You show me, that is the truth."

All these statements suggest only one thing: I have removed myself. I shall not intrude myself on You. I have no wish, no goal, no motive. I shall flow within you.

Therefore I say, faith is priceless, reasoning is fatal. To reason means: I shall decide, I am the judge. Faith means: You are the judge.

There are millions of underworlds
And infinite skies above.
The Vedas say millions have searched and searched,
Only to end in exhaustion.

Veda does not mean only the four books of the Hindus; rather it means the words of the sages, of all who have known. The word veda is derived from *vid*, which means

to know. It refers to the words of those who have known—
the Buddhas, the Jinas, the rishis, just as the original
Vedas, the Rig Veda, the Atharv Veda, etcetera, were the
words of ancient rishis, people who have known. Whenever a person attains, knows, his words become Vedas, as
will your words when you arrive. There is no limit to
Vedas; the words of all those who have known in the past,
all those who know today and all those who shall know in
the future, are Vedas. Vedas are the quintessence of
knowledge, of truth.

Nanak says: The Vedas declare that all those who set
out in search ultimately give up, exhausted and frustrated. It is important to understand this, because exhaustion and fatigue bear great importance in the life of
the seeker. You will not be prepared to annihilate yourself
until you are completely drained and depleted from exhaustion. The time comes finally when you realize that all
your efforts are meaningless, that whatever you try to do
you know that nothing will come of it. When your attitude
of doing reaches the last stages and you realize the use-
lessness of whatever you do, whatever you find, whatever
you attain turns out to be meaningless. Desire goads you
on, but even success proves flat and useless. Then you are
filled with deep sadness and melancholy because all the
endeavors turned to nothing. This is the point you must
reach before you can let go of your ego; not before that.

How could you let go as long as there is still the hope
of attaining something? Either a little more effort and it
will happen, or the direction is wrong, so you change the
method or the guru, and abandon temple for mosque, or
church for gurudwara. Until you are completely exhausted and thoroughly frustrated, until your dejection is
complete, you cannot let go of the ego.

Buddha searched for six long years. Perhaps never has
a human being approached the guest with such intensity.

He staked his all in each trial. Whatever he was told he did to the last dot. No guru could say that he was lacking in effort or resolve.

One guru told him to eat only one grain of rice per day for three months. Buddha carried out his instructions. He was reduced to skin and bone, his back and abdomen became one; he could hardly breathe he was so weak. Yet he did not attain knowledge, because <u>knowledge is never attained by doing anythi</u>ng.

Buddha did all that he was told, but the sense of I-ness persisted. He undertook fasts, repeated endless mantra, did penance, worked diligently at other practices, but deep within the subtle ego kept repeating: I am doing it. The fist was closed, the I was present.

The only condition to attain Him is that the I must drop. What difference does it make whether you are running a shop or offering prayers? In both cases the ego is involved; <u>it is you working or worshipping</u>. They are both the shop because you remain at the shop as long as the ego exists; there is a vocation, a job—that is the everyday working world of samsara. When the ego drops God begins; as you fall away and disappear He appears. <u>You are out, He is in</u>. <u>B</u>oth cannot <u>exist together</u>; duality has no place here. <u>There is room for only one</u>—either <u>you or Him</u>.

At last Buddha tired of it all. He had done all that was humanly possible—all to no avail. The hands were as empty as ever. He stepped into the river <u>Niranjana</u> to bathe. He had become so weak that he couldn't even wade out of the river. The current began to drag him away and he hadn't the strength to swim. He caught hold of a tree branch that was bent over the river; and there, while hanging onto the branch, he realized the fruitlessness of all his efforts. He had done everything that could be done,

but gained nothing. In the bargain he had lost all bodily
strength, and was so weak that he couldn't cross even a
river as small as the Niranjana. Then how was he going
to cross the ocean of existence? "All my efforts have
brought me only to this. The world has become useless to
me—the palace, all the wealth of the kingdom is like dust
to my eyes. Now I am so terribly tired and disheartened
that the spiritual search has become meaningless; even
liberation is useless." At this point Buddha came to the
realization that there is nothing worth achieving either in
the mundane or in the spiritual world. All is a sham; all
the running about is meaningless.

Somehow he got himself out of the river and went and
sat under a tree. At that very moment he gave up all
trying, all endeavor, because there was nothing to attain.
All lesser attainments had led to frustration and hope-
lessness. His frustration became total; there was not an
iota of hope. As long as there had been hope, ego persisted. Buddha slept under a tree that night. After endless
births this was the first night when there was nothing to
look forward to, nothing to attain, nowhere to go; nothing
was left. If death had approached Buddha this moment,
he would not have requested it to wait a while, because
there was no need; all hopes were dashed to the ground.

In total tiredness all hues of the rainbow of hope have
been rubbed away, all dreams are broken. That night
Buddha slept soundly; no dream disturbed him. Dreams
stop when there is nothing left to be attained, for dreams
follow on the heels of desires. Desires walk ahead, dreams
follow like shadows, because they are the slaves of
desires. No desires, no dreams.

Buddha awakened when the last star was about to
fade. But today was different—there was nothing to
be done. Everything had become meaningless. Until the

previous day there had been all that feverish activity—to find his soul, attain religion, God, so many things. And today, nothing! He just lay there. What else was he to do? He was looking at the fading star and, the story goes, at that moment he attained realization.

What happened at that moment? What happened that night that had not happened while he was straining every fiber of his body for six long years? What unique event brought about the realization of the ultimate knowledge to Buddha that morning? The answer lay in that complete exhaustion that Nanak was talking about. Buddha could do no more. He had reached the end of his body's strength, and with no result. The ego was crushed. All activities left him.

As soon as all effort ceases, grace descends; as soon as your hopes are shattered and all activities drop away and all struggling ends, the ego falls and the palm opens.

Do you realize, it takes no effort to open your palm, though it does require work to close the fist? When you do nothing, the palm opens of its own accord, because that is its natural position. You needn't do anything to open the fist. Just don't close your fist and the palm remains open. That morning Buddha did nothing—and the palm opened.

Kabir said: Things happen without being done. That moment Buddha did absolutely nothing—and everything happened! He was so tired, dead tired; he was frustrated. He had given up—and the ego fell away. As soon as the ego dropped God appeared.

Nanak says all the Vedas proclaim that those who set out to fathom His depth ended in utter frustration and exhaustion. And only when they were completely exhausted did they attain enlightenment. When you are completely tired then only will you attain Him.

Therefore the aim of all yoga is to tire you out. God is not attained through yoga; only the ego is tired out. No methods lead to God—just to exhaustion, so that you reach a state of perfect relaxation; so that when the fist opens there is no strength to close it again.

Many have been exhausted and disillusioned in their quest. The Vedas say that effort must lead to this state and then realization takes place. The *satgurus*, the perfect masters, say that God is attained by grace alone and not your endeavors. He would be small compared to you if He could be attained by your endeavors. He is infinitely greater. No sooner are you empty than you are filled.

When the rains come it rains equally on the mountains as in the valleys. The valleys get filled, the mountains remain dry. The mountains are filled and have no place for water, but the valleys are empty, so they fill with water and form lakes.

God showers on all alike. He shows no discrimination. Existence is the same for everyone, without any differentiation. There is no question of the worthy or unworthy, sinner or saint. God's grace showers on all alike just as the skies cover everything beneath. But those who are filled with themselves miss his grace, because there is no room within. Those who are empty inside become filled, because there is enough space.

When the I-ness falls He himself comes, and the I-ness persists as long as there is hope for attainment.

The holy books claim eighteen thousand worlds
But only one power behind all creation.

In this infinite expanse with infinite forms, there is only one hidden behind the many. If you concentrate on the many you will wander in the world; if you concentrate on the one you will reach God.

Take it this way: there is a mala with many beads but the string that holds them together is one. If you hold on to the beads you will wander, but if you catch hold of the thread you will attain God.

There are infinite waves on the surface of the ocean. If you do not concentrate on the ocean but get involved with the waves, you will keep wandering. For the waves will form and disintegrate endlessly; one wave will lead you to another, then another...and another. You will be like a fragile little paper boat, jumping from one wave to another, drowning in one then in another, suffering here, suffering there. You will not reach the destination because the waves have no destination; there is only change. The destination is eternal, ever-abiding. You cannot rest in the waves. You can rest only where all waves become tranquil. There you attain that which never changes.

Do you realize that the more changes there are in your life, the greater is your restlessness? This explains so much of the agitation in the world today, because there is constant change. Scientists say that as much change took place in the course of the first thousand years after Christ, as took place in the five thousand years before Christ. Within the next two hundred years as much change took place as in the previous thousand years. By the time we reach the present century the rate of change is fantastic—in five years the changes equal the five thousand years before Christ! And by the time this century draws to a close, the same change will occur in five months. It happens so quickly that you can hardly reach one wave before another comes.

Ask an old villager; he will tell you his village is almost the same as when he was born. But look at the towns, they are the blueprints of the future; nothing is the same on two consecutive days. In the West the change is reaching a frightening pace.

People don't remain in one place in America. The average occupancy there is three years. Since this is the average, actually half the people stay longer, and there are others who change places every two to four months. · Imagine every second month a change of place, change of atmosphere, of food, of clothes. With each change of season there is a change of cars, of clothes. The waves are increasing at a frightful pace, and they believe that the greater the change the more the enjoyment. In fact, the greater the change the greater the suffering. It is just as if you would uproot a plant every second day and plant it elsewhere. You do not have time to find your roots before you move again.

The greater the change, the more hellish life becomes. Therefore hell has become more intensified in the West. In the olden days the East was very tranquil because change was almost nonexistent; everything was static. In such stability it was easier to descend into the ocean, because the roots were well consolidated and each person could muster up the courage to dive deep.

Remember, if you keep floating with the waves you are a worldly person. If you begin to search for the ocean within the waves, by and by you become a sannyasin. To seek the eternal in the changing is sannyas. To grasp the unchanging within the changing is the art of sannyas. That alone is religion.

Nanak says that the writers of the holy books said there are eighteen thousand worlds. There are eighteen thousand existences, but the power behind all is essentially one. It depends on what you choose; both are open to you. You may choose the changeable that comes and goes; or you may choose that which is unchangeable, which never comes, never goes, but always is—on whose breast all change occurs, but which remains forever unchanged.

He who catches hold of this One, finds his life showered with bliss. He who grasps the infinitely changing finds himself passing from one suffering to another. He is never happy; he experiences merely a shadow of happiness in the process of change between two states of suffering.

How many times have you changed houses? How many times have you changed your car? When you exchange your old car for the new, the process of change gives you a momentary happiness; but this is how you felt when you bought the old car before, and this is how you will feel when you sell the present car for a newer model. And these are the same glimpses you feel when you change this wife for another, or one husband for the next. There is a momentary ray of hope.

When people are carrying a dead body to the burning grounds they keep changing shoulders when the weight is too much for one shoulder. For some time they feel relieved but the weight is the same, and soon the other shoulder tires and the weight has to be shifted again.

You are merely changing shoulders, as you change one wave for another. The way to attain happiness is to slip into the ocean through the wave. The waves are many; the ocean is one. There may be multiple existences, but the power is one. The One hides within everyone. The entire art of life lies hidden in this small verse—seek the One, grasp the string within the mala.

> *If anything could be written we would keep the account,*
> *But all estimates are destructible.*
> *Nanak says, He is the greatest of the great.*
> *He alone can know Himself.*

Nothing can be written about Him, because anything written can be erased, whereas He is forever. How can a perishable thing give evidence of the imperishable? All writings get lost. How many scriptures have already been lost? And those that exist now will be lost. How many words have been born and how many have dissolved into the emptiness? But truth has remained the same forever.

So the quality of the two is different. What can be written can be erased. If you learn the art of reading that which is not written—if you learn the art of reading a blank paper—you will be able to understand God.

It happened once in the state of Maharashtra in India, there were three saints: one was Eknath, and there was Nivruttinath, and a woman fakir, Muktabai. Eknath sent a letter to Nivruttinath that was only a blank sheet of paper; nothing was written on it. Nivruttinath opened the letter and read it with great interest, then handed it to Muktabai. She, too, read it with one-pointed attention. Then both were lost in ecstatic bliss. Nivruttinath handed back the same letter to the messenger saying, "Take this reply back to Eknath."

The messenger was very puzzled. When he had brought the letter he had not known the contents. He certainly didn't suspect a blank piece of paper. Now seeing the same blank paper sent then returned in answer left him confused. He folded his hands and turned to Nivruttinath: "Maharaj, before I leave would you be so kind as to satisfy my curiosity? When nothing was written, what did you read? And not only you, even Muktabai read that letter with interest, and you were both overjoyed. You read so intently that it seemed you did read something. What did you read? And now you are returning the same piece of paper without writing a single word!"

"Eknath sent word," explained Nivruttinath, "that if you must read Him you will have to read a blank paper. Whatever you read on a written paper is not Him. We agree with him. We have understood his message, and this is our message—that we have understood. What he says is absolutely correct."

Books have been written but God cannot be written. How will the books tell about Him? You wish to read the unwritten. Read the Vedas, the Guru Granth, the Koran; leave the written words and attend to the unwritten. Read the space between the lines, between the words, and remember what you have read.

If you read and concentrate on the written word you will become a pundit or a priest. If you read the unread you become a sage. If you concentrate on the written word you will acquire a lot of information; if you remember the unwritten you will become like a child—innocent, artless. Remember, the unwritten is the door.

Therefore, asks Nanak, is there a record or an estimation of Him that can be written? Has anyone ever known something about Him that he can tell? No information can be His information. Those who know become silent. If ever they say anything it is always an arrow pointing towards silence. If they have written anything it is always with the intent that you may read the unwritten.

No account of Him can be written. Whatever is written will disintegrate one day. No matter how much you may protect the books, they are bound to be lost. After all, they are made of paper and the words are ink. What can be more perishable than these? Regard them as paper boats. Those who ride the boat of the scriptures and attempt to reach God are sailing in paper boats that are bound to capsize and drown them. Don't ride paper boats. They are all right for children to play with, but not safe for undertaking a journey. And this journey is a great journey, perhaps the greatest of journeys that man ever embarks on, because there is no ocean greater than the ocean of existence.

No, scriptures will not do. Understand their message, the hint they give. It is only this: become empty.

But there is no end to man's foolishness. We promptly fill ourselves with that very person who tells us to be empty, cramming our skulls with such people, once again starting the cycle of changes. Our hopes, our expectations, our intelligence, offer no wisdom or understanding.

I must tell you a well-known story from the life of Alexander the Great. It is said that he was in search of the elixir of life, which once taken keeps death away. His plan to conquer the whole world was mainly in order to find this nectar.

The story goes that he ultimately found the spring of the immortal waters in a cave. Alexander entered the cave filled with joy, that now his lifelong desire was about to be fulfilled. He rested his eyes for a moment on the bubbling brook in front of him. Just as he was about to take the water, a crow that was sitting in the cave called out, "Wait, don't make that mistake!" Alexander looked at the crow. His condition was pitiful. It was difficult to make out that he was a crow. His wings had fallen off, his eyes could see no more, his whole body was in a state of disintegration. He was just a skeleton. Alexander asked him, "Who are you to stop me? What is your reason?"

"Listen to my story first, O king, then do as you see fit," said the crow. "I too was in search of this spring. I too discovered the cave and drank this water. Now I cannot die and I want so much to die. Look at my state: my eyes are blind, my body is old and withered, my wings have broken and I cannot fly, my feet have disintegrated, but alas, I cannot die! Look at me just once and then do what you please.

"Now I beg that someone should kill me, but alas I cannot be killed because I have drunk this nectar. Now I pray to God night and day to grant me death. I want to die somehow, anyhow!"

It is said that Alexander stopped and pondered, then he silently left the cave without touching the water.

If your desires are fulfilled you find yourself in as much difficulty as when they are unfulfilled. You do not wish to die. If you were to find this cave and drink the water from the spring, then you will find yourself in a dilemma—what will you do with your life now? When life was in your hands, when you could have really lived, you were busy looking for the nectar to escape death. You cannot live with the elixir, you cannot live with death, you cannot live in poverty, you cannot live in riches; you cannot live in hell, you cannot live in heaven, and yet you consider yourselves wise!

Bayazid was a Sufi mystic. He told God in his prayers, "O Lord, do not listen to my prayers; do not fulfill my prayers, because where have I the wisdom to ask for what is good for me?"

Man is absolutely without intelligence. He gets himself caught in the web of his desires and then wanders about within them. If his desires are not satisfied he is in difficulty. If they are satisfied he finds himself again in difficulty. Ponder a bit, go back into your own past and take stock of your life. What have you desired that has even partially come to pass? Has it given you happiness? Some of your desires that have not been fulfilled—have they given you happiness? In both cases you have had nothing but sorrow and suffering. You become involved with your desires, some that were fulfilled; and you are still involved with the unfulfilled desires.

What is understanding? What are the characteristics of wisdom but to ask for that which when attained, all sorrow and miseries end? On that basis nobody in the world except a religious person is wise. Only he who desires God never repents; whatever else you ask for ends in regret.

Keep in mind that all your desires end in regret and repentance, except the desire for God. Less than that will not do, because that is the goal of life.

Can you attain Him through the scriptures? Nanak says you will not find Him there. You will find mere words and doctrines, not truth. Where will you find truth? The answer Nanak gives is: He is the greatest of the great and He alone can know Himself. It means that you cannot stand away from Him and know Him. When you drown yourself in Him, then only can you know Him. The only path to truth requires that you become one with God.

We can obtain information about matter; that is the basis of science. The scientist examines and investigates matter from the outside and obtains knowledge of it. But nothing can be known about God in this manner. You have to go within, so deep within yourself that the boundary between Him and you is lost. You become His heartbeat and He yours. Where there is such oneness, there wisdom resides.

How can this come about through scriptures, through mere words? It can happen only through love. Therefore Nanak declares: Love is the key. If love for His name arises within you, if His melody begins to play within you, and you go mad in His love, then only can you know.

In the scriptures you will find a lot of material to discuss and debate. Don't confuse this with wisdom or you will miss the real thing. You will know neither God nor yourself, because the way to know both is the same. To know your own self, be one with God; then alone the wisdom to know is attained. To know God, then, become one with Him. You have to taste Him; that is the only way. All your debates and discussions without this experience will be childish and foolish.

When Nasruddin reached the ripe old age of eighty, he sent for his eldest son, who was about sixty. He told him that as it was quite some months since his mother had died and he could no longer stay without a woman, he had decided to remarry.

The son was worried—marriage at this age? He asked Mulla, "Whom have you decided to marry?"

"The girl next door," replied Nasruddin.

The son burst out laughing, "What a joke! Are you crazy? That girl is not more than eighteen years old!"

"You call me crazy?" the Mulla shouted at his son. "You fool! Your mother was barely eighteen when I married her. How does her age make a difference?"

All reasoning of man in connection with God is like that. It is always outside of the facts. For all purposes the girl is of a marriageable age... but the Mulla forgets his own age. Likewise you try to catch God from the outside with the help of reasoning and doctrines, but you do not give any thought to the fact that you have to go within yourself; you have to become a part of the doctrine.

The pundit, the learned ecclesiast, always remains outside. Knowledge is the goods he gathers, but he remains outside of it. He is very clever, very cunning. He does not risk the disruption of going within; he calculates from outside. But this cleverness ultimately proves to be great foolishness, because there is no other way to know Him.

It is just as if someone were to read treatises on love and assume that he knows what love is. Someone else reads about the dawn and feels he knows the beauty of day breaking. Yet another reads about flowers and considers himself an authority on them. This is no more than information. But the real encounter is with the rising sun or the dew-filled flowers! Then the sun is not outside of you; for just that moment you and the sun are one, when your hearts beat together.

And when you meet the flowers—when their fragrance and your very existence are intermingled—you are lost in each other, you are one. Oh, the bliss! This is the moment when your being and that of the flowers dance together, sway in the breeze; can you ever get this moment from a book? Impossible! When the experience with an ordinary flower cannot be obtained from books, how can the experience of God, who is the highest flower of life?

How can you establish a relationship with Him through doctrines? You will have to go within. Only those who are mad can enter, not the cunning; they are left out. For your cleverness, your cunningness is not genuine. It has always been true that lunatics have attained and the wise have lagged behind.

Nanak says there is only one way and that is to know Him. He is great and He alone can know Himself. You can never know Him unless you become one with Him and merge in His omnipresent power. To know God you must become God! There is no other way. Reach those very heights, those very depths, then only can you know. You have to be one with Him.

Those who praise, praise Him, but this does not bring about awareness. No matter how much you sing His praise, you still remain outside of Him. The distance persists. He will forever remain God and you the devotee. You will be repeating words and words, but never bridge the distance, which will only be increased. Prayers should not be said, they should be heard. Listen, do not speak. Be silent so that He may speak and you can hear Him.

Instead you keep on talking—not only talking, but shouting! Kabir had to say, "Is your God deaf? Can He not hear, that you have to shout so much? Does He not have ears? For whom are you shouting? Will your voice reach Him quicker?"

> Those who worship praise Him,
> But have no remembrance of Him.

The word surati, remembrance, is the quintessence of Nanak's practice. All saints merge into surati. The word comes to us from Buddha, who uses the Sanskrit word *smriti*. Gurdjieff calls it self-remembering, and Krishnamurti refers to it as awareness, a state of complete consciousness.

Remembrance is very subtle. It needs to be explained with an example. A mother is very busy cooking. Her little child is playing around. For all purposes it looks as if she is engrossed in her cooking, but her surati is in the child, lest the child fall, or go too near the staircase, or pick up something wrong to put into its mouth. She is busy in her work, but in everything that she does there is a persistent remembrance of the child. While the mother sleeps at night, no thunderclap can disturb her sleep, but let the child so much as stir, her sleep is disrupted and her hand goes out to the child. Surati persists even in sleep— remembrance of the child.

Surati involves a continuous remembrance, like the thread in the beads. Do everything that the world demands of you, but let your mind stay always with Him. Sit, sleep, walk, eat; no purpose is served by running away from the world. Go to work, go to the office or the shop or the factory. Dig pits...because money has to be earned; worry about your kids. All these webs of the material world are there, but through it all keep alive remembrance of Him. Let life go on outside as usual, but within let there be only He! Keep your relationship with Him always fresh and alive.

Nanak says there is no need to run away from the world. Attain surati and you become a sannyasin. Once remembrance is found, everything is in order. Of what use is your running to the woods if your surati is filled with the world? But this is what usually happens. People leave the world and flee to the forest—and think of home! It is the mind's way not to worry about where it is, but focus on where it is not. When you are here you think how wonderful it must be in the Himalayas. Then you go to the Himalayas and start thinking: "Perhaps I could have been in Poona. Maybe I have gone astray. The rest of the world stayed where they were. They can't all be wrong. What am I doing sitting under this tree?"

Even in the wilderness you will count your money and keep your accounts. The faces of wife and children will hover around you. You will be in the Himalayas all right, but your surati will be in your home with your family.

Nanak says: Stay where you wish, but let your remembrance be in God. Nothing is achieved by singing praises; everything is achieved by surati. All singing of praises is superficial, whereas remembrance is within. There is no need to shout aloud: "You are great, O Lord, I am a sinner. You are the redeemer, I am a beggar." Why shout like that? Whom are you telling? There is no need to ring bells and sing praise; what is needed is remembrance. Keep his remembrance; do not forget for a moment. Nurture His remembrance.

If you were to find a diamond, you would quickly put it safely away in your pocket. You might even tie it in a handkerchief lest it fall somewhere. Whether you go to the market, make your purchases or meet your friends, your remembrance will always be with the diamond. A faint low sound repeats again and again saying, "The diamond is in the pocket, the diamond is in the pocket...." Every now and again you will feel it with your fingers to see whether it is still there.

Nurture the remembrance of God within in the same manner. Now and then touch it inside to be sure it is there. While walking on the road, stop and look inside. Is the thread of remembrance intact? Is the flow continuous? While eating stop for a second and check; close your eyes and watch if the remembrance is flowing.

Gradually the experience will go deeper and deeper. Then the flow of remembrance continues in your sleep too. When it flows all twenty-four hours of the day, you will have made the bridge between yourself and Him. Now you can close your eyes and merge into Him whenever you please. The road is now made; the instant you close your eyes you are lost in Him. And when you return to the world from your meeting with Him you will be refreshed, filled with absolute energy, as fresh and light as if you have just had a bath. Therefore Nanak says that bathing in thousands of holy places takes place in surati.

Those who worship praise Him,
But have no remembrance of Him,
As rivers and streams know not the ocean
Into whose vastness they fall.

The rivers and the streams fall into the ocean, but that is not enough to know the ocean. The rivers and canals have no consciousness; therefore, though they fall into the ocean they are not aware of it. We also are falling into God all day long, but we are not aware of it. We move round and round and about Him but we know not. Again and again we fall into Him. In every death we fall into Him, in every birth we arise from Him, but we lack remembrance.

So we are like the rivers and rivulets. We fall into the ocean but are unconscious of the event. Without awareness we are unfeeling, unconscious. We move as if in a trance, as if under the influence of drugs, or in sleep, or caught in a deep weariness. The rivers and streams fall into the ocean but remain inferior, because they are unaware of what has happened.

We are going in and out of Him every moment. If you observe carefully and as your remembrance becomes stronger, you will realize how each breath you take goes into Him and comes back to you from Him. When the breath goes out of you, you go into God; when the breath comes in, God flows into you. In every moment, with each breath, He spreads all over you. And your joy can know no bounds.

With this experience you will get your first feeling of gratitude, of thanksgiving. Then only will you be able to say, "Your grace is unbounded." Then only will you be able to say, "Blessed am I," and then for the first time the light and splendor of faith in Him will descend. Singing the Lord's praise does not make one a believer in God, but remembrance does.

Even kings and emperors of great domains,
Who possess enormous treasures,
Cannot compare with the lowly ant
With remembrance of God in his heart.

The greatest of kings possessing wealth as vast as the ocean and whose splendor is untold, cannot equal a tiny, lowly ant who has acquired the alchemy of remembrance, who always thinks of You. The lowliest of the lowly became the greatest of the great on acquiring surati; whereas the greatest of kings remains miserably destitute without remembrance.

There is only one wretchedness—to forget God. There is only one wealth—to attain His remembrance. He whose surati awakens has acquired all that is worth acquiring, achieved all worth achieving. Then it doesn't matter if he has no cloth to cover him, or roof to shelter him. It doesn't matter how much wealth you possess, how many palaces, how many titles, if in the absence of surati you feel a miserable beggar within. The pain, the anguish of poverty will always gnaw at your heart.

Nanak says the only kind of wealth is His remembrance. The only kind of poverty is to forget Him. Ponder well over this. Are you rich or poor? Don't think of your bank balance, which is a deception, but open your internal account and see the entry labeled remembrance. You are rich to the extent of your remembrance. If there is none, then you have not yet begun to acquire wealth. What you amass in the outside world makes no difference.

When Alexander the Great was about to die he told his ministers that his hands should be left hanging outside the coffin. When they complained that this was not the custom and wanted to understand the reason, he said, "I want people to see that in spite of all my conquests I leave this world with empty hands."

People like Alexander die as paupers. The most powerful turn out to be impotent; but if even an ant is filled with remembrance, all the Alexanders pale in insignificance before it.

Who was Nanak? What was he? He had no wealth, no status, no kingdom, but how many kings faded into insignificance before him? Nanak became precious because of his surati. Kings will come and go but Nanak will remain forever. Fame and honor are made and destroyed; it is not possible to destroy Nanak, because he who takes shelter in Him who is indestructible cannot be destroyed.

Even if you are a lowly ant it does not matter; only let His remembrance forever be. Do not indulge in the madness of acquiring vast kingdoms, because it always happens that the more you are engaged in piling up outside wealth, the more you forget to remember Him; how else could you succeed? If you remember Him all outside wealth will be as dust to you; then the world's honor and fame will be of no consequence.

When little children gather colored stones, try to explain to them that they are worthless pebbles—they will still smuggle them home. The mother finds their pockets filled with this junk. These same children, once they grow up and their understanding develops, no longer collect these stones; they in turn tell their children not to indulge in this foolish game. But what about all the useless things they continue to collect?

Whatever you gather in the world holds significance and value for you as long as your understanding or remembrance has not awakened. As soon as remembrance awakens in you, you become mature. Then a flame of understanding is kindled. By its light you come to know that all you hold precious was mere rubble. You wonder why in heaven you went after it, why you were so mad about it. What have you attained by gaining this, you ask yourself.

Suddenly it all becomes meaningless and worthless in your eyes. Life is transformed the moment surati awakens. A revolution takes place within you. Your old personality dies and a new one is born.

The quest for this new birth is religion. Think about this. Seek within—is there a place, ever so slight, for surati within you? Some little corner? Is there a temple in you where remembrance vibrates? Do you hear some little melody inside singing His remembrance? Is that remembrance always inside you or do you keep forgetting? Or do you remember Him at all?

If you begin to contemplate these lines, the very thinking will provoke the birth of remembrance within, because as you begin to think, you will naturally start thinking of Him. The very thought that there is no remembrance of Him inside me will awaken His remembrance. As the remembrance appears more and more frequently, as the hammer strikes again and again, the mark goes deeper and deeper. Constant hammering writes a mark even on a stone; and so with your heart the mark is bound to be intensified.

Kabir said that the rope rubs against the well as it goes up and down in drawing water and it forms a mark on the stone. As the rope of surati rubs against your heart, surely it will form a mark; and the mark develops soon, because nothing is more tender than the heart. All that is required is for the rope to keep rubbing against you.

SUGGESTED FURTHER READING

AND THE FLOWERS SHOWERED TALKS ON ZEN

Commenting on 11 Zen anecdotes, Osho explores the spiritual search — speaking on emptiness and no-mind, knowledge and being, on belief and trust, repression and truth; on philosophy and religion, love and divinity; on death and disease, on happiness and living in the here-and-now.

IN SEARCH OF THE MIRACULOUS VOLUME 2

Guiding the reader through the seven bodies and their corresponding chakras, Osho talks on psychic phenomena, dreams, telepathy, hypnosis, color therapy, Dynamic Meditation, Kundalini, gurus and the Tantric dimensions of sex. "I am talking about very scientific things," He says, "not something belonging to religious superstitions."

BEYOND ENLIGHTENMENT TALKS IN BOMBAY

Osho responds to questions on topics ranging from religion to philosophy, from present-day politics to His own childhood experiences, from enlightenment to what lies beyond. These talks also provide a glimpse into the mysterious communion that occurs between an enlightened person and his disciples.

MEDITATION: THE ART OF ECSTASY

Emphasizing the "festive dimension" of meditation, Osho suggests a variety of techniques specially designed for today's seeker. He also provides detailed descriptions of each stage of Dynamic Meditation. Included is an appendix highlighting Osho's radical meditation techniques, as well as meditative and traditional therapies.

MEDITATION: THE FIRST AND LAST FREEDOM

A practical how-to guide, spotlighting over 60 meditation techniques — from Zazen, the ancient Buddhist practice of sitting, to Osho's cathartic Dynamic Meditation for the 21st-century seeker. In addition, Osho answers questions about the obstacles meditators may meet along the way.

THE GREAT CHALLENGE

This introduction to Osho's work includes the secret aspects of spiritual traditions, as well as talks on death, reincarnation and the scientific foundation of His revolutionary technique, Dynamic Meditation.

BOOKS ABOUT OSHO AND HIS VISION

IMPRESSIONS...
OSHO COMMUNE INTERNATIONAL

250 glossy color views of the Osho Commune International in Poona illustrating virtually every activity. Included are pictures of the While Robe Brotherhood, Osho's samadhi, Vipassana meditation in the covered walkway in Lao Tzu garden, therapies at the Osho Multiversity, creative arts events, evening events, the black pyramids, and the newly-created Osho Teerth Park.

All quotes in the book are taken from Osho's discourses.

THE CHOICE IS OURS. THE KEY TO THE FUTURE
BY DR. GEORGE MEREDITH

This small book is a brief outline of the state of the world as it is now. It pinpoints the problems facing mankind, examines how they were created, and offers a practical, immediate alternative — a basis for a new kind of world, a totally fresh beginning. Essentially a grand synthesis of communism, meditation and anarchism, the revolutionary insights in this book are drawn from Osho's vision.

> "In scary detail, Dr. Meredith has covered the challenges of the 21st Century and then, guided by Osho's philosophy, has envisioned an exciting, achievable future for all men and women."
>
> Robert Rimmer, USA., Author of
> The Harrad Experiment, Proposition 31

BHAGWAN: THE MOST GODLESS YET THE MOST GODLY MAN
BY DR. GEORGE MEREDITH
Introduction by Tom Robbins

Osho's personal physician for the last eleven years of his life recounts the events that led him to Osho, discipleship, and the unique experience of caring for the health of an enlightened master. In his introduction, American author Tom Robbins comments: "He maintains that irreverent sense of humor that characterizes so many sannyasins, often separating them dramatically from the rigid robots who worship by rote at the fee of more traditional holy men."

BHAGWAN: THE BUDDHA FOR THE FUTURE
BY JULIET FORMAN

In what Osho calls a historical document, a close disciple of twenty years describes the evolution of the communes in India and the USA. This is a detailed account of the master-disciple relationship, a story of trust and betrayal, and a record of society's reaction to the greatest iconoclast of all time, culminating in Osho's arrest by the American government.